THE EXECUTIVE SUITE—
Feminine Style

THE EXECUTIVE SUITE —
Feminine Style

Edith M. Lynch

amacom
A DIVISION OF AMERICAN MANAGEMENT ASSOCIATIONS

© 1973 AMACOM
A division of American Management Associations, Inc., New York.
All rights reserved. Printed in the United States of America.

This publication may not be reproduced, stored in a retrieval system, or transmitted in whole or in part, in any form or by any means, electronic, mechanical, photocopying, recording, or otherwise, without the prior written permission of AMACOM.

International standard book number: 0-8144-5320-1
Library of Congress catalog card number: 73-75674
First printing

With love and affection

to Peter and Carlyn Eileen Lynch

Foreword

Recently I was on an executive airline flight, and I was pleased with the number of women aboard. A few years ago, I was frequently the only one. That flight was notable not only for the many women in evidence but also for the presence of stewards. We have indeed come to realize that good jobs are good for everyone. By the way, a physician next to me whispered, "At last the airlines have realized that *we* like to look at an attractive face too!"

Women's role in society has changed, and, thankfully, industry is taking notice. Today, we find women, such as those interviewed for this book, in top management. There are many of us who work as labor relations experts, consumer affairs directors, personnel officers, retail executives, even presidents of companies, and who manage to combine this with family life, just as many men do.

Our society is realizing that women's talents are great and should not be wasted. Yet there are many people whose attitudes need chang-

changing. Unfortunately, a good number of these are women! Many of us lack confidence and do not think of ourselves as competent members of society. In fact, when we talk about equal rights for women, we are really talking about equal rights for every human being.

Recently I got a letter from the Commission on White House Fellows asking me to help them locate qualified women for the program. Over the years, only a handful of women have dared apply. Most executives, when asked to nominate candidates, think only of men.

The women's liberation movement frequently refers to women as "sisters" and appeals to us to recognize our "sisterhood." As you will note in this book, most management women are happy to teach younger women. They are willing to work together with other women to narrow the generation gap and to further women's careers. They are willing to look to the qualified people, regardless of who they are, and this book illustrates that many management men are too.

A number of other countries are far ahead of the United States in recognizing and using women's skills. Isn't it time that we realized the cost of wasting these talents? Men and women alike will have to work together to insure that all our people's abilities are developed fully.

Earning these rights for women does not have to be a grim, hard battle. The women in this book have proved that a career can be a stimulating, exciting experience that can add enrichment, fulfillment, and fun to one's life. As I told a young colleague recently, "Get with it. Be involved. You'll have the time of your life!"

Esther A. Peterson
Consumer Adviser to the President
Giant Food, Inc.

Preface

The need for an "inside look" at women's role in management was my main reason for writing this book. The tone of the book is positive in contrast to that of so many books published about women in the 1970s. It didn't start out that way, but the results of the questionnaire, personal talks, and formal interviews revealed a wealth of women working in many layers of management—from supervisors to presidents—whose accomplishments were many and whose outlook on the world of today is positive and encouraging.

I came away from this writing with a real admiration for women in management jobs. They are doing their work well, have few axes to grind, and most are willing to share their experiences so that other women coming along can benefit.

This book is mainly about women in the middle and upper levels of management, but there are a few who work around the fringes of these jobs, such as a management librarian or a skilled researcher in industrial relations, a few editors, and some young women who are on the first rung of management. These women, unlike some of their predecessors, have a definite plan as to where they will be in 20 years. Some of the others are consultants, lawyers, and doctors who still perform management functions, directly or indirectly.

To the surprise of some, there are five women who are staying home—a practice much frowned on by a number of women's liberation groups. One of these women is an officer in her husband's company, another helps run a 500-acre farm. The third, a well-educated home economist, manages a family of five plus many important outside activities. The fourth, a young cum laude college graduate with one child, spends her spare time editing and grading college master's theses and assorted free-lance projects. A fifth left a full-time supervisory job in a hospital to set up private practice so that she could raise a family.

Subsequently she became involved in a local hospital in a highly skilled leadership role.

Do they abandon their education and their management know-how when they elect to stay home? I don't think so. But it doesn't necessarily mean that they will stay there indefinitely. Three somewhat older women, in fact, are back in the labor market after 20 years away from it. One, a widow, is the director of employee services for a very large company, and the second a labor relations writer a third is a bank vice president. Before returning to work, all three spent their time raising a family and working in children's organizations and churches and doing volunteer work in hospitals.

The choice of staying home or working by all five of these women was not involuntary. Such women take their management skills and know-how with them to use in raising their families and managing both home and outside activities. Many times, as illustrated by two of the women who returned to work, they come back at equally high or higher levels than when they left. They may not have moved as far up the ladder as those who stayed on the job, but even that is a moot question.

The versatility of the women and the interesting positions they hold is a tribute to their own skills and know-how and to the farsighted, perhaps ahead-of-the-game men in management positions.

It bothers me that women must be told by other women how downtrodden they have been and that the only way to get ahead is to assert your rights. It bothers me, too, to see the choice of staying home downgraded and housework and homemaking labeled a terribly humdrum, sad existence. I have great respect for women, and men, who think that other people are intelligent enough to make their own choices. This does not mean that a woman should lie down and play dead when she is bypassed by someone else. The women who participated in this study did not get there by doing so.

Nor does it mean that there have not been and still remain many who underrate women's ability to perform management jobs. I hope that this book will help dispel some of the doubts about women's capabilities. I also hope that management decision makers will read this book and find that women can do and are doing essential management jobs and that right in their own companies are many women candidates who should be given a chance to prove themselves.

There have always been some women who have accomplished much in the male-dominated world. The young, perhaps partly because of the paths opened by women in this study, have many more opportunities. Well-educated, bright, well-trained in many disciplines, they have a multitude of choices, including the not-so-dull task of homemaking.

The future for the young women in the business world looks bright. This is in sharp contrast to the limited choices of teaching, library work, and nursing that women had 50 years ago.

There were many circumstances that made the women in the study the exception. Families where the mother was highly regarded as being as bright as the father and where both made the right decisions for their girls as well as their boys; schoolteachers and professors who encouraged women to develop their talent; husbands who recognized that their wives enjoyed the zest of the work world; economic pressures; and understanding management men (and a few women) all helped these women. The women, too, earned their reputations by producing, by sharing their part of the workload, and acting like managers.

Does this mean that all had the same peculiar set of circumstances or that they condemn those who didn't make it? I honestly think that, like men in similar positions, they recognize that their breaks have not all been "self-made" and that they bear both compassion and understanding for those who either by choice or otherwise have moved neither as fast nor as far as the more successful women.

Because the image of woman in management still is that of a slave-to-her-work-above-all-else, nonfeminine, step-on-the-neck, ambitious female, one without husband or child, and one of a semiskilled, at best, worker, I have tried to show the many sides of today's working woman manager. Her skill at managing her home, not an easy task, and her outside activities make one see the management woman as a person rather than a cog in a machine. Like her male counterpart, the management woman does not give up all her personal attributes and activities when she takes on more management responsibilities. Thus I have also tried to dispel some of the many myths about women on the job.

I do not mean to underrate or undercut the way women in the liberation movement are trying to make it easier for other women to move ahead. To me it is a different path—one that I have not taken and one that most of the women in the study have not chosen. I can only write about this movement from the outside and so perhaps have cast some unjust aspersions on activities that, taken by themselves, seem to me to be inconsequential, even harmful, to the advance of women in management. For example, neither I nor most of my colleagues get too excited if we are addressed as *Miss, Mrs.,* or *Ms.* This, however, is important to many women today, and I think they should be granted that courtesy and privilege if it is meaningful to them. I recognize this as a symbol of a much broader upsurge of feminine effort for equality, but to me there are better ways of advancement. I apologize if I have offended any of those who are more sympathetic to or involved in the women's liberation groups.

My view is that women in today's management world are intent on doing a good job and like many management men do not have either the time or the inclination to get involved in such movements. There are several women in the study, some not identified, who are either directly or indirectly involved. I have tried to report their views accurately. They, too, are doing fine management jobs, but have taken the time and interest to become involved in the feminist movement. It is their choice; to me that is the way it should be. There is no doubt in my mind that they have made the world more aware that women cannot be disregarded. Whether their methods are helping more than the solid achievements of the other women in the study is open to question. Probably the combination of the two approaches is making and will make it much easier for women in the future to be widely accepted as people with brains, ambitions, abilities, and management know-how.

I have tried to include all age groups so that the book isn't just a book for and about old fuddy-duddies who are preaching to the young. I have included the views of three young college students and those of four men. Unfortunately, I was unable to obtain much material on black women managers. Few answered the questionnaire, but a brief summary of informal conversations with a number of black women executives is included. The interviews with women on the Washington scene and with Joan Crawford give a different dimension to the book. I have read much of the literature of the women's liberation groups in an effort to understand their point of view and to present it according to my perspective. So the book, mainly introspective by a management woman about other management women, does have some outside opinions that should help women progress.

If I were to thank each person who helped me in my career, I would need many volumes. My own understanding family; my tolerant professors; my many, including the present ones, nonbiased bosses; and long-suffering peers and subordinates head the list. Added to that list are my many friends both in and outside the business world who have contributed so much to my understanding of management.

Very special thanks go to the women who filled out the long questionnaire. I hope I have done them justice.

Every author recognizes the help of those who stick with her from start to finish in getting the job done. To my niece, Jan Thomas, and to my ever faithful assistant, Clara Kushins—my warmest personal thanks and regards. I couldn't have done it without you.

Edith M. Lynch

Contents

1

WHAT'S IT ALL ABOUT?
The Role of the
Woman Manager in the 1970s

"Disgusted," "discouraged," "frustrated," "restless," "militant"—these are some of the words used to describe women of the seventies. "Ambitious," "well-educated," "capable," "adjusted," "cooperative" are other words used to describe the management women. Lost, however, are the descriptive words "meek," "mild," "sweet," "precious," and "loving," which were used in other years.

The Cries of the Liberationists

The literature written by women about women in a male-dominated world is usually bitter and filled with exhortation to the "sisters" to leave the kitchen and join the movement. The traditional conviction that a woman's world is her husband, her family, her children, and her home brings down their wrath. Sigmund Freud, once highly regarded by both male and female intellectuals, is now in disrepute. His male-envy theory just isn't bought by today's woman. The churches of the world are chided about their concern over modern birth control techniques. The feminists want "control over their bodies and control over their lives." [1] The literature pictures women as having been in bondage for 6,000 years or more. Some women are crying for action.

There is little doubt that the women's groups have called attention to the overall plight of women, but they have often not been able to delineate plausible steps for action. The reason for this may lie in the diversification of their forces. Women's groups range from the all-out liberationists to those working quietly and efficiently, often aided by intelligent men, to see that qualified women get equal opportunities.

Progress?

Women have come a long way toward achieving equality in the working world. There is still plenty of prejudice to overcome, but there is hope in the seventies that more progress will be made. Freed from the drudgery of housework by the miracle machines of today, plus better-planned parenthood, women now have more time than ever before to devote to work outside the home.

Progress has been made, too, on both a national and an international basis. It is no accident that both the political parties placed great emphasis on women's rights and prerogatives in their 1972 campaigns.

President Nixon proclaimed August 26, 1972, as Women's Rights Day, the 52d anniversary of the 19th amendment, which gave women the right to vote. The day was marked by meetings of women's groups all over the country with marches, rallies, and celebrations. In issuing a *Fact Sheet*, Mr. Nixon commented proudly about the progress of his administration. He said that more than 1,000 women had been promoted to or recruited for mid-level government jobs, including sky marshals, Secret Service agents, and narcotics and FBI agents, where women had never been considered before. There are also 118 women in policy-making government jobs earning $28,000 a year and up.

The United Nations is planning to proclaim 1975 as International Women's Year and "to devote this year to intensify action to promote equality between men and women and to increase women's contributions to national and international development." [2] The UN is urging member nations to upgrade the status of women.

Another fact of life is that passage by Congress of the Education

Act of 1972 assures women in professional, executive, and administrative positions that they will be treated equally.

All in all the seventies will see some startling changes in the world of work as well as in the social areas that seem to be of even greater concern to several women's organizations. The awakening of women all over the world to a reexamination of their role in world affairs, in the home, in government, and at work characterizes the seventies. Other minorities had their day in the sixties, but all predictions and overt actions point to this decade as the time when women and the rest of the world will decide what women's role really is.

Quiet evolution seems to be a thing of the past. Why the sudden clamor, the loud cries, the calls for action from the women's liberationists, and the repercussions as far as the halls of Congress?

Congress Passes a Constitutional Amendment

Some idea of the scope of the issue can be gleaned from the 1972 congressional debates on the passing of the constitutional amendment guaranteeing women's rights. Senator Birch Bayh of Indiana, in his fight to have the Senate pass the 28th Amendment, stated: "There is overwhelming evidence that persistent patterns of sex discrimination permeate our social, cultural, and economic life." [3] The magnitude of sex discrimination in the country today can be gauged by the simple, eloquent statement of Congresswoman Shirley Chisholm in testifying before the Subcommittee on Constitutional Amendments in May 1970: "I have been far oftener discriminated against because I am a woman than because I am black." [4]

Not that men succumb easily. In the same debate, the chief champion of states' rights and the old ways of running the world, Senator Sam Ervin of North Carolina, quotes from the Bible on the differences of men and women and has this to say about business and professional women:

> My finite intellectual strength does not enable me to comprehend why business and professional women—and this does not apply to all business and professional women by any means . . . , whose work is solely intellectual, wish to have a Constitutional amendment adopted which will rob their sisters who do work which is not entirely intellectual of the protections which the law throws around them against their will.[5]

The arguments on whether women should or should not be drafted took many pages in the *Congressional Records* of the last days of March 1972.

Newspapers and Magazines
Make Their Contribution

One begins to get some feeling for the impact of the feminist movement from national magazines like *Time*, which stated:

> Another New Woman has emerged, but she is, perhaps for the first time, on a massive scale, very much the creation of her own, and not a masculine imagination—an act of intellectual parthenogenesis. The New Feminism cannot be measured entirely by the membership lists of the National Organization and other liberation groups. It is a much broader state of mind that has raised serious questions about the way people live —about their families, home, child rearing, jobs, government, and the nature of the sexes themselves.[6]

When *Life* magazine (now defunct) gives its coveted cover picture to a "Dropout Wife" who left her home, husband, and two young sons for the companionship of two other women, plus her young daughter, one really begins to wonder what the whole world is really coming to.[7] The joy of watching your own children's growing delight with life is sacrificed for the questionable joys of being free. Some cannot see equality in the exchange of helping guide the most complicated of creatures— little children—for the mediocre accomplishments of many jobs. And yet this seems to be what many women of the 1970s are crying for.

Magazine or newspaper articles that make a big thing of a woman's taking a strange job or being elected to a board of directors are almost endless. The disturbing part about it all is that these facts make the news not to publicize the *talents* involved but to sensationalize the *sex* involved. Imagine a *woman* being on the board of IBM, Chase, Penney's, or Ford.

Those are only a few places where women have made news. When the venerable *New York Times* uses a column to discuss a woman's getting a job as a water boy at Utah State University, it seems we have come almost to the end of publicity on the status of women.[8] Perhaps a story that almost ties for the same spot is the one about the Canadian mother of five who became a stevedore in Sarnia, Ontario. She works side by side with her husband and 12 other men. There is also the street driller at Con Edison in New York who likes her work and holds her own with her male co-workers.

When a team of Yale University lawyers are strong advocates of the new Constitutional amendment, when the prestigious universities of the country have opened their doors to coeds, and when the women drive for and get backing from the federal government on preferential hiring and promotion, there begins to emerge a concept of the stirrings.

There are interesting sidelights, such as the "Male Chauvinist Pig Test" on Valentine's Day reported in *The New York Times Magazine.*

> Here are a few of the questions to test just how male you really are: Are you inclined to believe that topless waitresses are little college girls trying to make the price of tuition while bra-burners are despoiling the image of American womanhood? Or how about this one: When your wife can't for the life of her remember what she was going around look-ing for, is that what you mean by being flighty, but when you forget the kids at [a department store], is that merely [being] absent-minded? [9]

Or how about the quiz for the female liberationist in *The New York Times Magazine?* Here are a few of the quotes.

> Does the moral principle—"only among consenting adults"—apply as long as no one gets pregnant and seeks to pressure the other into mar-riage? [or] After cracking jokes about male chauvinists on a camping trip or beach party, do you automatically grab the cook's job, leaving him to gather the wood, wash the dishes? [10]

Government Edict and Personnel Policies

The nature of the change in the world of women is indicated by government edict versus personnel policies formerly promulgated by business and management. For example, the new regulations set forth by the Equal Employment Opportunity Commission (March 1972) say that an employer can no longer discriminate in hiring a pregnant woman. The same regulations would do away with such personnel poli-cies as differences in pension contributions and payments. Many firms now permit women to retire at 62 instead of the customary 65 for their male counterparts.

Worldwide Restlessness

The restlessness on the part of women is almost worldwide. Rus-sian women, long "liberated" to do heavy manual labor such as street cleaning, are now found more and more often in professional and scien-tific jobs. The press is filled with stories of African, Indian, and French women all striving for equality.

Here are a few specific indications of what is happening elsewhere in the world.

At the United Nations, for instance, Secretary General Kurt Waldheim appointed Mrs. Helvi Sepita of Finland as assistant secretary general for social and humanitarian affairs.

The *Newsletter on the Status of Women*, published by the United Nations, reports that the Costa Rican government plans to establish, in the Central America area, a center for the advancement of women. A national commission on the status of women has been set up by the Egyptian Government. Mrs. A. Ratib, professor of international law at Cairo University, has been appointed minister of social affairs. In France, a committee on women's labor was established in 1971.

In October 1971 the first European Conference of the Deutscher Frauenring considered the vocational opportunities for women in Europe. "The keynote speech was made by Evelyn Sulleret, the French sociologist. She stressed that the persistent traditional attitudes and practices determine the roles of men and women and condition the range of occupational choice and opportunities as well as remuneration and conditions. The resolution adopted by the Conference emphasized the importance of constitutional guarantees of the right of equal citizenship (for example, legal, political, social, and economic rights) to be provided by all member countries of the European Economic Community and the need for the application of the principle of *equal pay*." [11]

In Switzerland, in 1971, ten women were elected to the National Council (Lower House) and one to the Council of States (Upper House).

In the United Kingdom, Miss M. Head was elected chairman of the board of management of the National Chamber of Trade. She is the only woman, among 40 men, on the board and the first woman to hold the office of chairman.

In India, Indira Gandhi named Mrs. Nandini Satpathy to be chief minister of Orissa, India's problem state.[12]

An explanation of what is happening in China can be found in "Experiment in Freedom," by Bonny Cohen, in *Sisterhood is Powerful: An Anthology of Writings From the Women's Liberation Movement*. A review of the several steps in freeing women from tradition in China is interesting.

"The resistance put up by both sexes to women's rights was and is a continuing problem. For the Chinese Communists, ideology is always ahead of practice." [13]

According to Cohen, the Chinese realize that "a change in political institutions and ideology can come overnight. Changing human behavior takes generations. . . . The Chinese will keep trying to fight their past, two thousand years of female servitude." [14] China is not our model. Its needs and desires are very different from ours. Women are told what they should be and do—that's not the way it should be here. But Mao and the Chinese Communists do show us that society is changed by changing people's daily lives. Working side by side with men partially liberates women. "Freedom—however you want it—comes from new ways of living together." [15]

A report from the emerging African nations, based on a seminar on "Planning for Better Family Living" held in Yaoundé, Cameroon, in January 1962, states: "The issues throughout the Conference were the far-reaching changes beginning to rock the traditional forms of African life —and the role that women and women's organizations can play in harmonizing these changes with the specific needs of particular societies." [16]

The Working Woman—What Is the Picture?

Is the revolution justified, particularly in the struggle for management jobs and equal pay? It is high time to take a realistic look at the whole picture.

In 1972 there were 72,402,000 people in the civilian labor force. Of these, 24,370,000 were working women 20 years of age and older. Slightly over a million were unemployed.[17] To put it another way, approximately one out of every three workers in America is a woman.

Whether you ride the subways of New York, the buses of the South, or the car pools of the Midwest or travel anywhere in the country, you will see working women. In every city the sidewalks are flooded with women at lunchtime. Women executives riding the airlines of the world to their assignments are still somewhat rare, but they are there. Add to the working women who are visible in the streets those in the hospital corridors, behind the counters of stores, at the other end of the telephone when you are desperately trying to reach someone in San Francisco and you've forgotten the time difference, in the laundries, in the vast offices of the cities, in day-care centers, and in classrooms.

The stewardess in her glamorous half-waitress, half-public-relations job, the receptionist who greets your callers tactfully and efficiently, the woman who watches your children, and the most picked-on slave of all, your secretary—all are working women.

The real rub comes in the kinds of jobs women can attain. No one thinks twice about hiring a woman to clean a washroom, and most people expect to find a woman in the supportive role of a good secretary. When women try to kick over the traces and break into management jobs, however, tradition is against them.

The overall statistics on earnings for women workers published in the 1970 *Fact Sheet* of the Women's Bureau of the U.S. Department of Labor make almost every woman, and many men, cringe—particularly when differences in earnings figures presumably should be narrowing. The *Fact Sheet* indicates that women in full-time jobs earn only $3 for every $5 earned by men. The gap is *greater* than it was 15 years ago. From 64 percent in 1955, women's median wage or salary income as a proportion to men's fell to 59 percent in 1970—or a dollar figure of $5,523 per year as compared with $8,966 received by men. According to the *Fact Sheet*, for scientific personnel it was a little better. Women earned 76.3 percent as much as men for a dollar figure of $11,600 compared with $15,200 for men. Women professional and technical workers earned an average of $7,878 and men earned $11,806, or women earned 66.7 percent as much as men.[18]

In 1970 only 1.1 percent of the women in the labor force earned over $15,000 a year, while 13.5 percent of the men earned more than that. Only 5.9 percent of the women earned between $10,000 and $15,000 while 26.5 percent of the men earned corresponding amounts.[19]

Are government-employed women any better off? Here is what one prominent Washington woman lawyer says, "I feel that I have been plodding along in the practice of law like an ostrich with my head in the sand. I was actually shocked to learn recently that out of 10,000 U.S. government jobs paying $28,000 a year or more, 150 were held by women. I find that incredible." [20]

When one examines the discrepancies in earnings between men and women, after the initial shock wears off the big question is: Why the difference? Are women dumber than men? Can't they do the jobs as well? Psychologists tell us that women are just as smart as and in some areas smarter than men. Surely circumstances and customs have encouraged many smart young women to be satisfied with mediocre jobs. Why else would a young woman with an IQ of 140 or over be willing to work for a not-so-bright man?

The statistics reflect a bleak picture. There are many partial answers to such inequities but, overall, when one studies these statistics, it is easy to understand the flak coming from the women's organizations. Even more recently we hear the cry for "affirmative action" from our somewhat bewildered government, which doesn't quite know what to do with this hot potato, and the shrill voices of pressured congressmen and congresswomen trying to do something about the situation.

The Working Mother

In 1970 nearly 26 million children under 18 had mothers who were in the labor force.[21] Most of these children (nearly nine out of ten) were in families that had both a mother and a father. However, of 8.5 million black children under 18 nearly 7 out of 18 were in households headed by women.

These figures give you some idea of the scope of the issue of working mothers. These statistics are quoted here because in the study conducted for this book well over half the women in management jobs are mothers—many with young children.

Twenty Facts on Women Workers

A summary of where women stood in the fall of 1972 can be gleaned from "Twenty Facts about Women Workers," issued by the Women's Bureau of the U.S. Department of Labor.

1. Nine out of ten girls will work at some time in their lives.
2. Most women work because of economic need. Two-thirds of all women workers are single, divorced, widowed, or separated, or have husbands who earn less than $7,000 a year.
3. About 32 million women are in the labor force; they constitute 38 percent of all workers. Minority women in the labor force number 4.1 million; they constitute 44 percent of all minority workers.
4. Half of all women 18 to 64 years of age are workers.
5. About one-fourth of employed women hold part-time jobs.
6. Women accounted for three-fifths of the increase in the civilian labor force in the past decade.
7. Labor force participation is highest among women 18 to 24 and 35 to 54 years of age; the median age of women workers is 39 years.
8. The more education a woman has, the greater the likelihood she will seek paid employment. Nearly seven out of ten women 45 to 54 years of age with four or more years of college are in the labor force.
9. The number of working mothers (women with children under 18) has increased eightfold since 1940. They now number 12.2 million, an increase of 3.5 million in the last decade.
10. The 4.6 million working mothers with children under six in 1970 had 5.8 million children under six; the estimated number of licensed day-care slots is 774,000.
11. Women workers are concentrated in low-paying, dead-end jobs. As a result, the average woman worker earns about three-fifths of what a man does, even when both work full time the year round.
12. Unemployment was lowest for white adult males (4.0 percent) and highest for minority teenage girls (35.5 percent) in 1971.

White adult women	5.3 percent
Minority adult men	7.2 percent
Minority adult women	8.7 percent
White teenage boys	15.1 percent
White teenage girls	15.2 percent
Minority teenage boys	28.9 percent

13. About one out of nine families is headed by a woman; almost two out of five poor families are headed by a woman. About three out of ten black families are headed by a woman; almost three out of five poor black families are headed by a woman.

14. It is frequently the wife's earnings that raise a family out of poverty.* In husband-wife families 14 percent are poor if the wife does not work; 4 percent are poor when she does work.

15. Of the workers not covered by the Fair Labor Standards Act (FLSA), 45 percent are women. Fifty-six percent of all black women workers are not covered by FLSA.

16. The average woman worker is as well educated as the average man worker. Women have completed 12.5 years of school; men, 12.4 years.

17. Women constitute 39 percent of all professional and technical workers but only 17 percent of all nonfarm managers, officials, and proprietors.

18. Women constitute 75 percent of all clerical workers but only 4 percent of all craftsmen and foremen.

19. The median wage of full-time, year-round private household workers was $2,101 in 1970. Private household workers are protected by minimum wage legislation in only four states. They are protected by virtually no other legislation.

20. Fully employed women high school graduates have less income on the average than fully employed men with less than eight years of schooling.

The Woman Executive, 1973

A management spot in today's world is a pretty lonesome (but thrilling) place for a woman. What is it like in the rare world of women who earn over $20,000—to be one of the decision makers, to have the

---

* Classified as poor were those nonfarm families of four with total income of less than $4,000 in 1970.

Sources: U.S. Department of Commerce, Bureau of the Census; U.S. Department of Health, Education, and Welfare, National Center for Social Statistics; U.S. Department of Labor, Bureau of Labor Statistics and Wage and Hour Division.

perquisites of a window office and perhaps a rug on the floor, to be held in rather glum admiration by women who earn far less than you do? Is it harder for a woman executive than for a man to get along with others, to make one more move up the ladder? What characteristics have contributed to success? Why have some women succeeded where so many of their sister workers have remained behind? Answering these questions is sometimes difficult, but the women who were interviewed for this book were open and frank in talking about these issues.

Some of the women discussed a few of the social aspects of being one of the "annointed." Accustomed to being the only woman in groups of anywhere from 50 to 500 male managers, a woman becomes suspicious, or at least curious, when another woman attends the meeting. How did *she* get there, too? What special attributes does *she* have? When a woman executive asks for a seat on a plane or picks up her ticket, she is usually asked whether her husband will accompany her, or whether her boss would prefer a window seat. If she has an expense account, she is a rarity at the good restaurants and is dealt with somewhat superciliously at hotels. There is, however, a camaraderie among women executives—probably because there are so few of them. The older women executives, at least, have a healthy, sincere respect for each other because they know what it took to get there.

An Inside Story—A Woman Writes About Management Women

Men have written about women since the beginning of time. The sorrows of the world supposedly began with us when poor old Eve led Adam to his downfall. The early Greeks wrote both tragedies and comedies about us, Samuel Johnson had something to say about the sense of women, and much later Norman Mailer wrote about women in not-very-flattering terms. Ray A. Killian, in *The Working Woman—A Male Manager's View*, was kinder to women and gave us the pride of individuality. As he put it, "Management must recruit, supervise, and utilize the womanpower that is available today. The longer management delays in getting its house in order and providing realistic equality for women, the more needless time and valuable potential will be wasted." [22]

Despite all that has been written about women, the love songs, the diatribes, the long novels, the dirty-sex and the clean-sex books, little has been written from the real inside about management women. For the most part, women have been content with (or resigned to) secondary status and secondary pay. This book is *not* about such women. It is the inside story of women who have made it—perhaps not as far as they would have liked, but at least over the first high hurdles.

This book is based on the replies to a long questionnaire, requiring at least two hours to complete, sent to 100 women executives. Ninety-four took time to answer. Of the ten "no replies," a few had retired; Lillian Gilbreth was aging and has since died; and a very few said that business pressures prevented their completing the questionnaire.

The book was written with two purposes in mind. First, to remind male managers that women can do any management job and to review for them the careers of successful women executives. Since in most cases men are still the ones who decide on placement and promotion, it is hoped that the examples of the fine women discussed will give these men the courage to fill the next vacancies on their executive staffs with women.

It was written, too, for the young hopefuls. Gone are the days when the only respectable jobs open to women were those of teacher, librarian, nurse, or executive secretary. A myriad of positions have opened up for today's young woman. But she may still come up against some of the same problems that faced women who have surmounted the obstacles. The success stories in this book are included to make the cross-over easier for the next group of aspiring women executives. Because young women have made the cross-over more easily than their older sister executives, their experiences should encourage other young women who might have become disheartened with their first turndown. As one young woman lawyer put it, "We were given a blacklist of firms not to apply to because they just wouldn't think of hiring a woman."

Many young women and older ones too, are faced with choosing between home and work. Should even a temporary assignment as a housewife and mother offer a young woman no managerial opportunities? Some of the best executive material in the country could probably be found in many homes where the household is run like a well-organized executive suite. This alternative is mentioned especially for the young woman who too often has been told lately that when she gets married she could abandon hope of becoming anything but a minor executive.

It will be amazing—to some—to discover among middle- and upper-management levels the great number of happy, well-adjusted women with solid marriages and fine children. This practicable, rewarding combination is not rare among the women executives included in this book.

Positions Held by Management Women

What are the positions held by the women who contributed to this book? They range from that of president of a store, like Margaret Scarbrough Wilson, of Scarbrough's in Austin, to Sharyn Yanoshak, technical consultant to Cyphernetics, a computer company; from Marion Kellogg, consultant-marketing management development, General Electric, to Dr. Joan B. Berkowitz, a project director of A. D. Little, Inc. in Cambridge, Massachusetts; from Mary S. McMahon, director of Management Development and Communications, The Equitable Life Assurance Society of the United States, to young Jane Evans Sheer, president of I. Miller at 25. There is Coline Covington of *Glamour Magazine* and Maria Vescia, vice president of Airwick International, who is the first woman president of the International Trade Association. There is Betty Ann Duval, manager of personnel development of General Foods, who has helped many young men and women up the ladder of success. There is Esther Peterson, consumer adviser of Giant Food, with her distinguished background in labor and government. Many are officers of companies, editors, trade association directors, arbitrators, directors of community and consumer affairs, and technicians. The breakdown of the sample is shown in Table 1. (The women in the study are sketched briefly in Appendix D— a few preferred to remain anonymous.)

Something should be said about the variety of duties represented in the sample. Women executives, even more than men executives, have made their own spots. Duties have been added to make the job interesting and exciting and, like most management jobs everywhere, the challenges and the jobs are unique. So, even if there are five presidents and ten vice presidents, their duties vary all over the lot, and probably one would not want to swap jobs with another. Unfortunately the completed questionnaires cannot be included in toto. A copy of the questionnaire is in Appendix B. Illustrative statements were taken from several questionnaires. Although the information on them is only a shadow of what the women really do, a close examination of them would be an encouraging exercise for anyone interested in management—especially the role that women play.

The 95 women chosen for the sample represent a wealth of experience and know-how. Their personal concern with making the business world a better place for other women is not the usual blitz of bad language, name-calling, and affixing of blame for their hard climb to success. Their remarks are based on the day-to-day observations of capable, busy women. It is somewhat remarkable that there is not the hint of a whine among them, that they are an enthusiastic, gung-ho group, that life is interesting and exciting for them, and that they still are willing to face new challenges.

They are aware, and have scars to show it, of the "battle," or should we say "scuffle," of the sexes on executive row. They know the triple problems of being wife, mother, and executive.

Are there any characteristics common to successful women? Is

TABLE 1. Positions held by women responding to questionnaire.

Position	Number of Incumbents
President	5
Vice president	10
Lawyer	5
Treasurer	2
Tax expert	1
Arbitrator and labor relations specialist	7
Attorney	5
Trade association executive	4
Consumer adviser, urban affairs and EEOC	7
Teacher, professor	4
Assistant vice president	3
Store manager	1
Management development and organization planning director	7
Testing specialist	2
Training director	3
Personnel director	10
Employment counselor	2
Doctor	2
Government official	3
Director of nursing	1
Editor	4
Researcher (industrial relations)	2
Inhalation specialist	1
Other	3

there some magic touch that has given them their chance? Are their backgrounds the same? Are they the seventh daughter of a seventh daughter? Are they different from men executives—and how?

They come from small towns, farms, and big cities. Their fathers are farmers, executives, or tradesmen. Their mothers are often strong figures even though they have had to demonstrate their qualities in a role that was quite different from that of their daughters. Some of these executives are lone children, and some are from families as large as eight or ten.

For these women education was important. Even in the humblest of homes, the daughter was often given the same support morally and intellectually as a bright son. Not many attributed their success to just getting breaks; all talked of attention to the job and using their capabilities almost to the limit.

As to their intelligence—if the "cum laudes" and the "magnas" mean anything or if their reputations for quick wit mean anything—the women in the sample are ahead of the pack. All the indications are that they are smart—they have had to be to get where they are.

Can any of the business know-how gleaned by these women be passed on to other women aspiring to the top? It is hoped that a review of the behind-the-scenes, "hair down" reporting of the work experiences of women executives will accomplish this purpose and will be of interest and enjoyment to the reader—male or female.

2
MYTHS ABOUT
WOMEN MANAGERS

Women have been trapped by custom and by myths. Management, bound by the old taboos, looks past their talents in considering candidates for management jobs, and even the women themselves seem blind to their own qualifications. What are some of these myths, what do the management women of today really think of them, and how are they handling them?

Myth No. 1: Women Can't Take
Heavy Responsibility

The myth that women will fall apart if heavy responsibilities are foisted upon them should be dissipated. They are as fully aware of their responsibilities as men. Here is what Jane Evans Sheer, president of I. Miller (a job that she attained at the age of 25), says: "Remember, as you go up the ladder, you will be in the company of fewer and fewer women, so you will always be noticed in a crowd of men. Make sure that all that attention is focused primarily on your personality, intelligence, and ability—for to be respected as a high-caliber executive, your male peers must be able to recognize *the same executive characteristics in you as they do in their fellow males.*"

Or, as Marion Kellogg ° says, "Be excellent all the time. Every slip is remembered."

Some women do feel, however, because it has been drummed into them for so long, that they can't reach top-level jobs. Says Cynthia C. Wedel, "We have a reluctance to delegate responsibility. I think we tend to have a do-it-yourself complex. We sometimes have quite unwarranted feelings of inferiority if we are in a job usually held by a man."

Myth No. 2: Women Cry Too Much; They Are Too Emotional

"You can't have women around because they are too emotional."
"They think they can get anything if they cry."
"Heaven deliver me from a weeping female." Most of us have heard these cracks from management men ever since we entered the business world. It's a sad fact of life that most women do cry more easily than men, and even though I hate to say so, I've seen strong men give in when they shouldn't when a woman has turned on the faucets. Occasionally it happens in business, too, but in upper and middle management jobs tears are incidental or accidental. As one woman executive said, "Unfortunately, when I get carried away on a crusading point or I get very angry, I weep. When the president bawled me out last week, I also found the cursed tears starting to flow. I get provoked, but that's the way I am. I think, however, it is taking unfair advantage, and I don't think it has helped me one bit. I have to work twice as hard after such an episode in order to prove I'm not usually a weepy woman and am able to act like a man in a 'man's job.'"

This woman seems to be a "loner," however, for practically every other woman interviewed or questioned said that emotionalism is no more prevalent in women than in men executives, and the use of tears is strictly *verboten.* They cite the emotionalism of men shown in cartoons of the worried executive who lets off steam by screaming at his secretary or slamming the telephone receiver down in wrath.

All bad? Nonsense. Life would be fairly dull without emotionalism

° In general, only the name of the person quoted will be given; her title and company affiliation are in Appendix D.

and even a few tears when the going gets rough. But here is what some other women in business say to this question.

> It does not figure at all and should not occur. . . . If you have to fall apart, lock yourself in the bathroom (private, naturally).
> —ANITA GOLDBERG

> I think it is a myth. I recall few weeping women.   —BETTY DUVAL

> It doesn't belong there—unless it is a situation in which a man might weep.   —CYNTHIA C. WEDEL

> Would you make love in the board room? There's a time and place for everything.   —SHARYN YANOSHAK

> She gets big black wet marks—all negative.   —HARRIET WILINSKY

> All I can say is that a woman better not weep if she wants to get anywhere in business. There is no room for emotions that are normally expected from a female.   —MARIA VESCIA

> Such a practice should be nonexistent but unfortunately isn't.
> —ALICE KEHOE

> A weeping female—[shouldn't do it] in business if she's smart. If she does, she just supports this fiction of instability—and embarrasses the hell out of everyone around.   —EVA ROBINS

> If a woman weeps out of sympathy to others or due to some personal tragedy, it's normal, but weeping over office slights or job frustrations is not acceptable in my book.   —JEAN SISCO

And about the myth that women are more emotional than men, Eva Robins says, "Just that it's not true. More sensitive and aware of nuances—but not emotional in the pejorative sense. We all (men and women) live, hate, get angry, and so on."

Most other women don't necessarily agree about emotionalism among women versus men. Here are some opinions.

> Not so, I think most intelligent women are more logical than men.
> —MARYELLEN SCHWARZ

> Women are frequently accused of being emotional . . . because of their enthusiasm and impatience to get the job done. Men are detached, matter-of-fact, and slower at arriving at decisions and follow-through.   —RITA PERNA

Bette Heydrick has this to say about the emotions issue: "Most women have had enough years in the business climate to have strengthened their emotional control, and by the time they are ready for executive roles they are usually mature enough that their decisions are not based on emotion. Also, in many instances where employee relations are involved, a decision based on some emotional consideration might be favorable."

Myth No. 3: Women Ask for Special Privileges

Do women managers ask for special privileges because they are women?

"I don't want to start women up the ladder in management jobs," say some top management men. "They will work a while and then fall in love, marry, and want time off for raising babies."

Or, "Women managers want more time off because they must accompany their husbands on special trips or to special conventions."

"They want especially courteous attention even on the job. They want all the prerogatives of women without the responsibilities."

These are only a few of the gripes that men have about women managers. Are they true? Perhaps about some women, but not about most. It is true that many women want the best of home life and the best of the office, too. One privilege that women very often require and that is peculiar to their sex is time off for having babies. There have been promises (or threats) to have the doctor handy to deliver the baby at the office or to put in a playpen when the baby arrives. Rumor has it that there are a few such tolerant managements, but most of the time these remarks are made in jest. There is no question that maternity causes a few problems—and pleasures—in business as well as in the home. Most management women report, however, that their superiors have been more than decent in their maternity-leave policies. Good management people are cherished in most firms, and leave is usually granted with the special plea, "Don't stay away too long."

Even though we hear calls from the younger generation to stop the population explosion or to raise an underprivileged child rather than have your own, the desire for blood ties still runs deep in both men and women. Does this necessarily mean a long break in employment? Today's women are more like the Indian women who had their babies and went right on hoeing the corn. Maternity leave is planned carefully, and a leave of six months, five months, or only two months is not unusual for the busy woman executive. When women are really good at their jobs, this planned absence is not overwhelming. Men, too, are away from their jobs for long periods of time—the Harvard Business School management course runs 13 weeks, for example, almost enough time to have a baby and get back to work.

Until men start having babies or the artificial child is produced, women will need to take time off for this important function. Should this stop a manager from hiring and promoting a fine young woman? Do bright young men stay with the firm any longer? This is a question that management men should ask themselves. The women in management say, "Yes, we need a special privilege on this score, but aren't we worth it?" And their peers and their bosses answer in the affirmative. Of the 94 women who answered the questionnaire, 50 are married and 45 have children. Somewhere along the way they had maternity leave, and even though—or perhaps because—they have had children, they are handling management jobs competently.

Management women know that time off from the job must be planned carefully. Only emergencies or very special cases should require special privileges, and even then, if possible, the woman manager considers her work function. If a woman asks for special privileges because she is a woman, then maternity leave may be the one time when necessity requires it. The point to remember, say the women in this study, is not to make a big deal about it. Maternity leave should be fit into the normal leave practices of the company as carefully as possible. And the privilege should not be abused: A woman should not stay home longer or more often than is really necessary. Most women like sharing and comparing all the details of childbirth, but most men still can hardly stand this kind of chatter. And even though they are concerned about the health of a valuable employee, management men are more concerned about her being on the job when she is supposed to be. Women have been having babies for a long time. If a woman wants to keep her job, she should get back to it and tend to it.

When men talk about special privileges for women—especially when they are discussing the privileges that women expect—they are usually not thinking about maternity leave. They are thinking of the little pleasures of life that women traditionally have received and most women always have expected. The times have changed, however, and women, out in the workaday world, no longer are the sheltered flowers they used to be. Stories circulate about women who get highly insulted if men get up when they come into the room and who object strenuously when men let them into the cab first or so much as suggest that they are "girls." Often women have more money with them than the men they accompany, and frequently they are on expense accounts. Should they expect the same delicate treatment they have been in the habit of receiving? What is courtesy and what is good sense? This is where the difficulty arises in business etiquette.

How do the women in this study feel about such things as picking up the check, paying the taxis, carrying bags, and having men be over-polite? The replies are very mixed.

"When men jump up when I walk into the office or bounce up and down like Yo-Yo's, I get unhappy," says one woman executive. "But when I'm out at a business dinner or a work–social occasion, I like to be treated as a woman—my chair pulled out, help with my coat, and all the other niceties of being feminine."

If a woman is on an expense account and she can be unobtrusive, she acts like Nancy Knox, president of Renegades: "I believe the circumstances dictate one's deportment. In an appropriate business situation I have taken dinner checks and paid for taxis."

"I always volunteer to do so, then test the reaction," says Barbara Boyle, former manager of special programs at IBM, and now operating her own firm. "*Some* men's masculinity is endangered by a woman's assertions in many matters, so it's best to let them generally pay for the *small* items. I keep a mental tab, however, and good naturedly treat when it is acceptable and convenient to do so. It is extremely unfair for a woman to expect to always be taken care of. As far as chivalry is concerned (doors, bags, coats, and so on), I love it."

Playing it smart, Maria Vescia says, "If the male colleague and I are both on expense accounts, I would naturally straighten out expenses with him. I might let him take the dinner check and pay for the taxi but would settle with him later. If a man wants to open the door for me or carry my bag, that is great. I think it is fine for men to get up when I come into the room. I feel that a man should make some deference to a woman simply because she is a woman."

Some other reactions:

I think [being treated specially is] . . . great. I find I can always reciprocate with a small gift for birthdays or holidays if I choose.
—PATRICIA LEONARD

It is nice if they carry my bag, but unless we are on an expense account, costs should be divided or reciprocated. They have their expenses the same as I do. We are business colleagues.
—MARGARET A. GREEN

Yes, [I let them pick up the check] if they offer. Otherwise—Dutch, with no cute comments. —JANE M. ALEXANDER

Are such little things really asking for special favors? No, say most men and most women. Yet these are some of the things lesser men worry and fret about. Most men and women are mature and sensitive enough to know what action is appropriate at what time. And men enjoy being courteous as much as women enjoy their courtesy. Etiquette shouldn't interfere with business, but the little acts of considerateness between men and women make life pleasanter in the daily grind—just as good manners among men managers provide some relief from the jungle warfare of the business world.

When it comes right down to the job, however, women should not ask for special favors any more than a man should, except in rare cases. As Mary-Jane Raphael puts it, "If a woman takes an executive job, she will have to travel as much as any man holding the same position. (I travel well over 50 percent of the time.) What a woman must do is to organize her time so as to allow as much as possible with her family while at the same time fulfill all the responsibilities her job entails. This is really not difficult when you put your mind to it. In many ways, a woman can bring to her family life a greater understanding and worldly knowledge if she takes advantage to the fullest of what can be learned through travel."

Myth No. 4: Women Are Terrible Bosses and Men Don't Like to Work for Them

In our culture it is assumed that almost everybody, given the choice, would rather have a man than a woman as a boss—or, put another way, women make terrible bosses. Is this true? As in so many other cases, it depends on the individual, the circumstances, and the cultural background. When women are competent and understanding, men, as a rule, don't object to them as bosses.

Here is what Maria Vescia says about it: "Most men hate to work for women. Men do not like to take orders from women. This is inherent in the male mystique. It is the way they have been brought up in our society. Men still think they should dominate women and not be dominated by them."

Rita Perna says it well, too: "Good men do not hate to work for good women. Small-minded men are in difficulty because of their own small-mindedness, not because of women."

Mary Garzoni says, "Men do not necessarily hate to work for a woman boss. Some men hate to work for anyone. Some men like to work for women (reminds them of their mother). Some men resent working for women because they see the male role as being superior to the female role."

Carol Ivansheck makes this comment: "Probably the majority of men hate to work for a woman. Any man who doesn't want to work for a woman lacks confidence in himself and his masculinity. Men will be liberated when women are. These false fronts will be eliminated."

Here are some additional responses to the question of whether men object to working for a woman.

I don't believe a man objects to working for a woman if she is more competent and does not interject her private emotions on the job.   —PATRICIA LEONARD

Not particularly. Some do; some don't. Some feel we know our job and do it and either help or let them do theirs. A very limited number believe they can get concessions from us because of the male–female situation. These are the ones who end up our bitter enemies.   —MARGARET A. GREEN

Yes. [They] feel threatened. This depends a lot on cultural background. [It is] worse in Japanese and Latin–American men; but many Americans are very afraid of women.   —DR. HILDA PEDERSEN

No, men do not hate to work for or with women. It's a myth. But inferior men (as to quality of work or preparation) who want to get ahead nevertheless really seem to resent the good executive (male or female), and they will use this myth [to] . . . justify that resentment.   —EVA ROBINS

Many women bosses are conscious of the fact that they already have two strikes against them and hesitate to ask women who work for them—their secretaries, for instance—to do the ordinary things that a man expects to be done, such as going after airline tickets or making reservations at restaurants or running errands. It may be a real fault that the woman boss too often wastes her time on details that she rightfully should assign to someone who works for her.

If a woman (or a man, for that matter) gives credit where credit is due, then as a boss she is not resented. But just let her skip the credit line, and she is accused of acting "like a woman." A successful woman executive in New York was more heartily disliked than a man would have been in a similar situation because she claimed all successes as her own and attributed all mistakes to her subordinates. That is dirty pool in anybody's language.

Myth No. 5: Women Are Terrible Bosses, and Other Women Don't Like to Work for Them

What about women working for other women? Do women bosses show more than their share of bossiness to their female subordinates? The answer seems to be the same as in the case of male employees—yes and no. Ask the secretaries of some, and they will say, "A man boss wouldn't be so mean—he'd understand why I had to stay home." Maybe so. The feminine wiles of secretaries mean little to the woman boss—she can spot phony excuses better than most men. We women bosses may be a little more impatient than we should be with the foibles of the women who work for us. We've seen the tricks at first hand and perhaps are less willing to put up with them. Does this necessarily make us bad bosses? I hope in all sincerity that it does not.

More may be involved than skepticism and impatience. One woman remarks: "I've heard a great many women say they won't work for a woman. Perhaps it is that one woman feels more competitive with another woman and is therefore more resentful of organizational differences. Maybe the men—who have had more experience in subordinate–superior relationships—could help us all."

It would be wonderful if all women executives could have the reputation of Rhoda Stewart on this point. Dorothy Flynn, who has worked with Mrs. Stewart for a number of years, spoke about her boss in an interview:

"She is the most unselfish person I know. She is fair in her judgments. She has great administrative qualities. Contrary to many opinions about women bosses, she is *not* petty.

"She understands me better because she is a woman. Tricks that would work on a man boss just won't work here—she knows all the tricks.

"She understands that it is hard for a woman to get ahead in industry because she went the route herself. She really understands the importance of potential—especially among women. She knows that it is important to discern it and to use it. She keeps watching for opportunities for us to move ahead.

"She is aware of equal rights, asks and gets the same salary for women who are doing equal work with men. She does not look for loopholes.

"She leans over backward to give credit where credit is due.

"Besides that she is a beautiful woman. She has not lost her femininity. She is happily married.

"All in all, she is an exceptionally fine boss."

Among the nicest tributes paid to the new woman admiral, Alene Bertha Duerk, is that of a member of her staff. Captain Anna M. Byrnes, quoted in *The New York Times*, stressed that her boss was "very approachable—she doesn't stand on ceremony. She creates the atmosphere that makes it very easy to do your work." [1] The *Times* goes on to say, "This remark, combined with the general feeling of jubilance emanating from the Corps office today, seems to indicate that Captain Duerk has succeeded in communicating her personal philosophy to her associates."

Surely there are terrible women bosses who order their female subordinates about as if they were household slaves. But the ranks of such women bosses are getting thinner. The higher up the management ladder they go, the more concerned women are with human relations—maybe even more so than men. Men can sometimes get away with being tyrants, but women can't. No one smiles when somebody says, "She's a tough old biddy," but it's a different story when the remark is "What can you expect—*he's* only a bit eccentric."

Peggy Ogden's executive secretary says, "Working for a woman who is a successful executive is not essentially different from working for a successful male executive. One works *with* and for a person, and the relationship is satisfactory or not, depending upon the person and oneself."

Here are a few more quotes from subordinates of management women.

She's great. Better than a man boss because she is more understanding.

She does more than her share of the work—guess she is trying to prove . . . she's as good as people say she is.

My boss had been sitting buried in the controller's office for a long time. Someone discovered her talents and her background and now she is in our public relations department. This week she's off on a trip to Paris—on business. I think it's great. We've never had anyone in the department with as many wits or with as much understanding as she.

Myth No. 6: Women Can't Get Along with Their Peers, Especially Men

Do a woman's peers resent the fact that she is as good as they are, or even a bit better? Here is what one woman says about the peers of female executives:

"The higher up you get, the more apparent it is that top executive levels constitute a club. Most men nowadays grant women considerable ability, but they don't want us around on equal terms [in the club]. They are leery of us. We make them uncomfortable in this context."

And speaking of her peers, young Sharyn Yanoshak says, "The people I've worked with are intelligent and secure enough to help and subsequently recommend me. Many times a woman's real value is suspect because she is a woman. Therefore, all other things being equal, she must be better at what she does than a man in the same position. She is under pressure at first (especially if she is attractive) to prove she is good. Also she must use her femininity (along with her other qualities) effectively. I don't think a man has to use his masculinity."

In certain specialized technical fields, such as law, medicine, and scientific research, women are usually respected by their peers for what they know. The same is true in such new professional areas as consumerism and equal rights enforcement. In general, however, women have to be better than their male peers, as both workers and bosses, and must recognize the touchiness of the situation. Like Avis, they have to try harder.

Myth No. 7: Management Women Have Lost Their Femininity

The difficult question of having all the necessary drive usually exhibited by a fine male manager and still retaining femininity is discussed in more detail in Chapter 7. The following remarks give a general idea of the feelings of people in business on this topic.

The old version of a successful woman was one who took on all the characteristics of a man, including his dress. Pictures of women in business 50 years ago show lower-level workers wearing skirts and blouses and the few women managers (Lillian Gilbreth excepted) dressed in mannish suits with tie and cuff links to add to the illusion. Nowadays most women no longer strive to look like men. The pants suits of today are a far cry from the masculine attire of yore. Women usually dress well and choose apparel appropriate to the job.

Many people seem to think that swearing is a trait common to women managers and attribute it to an attempt to affect masculinity. Must women automatically quit swearing when they take on a management job? Is swearing really a male prerogative? And do women managers really swear any more than men or than their nonworking sisters? Just as there are a few men managers noted for their very colorful terminology, there are also a few women whose vocabulary is the talk of management circles. (There are rumors that Helen Delich Bentley, head of the Maritime Commission, can use words that even the sailors haven't heard.) Does this mean that a youngster coming into this field should learn a couple of fiery swear words in order to get the job? The answer is no, but she shouldn't forget the ones she does know because in a working life there are plenty of times when letting off steam (privately) with a few strong words may ease her tensions.

It seems that even though women take on so-called men's jobs, their peers and most men who are their bosses like to have them retain their femininity. Here is what the women said when asked, "What qualities, performance factors, and so on, make a female executive successful? What makes a *good* female a good female executive?"

Jean Moore attributes success in a woman manager to "perception (knowing when to and when not to), acceptance by men, being strong but not . . . aggressive."

Eva Robins says: "She must not try to look like or act like anything but what she is—trying to act like a man is silly. She must not throw around her 'femaleness'—comments about going home to cook dinner are unnecessary, and for her own sake, she had better not volunteer to sew on a button. She must be prepared for promotion—not give the impression that she has found a permanent niche and does not want to compete upward—and must be good at her job."

A woman psychologist says: "All-around competence in performance of job duties is basic, but beyond this a female often has to be self-assertive, make the right decisions quickly, and handle subordinates with firmness and humor."

Peggy Ogden recognizes that both men and women can have the same characteristics. She says, "A good executive spends a lot of time working at being a good boss. I have been fortunate to have had several good bosses in my career (some of them have been women), but without exception, the good women bosses saw themselves as bosses first and women second. Hence, they were able to work at being a good woman *boss* rather than a good *woman* boss.

"Conversely, I have had a few bad bosses, and sex had little to do with it. I'm convinced that on the subject of bad bosses, be it man or woman, a bitch by any other name . . ."

When asked directly the question, "Do you think you should still try to retain your femininity?" 90 percent of the women said yes, but with reservations. They said sex shouldn't make a difference on the job, but they could see no reason why they shouldn't retain their own natural manners or techniques. They thought that their male bosses seemed to like the fact that they had competent women on their staff, and it was an extra asset if they looked pretty, too. And practically all well-dressed, well-groomed, well-educated management women of today know the value of staying female or, as some of them put it, "thinking like a man, looking like a doll, and working like a horse."

Myth No. 8: Women Use Dirtier Tactics than Men to Climb Up the Ladder

Are women likely to use underhanded techniques in moving up the management ladder, as some people allege? Perhaps you can judge from the following remarks whether men or women are less scrupulous on the job.

Some jobs require constant travel by a mixed group of executives.

On one such trip a woman executive refused the advances of one of the men. Did he go home and forget about it? No, he spread the word back in the home office that Mrs. X really lived it up on the road. Worst of all, he made an anonymous call to the woman's husband, saying that his wife was misbehaving while she was traveling. Can you get much lower than that? Fortunately, most men don't like such tactics either, but if this woman hadn't been like Caesar's wife, then her career *and* home could have been really harmed.

Is taking credit for someone else's work a male or a female tactic? Since so many more women are in a supportive role, and so many more bosses are men, the person reluctant to give credit where credit is due is more often a male. Some women bosses do the same, of course, failing to give the men their due, and, as we have noted, women are more likely than men to be resented on this account. Perhaps more women will be guilty of such misconduct, when they attain top spots.

What about stepping on someone's neck to get ahead and apple polishing for the next promotion? Women claim that they have to be better in order to move up the ladder, that they have to get there on their own ability. But perhaps because men have been so reluctant to give up the management reins, women have had to become more aggressive. It is too bad that the women's liberation movement and the Equal Employment Opportunity Commission have had to shock management into taking a better inventory of the management skills among its women employees. Many now-successful women abhor the more blatant approaches and audacious demands of women's liberationists. However, many of them admit that their own way was a slow, hard process to reach the near-top rungs of the management ladder. Will the liberationists attain by demand what they are after? Not unless they can demonstrate that they really have the ability to do the job. Aggressiveness may help them get the jobs, but competence alone will insure that they keep the jobs. But if the aggressiveness displayed by overambitious women comes under the name of dirty techniques, then the women involved have probably learned them from some of the men with whom they have been associated.

The success of a career is probably the best indicator of the nature of the techniques used to achieve that success. The women in the survey attribute theirs to good education, hard work, understanding bosses, good timing, and luck. But if you have worked long enough, you'll have seen plenty of dirty techniques used as well. Some have been played out by masters at the game, and some seemingly have succeeded. Women's score versus men's on this issue? The men are ahead, but it may be because there are so many more of them. Advice to young women coming into the field (if you will take it): Stay clear of move-fast, step-on-the-neck deals. You may move up a few rungs on the ladder, but your perch is a very precarious one if you don't hold it by competence. Sounds old-fashioned, but you still have to live with yourself. Many executives with years of experience, some of it very troublesome, agree.

Myth No. 9: Women Can't Do Two Jobs Well—Either Home or Career Must Suffer

It is often said that you can't have two jobs and do both of them well. Can women be good wives and mothers and good managers, too? This question will be discussed in more detail in Chapter 8. The picture that one gets from the women questioned is overwhelmingly one of the manager who knows how to organize her work so that she can also be married. She seems to move with ease in both worlds—though some women, as pointed out in specific examples in Chapter 8, have preferred to stay home and manage their businesses from there.

The 50 married women in the survey think their marriages are great.

The management women who have children are especially proud of them. Because they have put much effort into making home relationships work, perhaps—and only perhaps—because their children are less neglected than those of many "traditional" families, who must put up with today's often unsettled home life. The women in management, because they are keenly aware of today's problems, are probably more concerned about their children than the average mother. (But no accusation of nonworking mothers should be inferred because the concern of parents everywhere these days is common knowledge.)

A few women in the survey are divorced, but what group of women today doesn't have some divorcées? Some of the younger women are looking forward to marriage, and those who are not married seem secure, too. The answer, however, as to the possibility of having both a happy marriage and family and a successful career is an unreserved yes.

Myth No. 10: Women Returning to the Job Market Are Unskilled

There is another management myth that women returning to the job market after having stayed home to raise their children must accept menial jobs. It is true that too many of them are bewildered and willing to take almost anything, but it just doesn't have to be that way.

Many management women wait until their children are of school age before returning to the job market. As Ray A. Killian says in *The Working Woman—A Male Manager's View,* "The most stable employee is the woman over 35, married or single, who is career-oriented. Modern women often marry immediately after completing high school or college, have fewer children, and usually do not have any more children after 27. This means that the youngest child is ready for school when the mother is only 33. According to statistics she still has 32 years of potential employment before retirement." [2]

Does this mean that a woman must start from scratch if she comes back to the job market? Not necessarily: She starts where her skills are. If she has gained a considerable reputation or has very special skills, she can walk back to a position whose level corresponds to her experience. There is no use kidding young people and saying that six or seven years away doesn't make any difference—because it does. And if a woman waits too long—20 or 30 years—she had better have very good qualifications or she will find returning to work very hard.

Special skills in writing, communications, mathematics, data processing, teaching, or personnel, for example, will help a woman get back into the market in a job that is at least a few steps up. If a woman marries young and has no special business skills, she'll start at 33, with perhaps maturity in her favor, at a job other women begin at 20 or 21. But the woman with foresight will not have wasted all her time at home. Some of the skills employers are looking for she can acquire on her own. She can also find schools that will help her brush up on her skills. Some smart suburban women have even organized seminars for just that purpose. A management man starting a new company or store in suburbia would do well to canvass the area for topflight women *managers* as well as typists, secretaries, and factory help.

Myth No. 11: Young Married Women Can't Take Management Jobs Because They Will Move with Their Executive Husbands

This myth does have some substance. Young women married to ambitious young executives will usually leave their own jobs the minute their husbands' jobs require a change of location. Nevertheless, it sometimes works to management's advantage to find out in advance what the case really is. A potentially good young woman manager was almost passed over because of her youth and because management knew she was married, but it turned out that her husband was a writer and could move almost anyplace. In another instance the husband was a professor who could get a job almost anywhere, and in still another the woman held a higher-level job than her husband, so he could find another job more easily than she could. The point is that the potential woman manager deserves the courtesy of a discussion of this topic. Her boss shouldn't assume she can't pick up her household and move to wherever the new job may be. By keeping in mind the differences in the family situations of his female employees, a manager has nothing to lose and much to gain.

Most negative conceptions of women managers, then, are really just *myths*. They effectively keep vast numbers of women out of top-level jobs despite the fact that they simply don't apply to modern women in today's fast-paced management world.

3
EXPLODING SOME
OF THE MYTHS

In Chapter 2 we talked about the myths surrounding the management woman. Now we will try to tell you what the management woman is really like. From what we can determine from personal observation, the remarks of other executives, and primarily from the remarks of women themselves, she is a down-to-earth, hardworking person. When we analyze some of her characteristics and work habits, many of the myths fall apart.

"Woman Talk"—Do Management Women
Have Time for It?

"Woman talk," conversation that deals with diapers, dishes, and the minutiae of clothes, food, and bargains, is not the province of the woman executive. Like her male counterparts, she is too busy doing her job. Long telephone calls or conversations on extremely personal matters may happen more often among women clerks than among men in similar jobs, but women in the executive suite can't take time for such trivia —or at least not very often. Incidentally, have you heard men executives boasting about their skills in the kitchen or on the golf course? Same thing, isn't it? Perhaps people on the clerical and routine level are more interested in outside activities because they find their jobs somewhat dull. It is sometimes a hard bridge for a secretary or administrative assistant to cross over—to leave her friends in their effervescent environment and take on a more sedate role in the management circles.

Gossipy? Who isn't interested in what goes on in the office? Again, think of where you heard the latest information on the new female assistant. "Why, did you know she was in his office with the door closed?" or, "Let's take bets on how long she'll last." Man or woman? Men are the first to notice, too, when old Joe starts to slip. "Did you know he's getting senile?" is more apt to come from a man than from a woman. As cruel as gossip can be, it is not applicable to women alone. The line is thin between gossip and news—but to accuse women of being in the gossip business to the exclusion of men is a gross fallacy.

Other Characteristics

Are women more vicious than men? Will they step on anyone's neck to get ahead? Does setting your goal high or reaching for the stars (which one executive describes as her reason for success) brand you as overambitious? Anyone who has been in the working world for any period of time knows that there are some eager beavers, men and women, who are overambitious, who will do a bit of neck stepping. From a review of the questionnaires, the conclusion seems to be that women are more anxious to succeed on their own than to depend on favoritism, false pretenses, or dirty pool. As one of them says, "I couldn't afford either morally or businesswise to have had to reach this spot on the heads of those I bypassed."

So-called overambitious women are said to have ruined many men or at the very least to have made their lives hell on earth. But the "ruin" of these men rarely can be attributed to a woman co-worker. Most likely nonworking wives make their husbands' lives miserable by perpetually needling them to achieve more social prestige or more material possessions. Frequently, these women are unfamiliar with the perplexities of the job world and cannot understand why they can't have what they want. Working women, on the other hand, know the job world very well and are less likely to drive their husbands to ulcers.

But there may be another, infinitely more important reason why a working woman does not make unrealistic demands on her husband. When a talented woman is able to achieve personal fulfillment in her career, she has no need to seek substitutes for such fulfillment. But women forced into the traditional role of housewife and mother, with no opportunity for self-fulfillment, see no other way to vent their frustration and latent anger. Often they erroneously see material gain as a way to achieve their pent-up needs for social and intellectual fulfillment and have no choice but to demand substitute symbols of success through their husbands' achievements.

Some women claim that they failed to reach the very top because they have been conditioned to playing second fiddle, to being told what their place is. For the most part society has reinforced this conditioning. Therefore, how can they be accused of being overambitious? As one executive puts it, "Women just aren't supposed to know too much about business." And another, "I never figured I would get as far as I have. It seems almost accidental that I am now a vice president. I find no such reluctance among the younger women executives I know. They want to know where they are going, how they are going to get there, and can't we double up on the timetable."

In the current management setup, where goal setting is one of the characteristics of our time, now *young* women demand and are getting the same treatment as young male executives. Why shouldn't they be told why they do or do not meet what is expected of them? If women are to take on men's jobs, then they must take on men's responsibilities too.

One of the strongest factors keeping women from moving up the management ladder is their reluctance (or inability because their traditional role has followed them to the office) to cast aside home responsibilities. "There have been times in my career when I had to make my choice about giving more of my time to the office and neglecting home. I had to choose home and perhaps missed at least one promotion," says one executive.

Are women perfect? Not by a long shot. Here is what one outstanding woman said, "Women have a lack of confidence, have arrogance when they do get promoted, fail in knowing how to work with people, attempt to be sexy instead of taking care of [business]. One subordinate said of his woman boss when she was promoted, "We can't get past the three secretaries she now maintains. She's surely different from what she used to be."

Do women depend on their looks to help them get ahead? There are good-looking women who really depend on their looks to get themselves noticed, particularly on the first big job. Being good-looking is surely an asset for woman, just as it is for a man. As one young executive says of his extra-charming, bright young assistant, "She gets their attention, surprises the client on how smart she is, and then I move in and help clinch the sale."

Or as another good-looking girl puts it when asked why she had made it, "Personality and *looks*, sincerity, listening, and being kind seem to have helped me."

"I think the ability to 'turn on' a male can really get you . . . recognized and then promoted," says another.

Sex on the Job

What about sex on the job? Help or hindrance? Here is what the women say.

> Boy, do I work with squares. Ours is a very unsordid executive suite. I really don't think our president knew whether I was male or female for the first ten years I worked there. If any man tried to imply that I needed him to get ahead, I'd toss him (or the job) over my shoulder. Even though "the boys" treat me like one of them (or their pet poodle), basically I like the respect they show me. I know that they are proud when we are out together at a business function and I look and act like a woman.
>
> —VICE PRESIDENT

> I won't say it hasn't been tempting; however, I want a permanent arrangement, so I don't want to get involved with a married person. I have a wonderful time and relationship with many men— basically end up knowing their families.
>
> —DIRECTOR OF MANAGEMENT DEVELOPMENT

> I have no problems as far as sex is concerned. I feel romantic involvement is asking for trouble. Romance and love can very easily turn to resentment and hate. If you want to get romantically involved, do so with someone other than a colleague.   —PRESIDENT

> Remember that involvement in business courts disaster. Feminine wiles can stand one in good stead if used with discretion—to make a point. The feminine charms should not be submerged, but used to good advantage for business. Top-level executives generally accept a woman for her professional talent and ability—not her sex.
>
> —PRESIDENT

> A good sense of humor gets over some rough spots in this area. Most of the men I meet are married, so if I feel they are heading in directions I'm not interested in, I start to evidence great interest

in their children—children can be a very "diffusing" topic of conversation. During business hours, I try to keep my business and social life separate. I don't, for example, bring dates to our office parties. —ANONYMOUS

Fortunately, I've never had problems. As for a romantic involvement, I would feel that it can be accomplished if both are mature, well-adjusted individuals who don't expect the impossible in said relationship. —ANONYMOUS

It's just different for different people. I have known of affairs which were very stimulating and fruitful and made both people work at a very high level. Naturally, they can also be disastrous. Depends on the participants. —ANONYMOUS

The consensus still seems to be: "Don't mix business and pleasure." When the romance cools, it is difficult for either party to continue to operate.

Working with male colleagues is lots of fun. Most women admit it gives an extra, nice touch to the job—it lightens the going when things get tough. The underlying sex challenge and appeal don't disappear just because you are working together, but if you really care about your job, to get seriously involved with a colleague is playing with fire. Leave the escapades to someone else; don't be the one to give management women a bad reputation.

"And if you do get involved, for Heaven's sake, keep your mouth shut," says one woman executive who eventually married her boss. "We were in love, but I honestly don't think it showed at the office. In fact we both worked hard to destroy any sign of partiality."

So, if you have women executives on your staff or if you want to promote the young ones, you can be assured that most of them, if they are smart enough to do the work, will also be smart enough not to foul up the works by getting involved in sex on the job.

Pet Names for Women

Men often think they are paying us compliments on the job when they give us pet names like "broads," "dolls," "babes," "girls," "chippies," and "dames." Many times these words are meant to be somewhat endearing terminology, but it seems that most women executives don't take them as such. It is a little surprising how serious most of us are—can't take a joke when it's meant that way. The trouble is, too often these terms are evidently not used in jest, or at least the women don't think they are.

Some "girls" take these remarks in stride and some don't. Here are some of the reactions:

I think it's cheap and common. My male colleagues know better.

No one says that to me any more and it makes me a little sad— guess there is too much of a gap and they don't kid me any more.

I feel that this depends on how the expression is used and in what vein it is said.

I don't care—mostly I grin—I think they are like kids showing off.

I have heard them so long that I guess I tend to accept it as part of the vocabulary. They seem to need it.

To me it depends upon the person and how he said it, and the time and place. If I objected to any particular expression, I would tell the man so privately.

I don't care. Where's your sense of humor?

Behind Every Successful Man Stands a Good Woman

Occasionally from a public platform an orator talking about a great executive will say that often a good share of the credit goes to a subordinate who has shored up her boss all along. In ringing words he'll intone, "Behind every good man there is a good woman." Again, it sounds great the first time, but the second time around you begin to think you would like some of the real credit in better recognition, in title, and in cold, hard cash.

Some of the women's reactions to "Behind every good man there is a good woman" are:

Behind every woman, too.

Very often and vice versa, too.

Most of the time this is true. Shall we also say that a bad woman can help to break a man?

I don't mind. I'm proud to help my boss. I think he is wonderful and I'm glad to be his chief assistant and backer.

It's a gallant expression—I think it is true.

If you really want to make a woman executive unhappy, just tell her she doesn't belong in the office. Start longing for the old days when her place was in the kitchen, and be prepared to get hit over the head. If you imply that she's so good at everything that you expect she's good in the kitchen, too, that's a different story. Here's how the women react to the saying "Women belong in the kitchen."

> *This is an oldie.*

> *Just because you're an executive, it doesn't mean you can't be good in the kitchen.*

> *Up to a point women should enjoy being in the kitchen, but she should be there because she wants to be.*

Personal Characteristics That Have Held Women Back

Here is how the women answered when asked, "What do you think are women's chief hangups on the job?"

> *General sensitivities, which women find harder to submerge than men.*

> *Lack of perspective. . . . Imagined discrimination. If she's dumb enough, trading on her sex.*

> *I found that the worst hangup a woman has is emotion and jealousy.*

> *The conviction that they will be discriminated against. Anybody, man or woman, who carries around a sense of outrage at what might happen, invites the happening. Also I think women generally have not let management know that they consider themselves prepared to—and capable of—moving up. Women too often have latched onto a male executive (the "boss" complex) and have failed to see themselves as individual producers.*

> *Oversensitive reaction to situations, tendency to become defensive, fear of being named an overaggressive female—so there is a tendency to not be as aggressive as you might want, tendency to avoid real "confrontations."*

> *Many of us have been confused by years of propaganda to the point where we don't know what our proper role is, what we want to make of ourselves. Thanks to the mass media some of us even rather like the idea of being chiefly a 'sex object.' Also it is unfortunately the truth that most women react emotionally both to crisis and criticism (more than men do), although it is possible to train oneself not to.*

> *I think the answer would be that they have to adjust to the fact that most men think they are a little better and a little more capable than most women.*

A lack of direction as regards career aspirations. A false impression that speaking up or taking a leadership role will be considered aggressive or unfeminine.

Taking things personally on the job.

False notions that the young and pretty girls get all the best breaks—tendency to be petty about unimportant details—hesitancy to take the initiative in getting the responsibilities and/or promotion—having a tendency to want it handed them because they "deserve it"—chip-on-the-shoulder attitude of "women are discriminated against in business"—defensive attitude about personal matters (home, children, boyfriends, and so on).

Feeling they are inferior to males and cannot succeed as well as a male. Thinking their place is the traditional one of getting coffee and doing the dirty work. Because they think that way, they are not hard workers, but giggling flirts and not worth promoting.

Many women are not tuned to delegate responsibilities—they feel they have attained their goals through sheer "guts" and will not give up the reins, even though occasionally they may be wrong.

Wondering if my decisions and reactions are truly as objective as I think they are. Feeling guilty at hiring women rather than men even when [the women] are better qualified. Yet men hire men and nothing is thought unusual about it.

By an examination of these answers, taken at random, you see that women are aware that they have personal "weaknesses" that keep them from pushing too hard, are aware of the sensitive spot they play in today's topsy-turvy world. They are too much aware of the traditional role which is expected of them. It has been hard to break the mold, as you can tell from the above remarks. However, women have succeeded in spite of these hangups.

Men's Hangups—Are They Worse Than Women's?

Perceptive women try to understand why their men bosses or colleagues act the way they do. Most women understand that the boss has his hangups, too. He worries about his job and his image, and it seems nothing can scare the pants off him quicker than a smart woman who lets it be known directly or indirectly that she is after his job. The insecure men are discussed here by the women who work with or for them. Secure executives, men and women, are not afraid of being "overthrown" and encourage their women subordinates to move up the ladder. Here is how the women view the problems of their bosses. Some of the comments are harsh and some reflect understanding of the male ego. Here is what they say in answer to the question, "How do you view the hangups of the men (vis-à-vis women executives) who are or have been colleagues or bosses?"

This is difficult to evaluate, but it has appeared as though many of the men I worked with in the past have felt threatened, and perhaps subconsciously resentful, to find any woman reach a supervisory level. I believe most of these men are themselves victims of the culture that has for so long caused them to downgrade women's work. Their attitudes are inbred, but many of them are making genuine efforts to develop open minds on the subject. A few find it almost impossible to change. I have been fortunate in that none of my supervisors to date have had any hangups toward me as a subordinate and, as individuals, have not discriminated against me.

Petty. Bad-tempered. Poor communicators, inconsistent, poor delegators.

Fear of a woman having the upper hand.

Male executives recognize females as top-notch assistants but won't let them into the mainstream of an established organization. They regard a competent female as "special."

I always prefer a man who is ambitious and self-confident; he is going someplace. When he is secure, he is ready to accept all the help I can give him. When he is insecure it presents a problem, for he's uncertain about any help he receives unless it is from someone less strong than himself.

Masculine ego—not feeling comfortable in a situation in which a woman has more knowledge than the man. Even though the man may know that the woman has more information or knowledge, he may not want to be in a situation which to him seems inferior. Some men are scared of smart or capable women.

Reluctance to delegate responsibility, distrust of women's ability to keep a secret, fear that she will learn too much about his business and become a threat to his position, procrastination, feelings of inadequacy or discomfort if she has more education than he.

Since 1962 (now that I think about it) I have been the only woman professional in the areas in which I worked. In that period only one man evidenced the "barefoot and pregnant" syndrome.

I think a man has to be very secure in his own personal strength and job abilities to feel comfortable in working with a bright woman, to say nothing of encouraging her to advance. It's a two-way relationship. Her advancement might mean his being pushed aside—survival of the fittest. I've had good bosses except in one flagrant case. Mostly they placed me where I could enlarge my sphere laterally instead of rising. My pay raises reflected a "dual ladder" approach.

Fear of "unreliability" of women. Fear of waste of education. Find women difficult to deal with. Resentment of absences due to pregnancy, family commitments.

A need to overprotect a woman—not promoting her until she is overqualified for the position.

Not taking a woman's views seriously—except on social or feminine matters.

I have found that men, particularly those who are insecure or unsure of themselves (professionally or personally), are uncertain about how to take women in their world. These are the type of men who would never let their wives work or who are just uncomfortable with women in general.

Here are other prejudices the women had encountered.

"A woman's place is in the home." Why isn't she married or at home raising a family?

Every woman has some man supporting her, so she doesn't need a well-paying job.

An attractive woman will marry sooner or later and choose home-making rather than a career.

Women are not promotable.

An able woman can't find a better job elsewhere—hence she'll have to take her lot here and like it.

Then every once in a while you find a woman like Cynthia Wedel, who says, "I seem to have been unusually lucky because I've worked with many men—subordinates, peers, and bosses—who really seemed quite free of hangups."

Another woman says, "Competitive urges increase in spades if women are in competition for the same job. All this melts if the woman's job is subordinate to his."

Thinking and Acting Like a Man

It seems, too, that men more than women, perhaps because men are insecure, will lean more on the old excuses to describe their women colleagues. Most successful women have heard the so-called complimentary phrases (which supposedly bring them in closer rapport with their male colleagues) hundreds of times. When you are young, the first time you are told that you think and act like a man you get all choked up and think, "Gee, he thinks I'm great." Now, after all the years, the compliment is pretty timeworn and you look at the man who is saying it and you are not so sure. It evidently is one of the clichés that the new women executives dislike the most. Times change and most women don't think it is such a compliment any more. Here is what the women executives said when asked, "What does it mean when a male executive says that you think and act like a man?"

> *This is supposed to be a compliment?*
>
> *Naturally men think they have better minds than women. Actually, the training that a woman receives today in college and business enables her to think in the same way that a man thinks. This is due, however, basically to training rather than to the sex of the individual.*
>
> *No resentment. He is saying that you're hard-nosed, tough, a clear thinker, and objective. He believes he's being complimentary. He's suggesting you are logical and well-organized in presenting thoughts.*
>
> *Obviously a compliment is intended and, since we still live in a somewhat chauvinistic male world, the wise woman accepts the compliment graciously.*
>
> *He is enchanted with himself. What he means is, "She thinks like me." And obviously he thinks that's great. Whenever it's been said of me, I've asked, "Which man?"*
>
> *He thinks this is the ultimate compliment because he is convinced that male thinking is always superior, more logical, et cetera, et cetera.*

What Can You Expect—She's a Woman!

Another phrase often used in the executive suite, especially after a woman has made a foolish mistake, will make female managers crawl the walls. If a man says, "What can you expect—she's a woman!" you would like to haul off and sock him one. But being the polite, refined lady executive that you are, you keep your physical violence under control, but that doesn't keep your temperature from rising. Most of the women executives questioned feel strongly about this unfair accusation;

they usually take the irritating remark in stride but certainly don't like it. So, men executives, don't throw this one at us too often or you'll stir up deep-seated resentment.

Here is how the women reacted to this remark—

This statement could only be made seriously by an extremely chauvinistic, narrow-minded, unintelligent individual, whom I could no longer respect.

When that is said by a man, he is clumping together all general weak characteristics about women he has been brought up to accept.

Haven't heard this in years! Patronizing is much more sophisticated these days. [The attitude is] *still there, though.*

This phrase is frequently used by men if a woman executive makes a mistake. If a male executive made the same mistake he would not receive the same criticism. In other words, female executives can't afford to make mistakes.

Seems to me this is an unfair and biased declaration and one I, personally, would dismiss as childish. However, it is this type of demeaning statement that encourages militant and radical movements among women.

Women Should Do the "Feminine" Chores

It has often been said that it is the little, irritating things about the male–female office relationship that cause the most trouble. Some women take themselves so seriously that any act that smacks of discrimination makes them belligerent. There are wide variations of opinion among women about being asked to take notes at a meeting or to do some of the other "feminine" chores. "They wouldn't ask a man to do this" or, "I have to get the coffee ready and pour it—do they think I'm a servant?" are two typical reactions.

Despite all the indignant remarks from the women, there is a time when it is proper to take on these chores.

When it is your job to see that everything goes well at a meeting, you had better see that these details are decided ahead of time. There is no sense in making a fuss in public over your hurt feelings at doing such a demeaning job. If your scene making detracts from the business at hand, then it is not surprising that your men colleagues are taken aback. There are ways of getting around these chores, as so many of the women's answers indicate. Men bosses, however, remember that these little things are the ones that may irritate your women executives the most. Better find out ahead of time how they feel. It may save you much embarrassment and hard feelings.

Here are some of the responses to the question "What is your reaction if a male executive suggests that you take notes (or serve coffee) at a meeting?"

Indignation—at being forced to assume an inferior service-type role. If I volunteered to do so, fine!

[I say I'm] happy to do it. I ask for a . . . tip.

It's very important to move him off that image of you, but with grace. One way is to say, "I'll do it this session and then let's take turns." Be sure also never to offer—it does only harm.

There are a few gracious women who act out the "role" of hostess at any meeting without losing the respect of their male colleagues. This goes for serving coffee but not taking notes.

No! This is demeaning and the man who asks it is neither perceptive nor sensitive, unless your job is to take notes and serve coffee. Suggestion: Ask if it is your turn to do it and get the chore rotated among all attendants.

I tell them that even I can't read my notes when I get done. This gets a good laugh, but they get the point. I take my own notes anyway—I don't want to miss anything.

Doesn't really bother me—the younger women tell me it should.

I would probably grin to myself and do it. Men are used to having women take notes. Men are used to thinking of women as secretaries. There would be no point in refusing and creating a scene. Nothing could be gained.

It doesn't happen very often. When it does, I don't mind. In fact, I kind of enjoy doing the little feminine things (as long as men still treat me as their equal). I think men ask women to do these things for the same reason that women let men open doors for them.

I'm president, so the men never suggest it.

If everyone present is more or less on the same executive or professional level, I try very gently and tactfully to point out that it is someone else's turn, and suggest that perhaps Mr. So-and-So would like to take care of these chores for a change. I do so because I am frequently the only woman present at such top-level meetings and it has always been assumed in the past that I would take the notes (or serve the coffee), and I believe most men have been quite unconscious of the fact that they have automatically assumed I would do these chores. If one handles this type of situation with humor and in kindly fashion, I have found it takes care of itself. Everyone laughs and then one of the men present "volunteers."

Personal Characteristics
Leading to Success

Cynthia Wedel sums up the personal characteristics that make women successful: "Self-assurance, a sense of humor, willingness to give and take criticism, honesty in dealing with people, tough-mindedness, not looking for or magnifying slights or prejudices."

Judith Vladeck puts it this way: "Knowledge of the job, willingness to make decisions, willingness to be wrong, and ability to delegate."

Alice Kehoe says she must have these characteristics: "Fairness— an ability to see both sides of the question or performance before making a judgment, understanding of the personal load and capacity of the particular employee, and finally ability to perform at many levels (and her willingness to do this when needed). Most employees respect a working boss."

Betty Duval calls it "swinging with the punches" and being sensitive to the needs of others.

Mary-Jane Raphael says it this way, "I've reached my present job level because I have worked hard, I have done my job well and had good friends from whom I tried to learn as much as I could. I treat each day as a learning experience and hopefully will continue to do so the rest of my life. I believe my primary assets to be intelligence, dedication, ambition, patience, respect for my superiors and colleagues alike, ability to get along with people, a sense of humor."

Here is what others say on the subject:

A man can succeed if he is good; a woman must be excellent.

She has to be as intelligent and unemotional as a man; she can not flirt or cry. A woman is sensitive to other people; she is practical.

She has to be superior in every way—man can be mediocre but have the correct credentials or mentor within the company. She has to subtly make sure the right people know what kind of job she is doing and has been doing. She has to be feminine when that is required and a powerhouse without [appearing to be] one.

Work harder than male executives, who may have spent much of their thinking time on a wider view of what is expected of them. Do a lot of forgiving: she's poaching on their territory, and must expect them to fight back. They fight other men, why not a woman?

The ability to be objective above pettiness on the job—to be able to delegate work—and responsibility for projected projects which may go awry on the job—to meet a challenge with boldness and ride with it!

I have seen nothing thus far to change my opinion that in order to be successful as a woman executive or professional, it is nearly always necessary to work much harder and longer than men in similar positions. Men are permitted to exhibit emotion on a job, but a woman shows emotion at her peril. A woman executive has to be dignified, always well dressed, efficient, tactful, understanding, diplomatic, self-sacrificing, perhaps even self-effacing under certain circumstances. If she has too much "drive," or is too aggressive, she can destroy her career because most men in positions of authority heartily dislike these traits in a woman, although finding them acceptable and desirable in other men. In addition, it is generally necessary for a woman executive to be overqualified for the job in comparison with the qualifications expected of a man for a similar position.

Be better prepared. Learn not to always show the preparation too openly with males. Not fall for women's lib per se [without first studying its philosophy carefully].

Do women really have the qualities Bette Heydrick talked about earlier? We honestly hope so. Here is the way she says it: "Women have natural diplomacy, loyalty (women tend to remain with one company and in one location because of family ties, roots, and so on), background in human relations (from rearing children, working with club groups, organizations); women are natural planners and organizers, and once they set standards or objectives are persistent in working toward them. Gentleness of manner (a woman's presence often brings out the best in men), ability to divide her attention between several things, not losing sight of any."

Many men will vouch for a woman's tenaciousness on a pet project. They complain that women won't let go. Some women have been accustomed to using the flank approach (no snide remark intended) to get what they want from their husbands and will use the same tactics at the office.

Men seem to accept such tactics better at home than they do at the office. Often, unfortunately, women don't see the whole perspective and emphasize their own pet projects too much. If men managers were more willing to explain the whole, maybe they wouldn't experience this persistence of *some* of their women managers. Some managers have even had the gall to insinuate that just because you are concerned you are nagging them.

Another woman says, "The more I work and observe other really successful executives, male or female, the more I'm convinced that the old virtue of integrity—the willingness to stand up and be counted for what you believe is right—is an absolute must. I'm not talking about the fast-buck, floating executive, but the one you can count on for good sense and honesty. May sound old-fashioned, but try working for a bunch of cutthroats and you'll double your respect for the person with integrity. Interestingly enough, he or she is the successful one in the long run."

Or, as one man puts it, "I've grown to really respect the talents of other people. I find women are just as bright, just as talented, just as honorable, and just as human as the next capable executive."

It is to be hoped that more and more management people will say the same as time goes on and that the condescending manners toward women because of any false impression of their personal characteristics will become a thing of the past. Just one sniveling, overambitious, loud-mouthed, ill-prepared female who tries to make it by using her emotion-alism or demanding differential treatment on the basis of her sex can do much to set us back a good many years. Women in management jobs still can't afford the luxury of having as many inept members in manage-ment as men can. It's still, unfortunately, a testing period.

All in all, the humanistic, personal characteristics of men and women can't be left behind when these managers enter the executive suite. If the office becomes devoid of all humor, if there are no rumors or even some gossip, if it is all work and no play, then the business world must be on the downgrade. A lively, progressive office is bound to have its human side, and both men and women executives want it to remain that way. It is going to be rough if everything is dehumanized—no fun and not so much accomplished either. And just as among men, you'll find all kinds—good bosses and lousy bosses; kind, decent human beings and vicious, mean characters; intelligent and dumb individuals. It is hoped that the more positive balance will be achieved.

This doesn't let men or women off the hook in trying to improve their personal habits on the job. This chapter has revealed a few of the secret sore spots, which, hopefully, can be healed.

4

UNUSUAL JOBS FOR WOMEN

Management, which has been traditionally male, has conceded that women are needed to fill the numerous tedious, time-consuming, necessary jobs in factories, offices, hospitals, and education. In factories you will find women on drill presses, assembling the minute parts in radio plants, and in the clean rooms of missile plants where assembly of parts is done under a microscope. In offices the majority of clerks and secretaries are female. Nurses, nurses' aides, and cleanup women are essential units of the hospital workforce. And who among us remembers our elementary and high school days without remembering our favorite female teachers? We have not yet come to the decision to have many women street cleaners or heavy laborers, as is the case in some countries. Facts, as they stand today, indicate that women as a class have been relegated to the less responsible positions and most often to the menial jobs in our society.

Top executives, plus the general public, have been loath to concede that women can perform equally as well as men in management jobs. Among the management positions there are some that are real male bastions, and rare is the man who admits that women should invade it.

Men are sometimes willing to admit that perhaps women may be able to do some of the "nicer" jobs that still reflect the old concept that women are really soft, gentle creatures. These jobs usually are second-line positions in jobs dealing directly with people—like working in personnel, doing statistical research on personnel problems, editing the company house organ, or serving as administrative assistant to a hotshot male. In the medical field there are still few women doctors or heads of hospitals and in education still comparatively few who hold full professorships.

One of the most extraordinary women who contributed to the survey is Helen Delich Bentley. Her very unique position as head of the Federal Maritime Commission makes her the top-appointed woman in the Nixon administration. She runs a 285-person independent agency, which is responsible to Congress and the president. No woman has ever held this position. Dr. Bentley really breaks new ground in not only being head of this important government agency but also heading up a domain that has traditionally been managed by tough, hard-talking, hardworking, smart men. Dr. Bentley's excellent work has been reported in the press.

She came to the Maritime Commission with a fine executive background. As a managing editor of the *Baltimore Scene,* she was well-known for her integrity and her ability to deal with the hard facts of life. Her background in newspaper work made her well aware of the toughness of the waterfront, but she never backed away from the difficult assignments. The same can be said of her today.

By her assignment in a "man's" field, she breaks new ground for herself, but also provides an excellent example that can and should be followed in appointments of this nature.

The jobs women can do—and are doing—offer objectives as wide as women want to make them. True, there may still be some difficulties in breaking into the "man's world," but there is room for women of talent and perseverance. This chapter and Chapters 5 and 6 do not contain all the names of the women included in the survey. The positions are examples of what women can do (1) in jobs traditionally male, (2) in jobs where you do find some women but they are outstanding in their specially gifted way of handling the job, and (3) in jobs where they have given the extra turn to the traditionally woman's job so that it is unique and new all over again. The division is somewhat arbitrary (you may think that some jobs are in the wrong chapter), but any way you look at it, reading these chapters should open your eyes to the talents that abound among women as well as men. It is tragic if women like them have not been able to exert their talents because tradition has led them, perhaps unconsciously, to lower their sights or because management has been unwilling to recognize the management skills of women.

Labor Relations

The role of the union leader, although the image is changing, brings to mind the tough old master, George Meany. Thinking of management men in this field conjures up an image of an unyielding, hard-nosed bargainer who smokes and swears his way through long, last-ditch night sessions, announcing the final settlement in the early morning hours. For most people it is hard to picture a woman who can hold her own against a tough labor leader. Will she be able to sit down and negotiate with a clear head and not "give the store away" through some mistaken bleeding-heart notion? Her feminine wiles, used with such success elsewhere, will not, or so it is thought, be a match for the hard-nosed, well-informed, tough union negotiators.

When one examines some of the settlements that haunt management or that have eventually led to the close down of stores, plants, schools, and hospitals, one would think that men would be willing and eager to get any help they can. Times are and have been changing in the labor relations field. It takes a well-informed, smart, skillful, non-squeamish individual to bargain on either side of the table in the complicated world of today. The table-pounding, tough old negotiator who often bargained more from his wits and emotions rather than with facts is more or less a creature of the past. There are a few women, and they can match the best among the men, who have entered the field on both managements' and unions' sides.

There have always been a few hardy women pioneers in labor relations—among them the late Eleanor Herrick, of the defunct *Herald Tribune,* who had a reputation of being as tough as any man. Cigar smoking and ash dropping were part of her style. Her sharp wits and her tough talk were also part of the legend.

Another of the early women in the field was Anna Rosenberg, who still practices law in New York. The diminutive Mrs. Rosenberg has been the confidante of presidents and high political figures. Her successful efforts at mediation and conciliation in the labor field are numerous.

In today's management picture there are several labor relations experts throughout the country, but none are more successful than the women negotiators included in this survey.

G. G. Michelson, senior vice president of Macy's, New York, is vice president not only of labor relations but also of consumer relations. In addition, she has recently been appointed senior vice president for all personnel. She is recognized throughout the country as a fine negotiator and labor relations expert. A woman of charm, fairness, and fine intellectual capabilities, she has received numerous awards for civic and educational efforts, especially for working with minority groups.

In bargaining with the Department Store Workers, AFL-CIO, Mrs. Michelson faces the challenge of an around-the-clock bargaining session every two or three years. This is a traumatic experience for everyone involved. Strategy must be planned, information gathered, and techniques studied. When the direct welfare of 8,000 employees (those covered by the union contract) and the indirect influence on thousands more is measured, then there is some concept of the burden of responsibility borne by Mrs. Michelson in dealing with the union. Management's decision to withstand a strike is always a rough one. In 1972 that decision was made, and pickets lined the block yelling insults loud and long at passers-by and those entering to shop at the store, which was being run by supervisors, executives, and their families. The behind-the-scene maneuvering necessary to bring an eventual settlement had to be done with finesse and strength. Such a job was not for a soft-hearted woman, but for an intelligent, well-informed executive. Mrs. Michelson fully meets those qualifications.

The bargaining does not end her dealings with the union. The administration of the contract, including the top step of the grievance handling, the constant watching of practices, and the training of others in labor relations are only part of Mrs. Michelson's other duties.

Eileen Casey, called "Case" by her peers in industrial relations and sometimes "the lady negotiator of the East," has earned her reputation for knowing what she is talking about in the labor relations field. Her white-collar bargaining was preceded by years of blue-collar bargaining with the IUE at Teleregister Corporation. Currently she is personnel director of the Group Health Incorporated of New York and bargains with the white-collar union, Office and Professional Employees, AFL-CIO.

White-collar unions are usually envisioned to have extra brainpower. Although in some cases this attribute may be mistakenly granted, Local 153 is led by one of the most aggressive and best-known white-collar union leaders in the East. There is probably some truth to the statement that it takes someone smarter than he is to come out ahead in negotiations. Because white-collar unionism is still a rarity, gains made by this union are touted in other organizing campaigns. But bargaining at Group Health has not been a giveaway that could act as a real incentive for every white-collar employee in New York City to join a union. Bargaining has been tough, fair, and aboveboard. Miss Casey sits across the bargaining table as management negotiator and sweats out the late-night, early-morning sessions before the contracts are signed. Drives by rival unions, tough arbitration, day-to-day sticky jurisdictional disputes are only part of her daily job.

Jean Sisco, vice president of Woodward & Lothrop is another woman negotiator who also bargains in today's complicated labor climate. Mrs. Sisco is well aware of today's Washington scene and its influence on labor relations. She has the rare combination of being as well informed on advanced human relations as she is on labor relations. When she sits down to bargain, she brings a breadth of vision that has made her position unique.

These women are a far cry from the old stereotype of the rough-talking, and not very sociably acceptable labor relations negotiator. They have steel-trap minds, but have been doubly blessed with good looks and charm, plus an inner assurance of knowing that they do their job well. They negate the idea that women have no place in labor relations. They are equally at home on the ballroom floor, on the sales floor, in the concert hall, in the halls of academe, and in the kitchen or entertaining at home.

Labor Law

Labor law is one of the most interesting and exciting areas of the law field. How do women rate in this no-woman's land? Again, the representation is fairly slim, but the ones who are there are doing an excellent job. It looks, too, as though this field should prove extremely fascinating for young women who are looking for not only an interesting but also a lucrative field. Men who are responsible for hiring and promoting in the labor field should not overlook the fine young women labor lawyers who are appearing on the scene.

Unique among the women labor lawyers in New York City is Eva Robins, labor mediator par excellence. In March 1972 she set up her own office as a full-time arbitrator. Because she has been well known in the field as a fine lawyer and a solid practitioner, and is uniquely experienced as an arbitrator and mediator in difficult labor disputes, her reentry into full-time dispute settlement activities, in the public and private sectors, keeps her busier than ever.

Miss Robins's previous job was head of the dispute settlement procedures and deputy chairman of the Office of Collective Bargaining (OCB) of New York City. This brought her into the thick of the messy collective bargaining situation of the big town. One doesn't have to live in New York to hear about its collective bargaining impasses. Subway workers, teachers, welfare workers, social workers, garbage collectors, firemen, policemen—you name it. Everybody, or so it seems, on the city payroll is unionized. Given just so much of a budget to be distributed, countless political situations, irate taxpayers and visitors, mediation and conciliation in touchy city situations is not easy. Miss Robins's duties included mediating major labor disputes; administering the arbitration, mediation, and impasse procedures of OCB; and acting as dispute settlement specialist in matters requiring board decision. In a city like New York there certainly was enough to keep her active and busy. She speaks of this experience as being educational, exciting, and frustrating.

Prior to her city job Miss Robins was staff mediator at the New York State Board of Mediation and assistant vice president and assistant director of industrial relations for the Pioneer Ice Cream Division of the Borden Company. Her list of successful mediation in everything from heavy industry to hospitals speaks not only of her versatility but also of her capabilities.

G. G. Michelson, Eileen Casey, and Eva Robins have reached their current status with years of solid accomplishment behind them. Fairly new among labor attorneys on the management side is Jacqueline Delafuente, urban affairs counsel, F. W. Woolworth Co., a pretty, aggressive, intelligent, and ambitious graduate of Fordham Law School. Like so many of the younger management women, she started several notches up the ladder than the earlier women in the field. Miss Delafuente takes the responsibilities of urban affairs counsel in stride. Her work includes many facets of the labor relations field and requires the same travel assignments to Woolworth stores across the country, the same court appearances, and the same long hours that are required of a man. Miss Delafuente asks for no special concessions because she is a woman. Her colleagues at Woolworth speak highly of her and are proud to have her with them at management meetings.

Betty Southard Murphy in Washington, D.C., came close to being appointed the National Labor Relations Board (NLRB) general counsel in 1971. Evidently the country wasn't quite ready for a female in this spot despite all the management support from top male industrial relations experts. The competition for this appointment brought out some of the best male labor lawyers in the country. The fact that Mrs. Murphy was considered for and almost won the appointment indicates some progress. Perhaps her attempt will make it easier for the next female candidate.

Mrs. Murphy, now a partner in the law firm of Wilson, Woods, and Villalon, has pleaded cases on both sides of the industrial relations scene—both for management and for unions. She is active in all Washington, D.C., courts and has argued or appeared in 9 of the 11 U.S. Courts of Appeals. She has tried cases in the courts of Maryland, Massachusetts, Maine, Georgia, Louisiana, Florida, and Washington, D.C. Her previous jobs included work in the enforcement branch of NLRB, work with the United Press International, and freelance reporting in Europe and Asia. Not bad for a 41-year-old, happily married mother of two.

On the union side of the picture, few women are more highly respected than Judith Vladeck, a partner of Vladeck, Elias, Vladeck, and Lewis. This law firm specializes in the representation of unions in labor–management relations in addition to handling general legal matters. The very fact that a male management attorney recommended Mrs. Vladeck for inclusion in this survey speaks volumes. G. G. Michelson also speaks of her as a "wonderful, bright, and charming person with much talent."

Mrs. Vladeck's work has included cases representing textile unions, hospital workers, and office and professional workers, among many others. In addition to her law practice, Mrs. Vladeck shares her knowledge with others in her course, "Working Women and the Law," at the Cornell School of Industrial and Labor Relations.

She has the rather unique experience of working with her husband as a partner in the same law firm. A proud mother, too, she leads a full life.

Government Lawyer

It is interesting that labor relations has become such a complicated process that labor lawyers are needed on both sides of the picture. Labor law is not a simple process—living within the law makes it necessary to have both the knowledge of and the ability to apply the law. Both sides need the extra skill provided by the women discussed above. In addition, the people who often start legal proceedings are government lawyers for the aggrieved.

There are some very talented and able women lawyers both in the Wage and Hour Division of the U.S. Department of Labor and the Equal Employment Opportunities Commission (EEOC). Equal pay for equal work, for example, is one area where women government lawyers seem to put more than ordinary zeal into their work. Despite loud cries of "unfair" and distress over large fines by employers, these women are pushing management to get their houses in order on the equal pay issue. The same can be said for the women lawyers on the EEOC staff who not only have been active in the enforcement field but also have helped prepare guidelines concerning equal pay regardless of sex that have many employers very disturbed. Acting with the courage of their convictions, these women are often thorns in the sides of male managers. They are not underestimated by executives and in fact receive a certain degree of respect—if not approbation. They do represent a good cross section of women in good-paying (if not top) jobs.

So much for women in labor relations. The representatives discussed above are only a sample of the talents and versatility of the women in this field. In the past it might have been a man's world, but it is one world that has been invaded by a group of capable, smart, and attractive women who have become respected, cherished, and, even though at first somewhat grudgingly, accepted by their peers. No doubt many more women will enter this interesting and exciting field in the future. Labor relations and labor law are certainly getting no simpler. Indications are that, unless there are drastic surprises, the government agencies, labor unions, and industry will gobble up all the capable lawyers in this field for a long time to come.

A fine lawyer in a slightly different field is Jane M. Alexander, who has combined her law with government duties. She holds the responsible position of director, Bureau of Foods and Chemistry, Pennsylvania Department of Agriculture. Her background includes private law practice in the firm of Alexander and Alexander. Mrs. Alexander handles home and job responsibilities competently. Married for 22 years, she has four children ranging in age from 14 years to 21.

Sales Estimator

As sales estimator for Avon Products, Inc., Wendy Duval has a job that ordinarily would be held by a man. This job entails sales forecasting for the year ahead for an important phase of Avon's products. She is familiar with sales histories and trends and comes up with reliable, dependable forecasts. Personnel work gave her a start up the management ladder.

Line Executives

Perhaps women can hold supportive staff roles, but how do they perform as line managers? A long-held myth purports that women get fouled up when they get into jobs where the action is, where they give the orders, where production is important, and where mistakes are costly and the competition is keen. Is it possible for women to perform well in the day-to-day, decision-making, direction-giving, "hard" line jobs?

Store President

"Yes," says Margaret Wilson, chairman, president, and chief executive officer of Scarbrough's Department Store, Austin, Texas. In addition, Mrs. Wilson is on the boards of the National Retail Merchants Association and the American Management Association, and is the president of the American Retail Federation. She is active in the Young Presidents Association, whose members, practically all of them men, assumed presidencies when they were under 40. (Being under 40, and a president, is one of the qualifications for membership in the organization.) Even though retailing probably has more women in management jobs than most other industries have, men still sit behind most executive desks. Mrs. Wilson, the exception to this rule, has proved her capabilities by doubling the sales of her store in the comparatively short time she has been president.

It is true that Mrs. Wilson's father owned the store before her, but there are many women who would have shirked the responsibilities of making a go of a store in a highly competitive industry. When she assumed the presidency, she pepped up the place considerably—paint and a general cleanup were first in order. Then a beauty salon and a designer's shop helped set the modern trend.

Margaret Wilson is not a stay-behind-the-desk executive. When you call Scarbrough's you may find that she is off to France or Alaska, or walking through the store aisles. Just like her successful male counterparts in other stores, she knows the importance of personally checking on what is selling. She keeps up with the trends—knows what customers are demanding and how to meet their needs.

An important key to Mrs. Wilson's success may be her insistence on keeping pace not only with merchandising trends but also with the behavioral sciences. The Grid® approach, the assessment center, the AMA Management Course, and Theory X and Theory Y are all part of Mrs. Wilson's working tools. She makes practical applications of the latest thinking in the behavioral sciences, turning long-hair theory into personnel practices that keep her store a leader.

In 1972 Mrs. Wilson was appointed to three leading advisory posts. She was appointed to President Nixon's Commission on Personnel Interchange, was appointed to the New Communities Advisory Board of the U.S. Department of Housing and Urban Development (by former

Secretary Romney), and is a regular member of the Conference Board. In addition, she is listed in *Who's Who in America* (1972).

One example of this practical use of management theory is her progressive approach to employment. Mrs. Wilson hires students and teachers (and their spouses) of the University of Texas, aware that many of them will be with her for only a short time. She also knows that, while they are there, they will furnish enough innovative ideas to well warrant the turnover costs.

In the chancy world of retailing it takes a smart person to keep the profit figure moving up. It is a close-margin industry, and carrying out the top responsibility for running a store profitably is no easy task. Catherine Case, president of Gidding Jenny in Cincinnati, is responsible for the management of 11 stores. She reached the top by gradual steps, from saleslady to buyer to merchandise manager and then to vice president of merchandising. The line jobs along the way gave her an intimate knowledge of store operation, merchandising, and market intricacies.

Vice President–General Manager

Vice president and general manager—this title carries much prestige and you would expect the incumbent to be a man with high-pressure tactics. Instead, in this spot at elegant Bonwit Teller sits Helen Galland, general merchandise manager, who in her words is "responsible for and supervises every aspect of buying, selling, making a profit, control, and promotional activity of the total company." An easy job? Of course not, but an exciting one. It is demanding, time-consuming, and difficult, but Mrs. Galland handles it well. Having worked for six presidents in 21 years, she learned much from each of them. Adjusting to a new president on an average of once every three years takes some agile brainwork. Too often when a new president assumes the top spot, he moves many of the subordinates around and often out. It takes real staying power and ability to last through six presidents, to retain their respect, and to admit having learned something from each of them. Incidentally, one of them was a woman. Mrs. Galland knows her trade, too. She started as a buyer and moved up to her present position through the merchandise route.

Store Manager

Not all store managers come up through merchandise; almost all of them come up through operations. Managing a multimillion-dollar operation with almost 200 employees is certainly no job for a babe in the management woods. Yet Peggy Ogden efficiently manages Ohrbach's successful Westbury store. Miss Ogden came to her line job as manager via the personnel route. People-conscious as well as merchandise-conscious, she presents an ideal combination to run the store well. Does she do it better than a man? She'll admit that she works hard enough, or even harder, so that she will be as good as or better than any man who holds a manager's job.

Company President

Are all women presidents found only in retailing? Not by a long shot. Arneta K. Dow, president of Dow Sales, Inc., Branford, Connecticut, started her own firm as a hobby. It was a long jump from being a business administration teacher and supervisor of arts and crafts in another firm to starting and successfully running a firm of her own. Mrs. Dow actually owns three corporations—and is president of all three. She avoids any sex problems in her operation by hiring only women. It is a unique idea, and it is working well. Would she hire males? She has hired many as salesmen, and I expect that, rather than risk EEOC charges, she would hire males if they applied for production jobs.

Treasurer

Pretty, vivacious Catherine Cavalli is controller for the National Retail Merchants Association and treasurer of NRMA Enterprises, a trade association with more than 26,000 stores scattered around the world. South Africa, New Zealand, Sweden, Paris—the dues and orders come in just as they do from Abilene, Fargo, Chicago, New Orleans, and New York. Whatever the amount, this versatile woman really can add, subtract, and figure the intricacies of budgets.

Alice Rohloff is treasurer of Rohloff Brothers, Inc., a comparatively small agricultural firm in Ohio that dehydrates and markets alfalfa products around the world. In addition, the company farms approximately 2,000 acres of rich Ohio dirt to produce its own alfalfa. Mrs. Rohloff has kept the books while running a successful home, bringing up two fine children, and having a husband who thinks she is great and gives her well-deserved credit for helping run the business successfully. Starting the business from scratch with one truck took lots of courage and hard work on the part of Mrs. Rohloff and her husband. She is an excellent example of the valuable contribution women executives can make toward building a business.

Director of Nursing

Too often a skill is isolated, and administrative and supervisory duties are not combined with technical job know-how. Mrs. Alice Ready Kehoe, director of nursing at the Clinton Nursing Home in Long Island, N.Y., is a registered nurse with the combined administrative and nursing skills necessary to carry out her responsibilities. As president, Mr. Kehoe never underestimates the part his wife plays in making Clinton a humanitarian as well as up-to-date, efficiently managed geriatric home.

Voluntary Services President

Some of the line jobs that women hold are in the voluntary services. Cynthia C. Wedel is the associate director of the Center for a Voluntary Society in Washington, D. C., which works with all kinds of voluntary organizations across the country. She shares the duties of the director of the center—the decision-making, consulting, writing, and training responsibilities.

Probably the most exciting of Mrs. Wedel's achievements was her election to the presidency of the National Council of Churches, a policy-making spot never before held by a woman. The level of the responsibility for policy making may be a step away from the level of responsibility given to a general manager, but the relationship in this case is so close that it merits inclusion in the top management roles that women play.

Mrs. Wedel assumed this position ahead of many men candidates. One of the most sensitive situations can follow such an election. Will the defeated candidates cooperate, or will they do the equivalent of sulking in the corner? One of Mrs. Wedel's most talked-of characteristics is her ability to have unlike groups work together for a common cause. She is said to have gracefully smoothed the waters, so that she has not only the full cooperation of the staff but also the support of those with whom she competed. Her important role will help influence American church life in the years ahead.

Director of Publications

Still another exciting job is held by the director of publications of a $2- to $3-million a year publishing operation. Preferring to remain anonymous, the woman who runs this operation does so with excellent management skills. Her job encompasses not only helping select the books to be published but also following them along until they are printed and sold. In addition to books, there are periodicals, studies, and programmed instruction manuals to be followed through from start to finish. An exciting job for anyone—but especially for a woman who has come to her present position step by step, from secretary up to editor in chief and finally to director.

Heavy-Industry Executives

It is true that you will probably find top women line officers primarily in banks and in stores, but again some women have proved themselves capable of managing in "tough" industries.

There is Maria Vescia, vice president of Airwick, International in Carlstadt, New Jersey, who in August 1971 was also elected president of the International Executives Association. No one ever dreamed that a woman would hold the presidency of this 55-year-old world trade group. At Airwick, Mrs. Vescia is responsible for marketing and sales in Latin America, the Caribbean, Japan, Taiwan, and the Philippines. She is credited with having increased the sales of this multimillion-dollar company to these areas by 70 percent in 12 years. Her thrilling job takes her to these countries fairly often. The very fact that she speaks both Spanish and German fluently and has a working knowledge of Portuguese, French, and Italian is indicative of the special talents that today's women bring to management jobs.

Rhoda M. Stewart, vice president of the Administration Services Division of the Chemical and Plastic Group of Borg-Warner Corporation, is a woman on the move, too. She mentions a trip to Australia as casually as some of us would talk about taking a trip on the Staten Island Ferry. Miss Stewart says good women managers are as competent as good men managers. And she herself has proved that a good manager is a good manager, regardless of sex. A *Saturday Evening Post* article, "Is There Room at the Top?" said about Miss Stewart: "[She is] a fragile and elegant lady. It's hard to imagine Miss Stewart, who looks like a gently nurtured product of the Old South, bossing a fleet of truckers or out selling styrene; nonetheless these things are and have been a part of her job during the 30 years she's worked for [the corporation]." [1]

Miss Stewart has come a long way since joining the company in 1937 as a temporary clerical worker. At this writing (when this book is published, she may have even more duties) she has managerial responsibility for domestic and international purchasing in seven states and five foreign countries, and supervises an incredibly complicated inventory control system as well as traffic, distribution, and some sales. Like many other successful women executives, Miss Stewart claims her sex has been an asset rather than a hindrance.

A Young President

Many of the top women in the survey have reached the top only after many years of work. Like the majority of men, experience and brains have been the answer. Every once in a while a bright young person comes along who has all the finesse and know-how necessary to run a top spot. No one questions either the ability or the success of Jane Evans Sheer, president of I. Miller in New York City. Named president when she was 25 and not too long out of Vanderbilt University, Mrs. Sheer has done a superb job as president. Now at the ripe age of 29 she is recognized as a leader in her field. She knows style and she knows merchandising. In addition, she is a good speaker, is proud of her company and of her family life. She is an outstanding example of a young executive who is really on the move. It is interesting that none of her co-workers, her subordinates, or her bosses underrates her. They both respect and take pride in their lady president.

Production Manager

Mildred McLean, advertising production manager at the General Learning Corporation, is another well-known line manager. In a field dominated by men, her duties have progressed consistently since she served as personnel director at Martindale-Hubbell, law publishers in Summit, New Jersey.

In addition to doing a fine job in her own right, Mrs. McLean has been dedicated to furthering the advancement of women in business. She has worked hard in a practical yet inspiring fashion. She has served on many committees of the New Jersey Federation of Business and Professional Women, acting as president in 1968–1969. Among her honors is an appointment by Governor William T. Cahill to the New Jersey State Commission on Women in the Department of Community Affairs. In December 1971, she was named charter chairman of the New Jersey Commission on Women. She has received many honors and is a popular worker with other women in furthering the careers of women. She is listed in *Who's Who of American Women*. Mrs. McLean has also contributed to many aspects of community life. She is a rare woman, one who takes time to help younger women attain many of their goals.

There are many more women who should be mentioned, but those discussed here illustrate that women can and do hold jobs customarily held by men. The women included in the survey demonstrate that women are excellent presidents, line vice presidents, and managers and that they also are competent and comfortable in labor relations and finance. A review of their talents is overwhelming. In fact, their super-capabilities would scare you if the rest of their lives weren't so human, so lively, and so filled with excitement. Most of them seized opportunity as it went by and climbed the ladder the hard way, step by step. A few had family connections; some inherited a firm or helped their husbands in their businesses. But these women, too, have fully utilized their talents to enhance rather than hinder the enterprise.

This chapter has indicated the versatility of the jobs capable women can hold in the traditional men's areas. In later chapters we will look at the personal side of their lives, including their opinions on some of the hangups of both men and women.

5

ARE THERE "WOMEN" JOBS IN THE MANAGEMENT HIERARCHY?

One management conception has it that there are women jobs and men jobs. Often women are supposed to excel in the "people" jobs—those concerned with dealing directly with employees or customers—or in support jobs as personal assistants to males in more responsible jobs. As one woman put it, "The men expect us to carry on in the roles of their mothers, grandmothers, and sisters in almost a family kind of dealing with the people problems of running the business." Women are expected to be helpers—secretaries, typists, and clerical workers. Often, too, they are in any job in the company where the "people" function is important.

Women in the Personnel Function

It's taken for granted that women will be found in personnel jobs. No one lifts an eyebrow at the beginner sitting behind the interviewing

63

desk, at the girl who is doing the record keeping, or even at the woman personnel manager. There is a feeling that women can do these jobs, that they understand people better. According to tradition, women are supposed to be more understanding and sympathetic. Part of this misconception that only women can do personnel work stems from the old idea that personnel is a do-good operation. It is supposed to be a "nice" job. There is no dirt, no mess, and no sorrow—or so the story goes.

In today's world the top manager of the people function can be a "nice" person. She can usually go to a fairly decent office and she can "like people." These are all things that women are supposed to want out of a job. If a woman has only such minor ambitions, however, the top spot in personnel is really not for her.

Today's top personnel job has no time or place for the professional do-gooder. The management of people is as important as or even more important than the management of things. As such it demands high-caliber, positive, and practical people who can produce tangible results. Anyone familiar with the personnel function knows that a person in the top personnel job must care deeply about people in the true sense— appreciative of talents, know-how, and ambitions, and tolerant of foibles unless they stand in the way of doing a good job. Misplacement or waste of talent and hindering someone from reaching his or her potential are crimes that industry can no longer afford.

In companies that are in tune with the times the whole personnel function has been upgraded. No longer is the job relegated to poor old Joe, who can't do anything else, or to the sweet, little-educated female who happens to profess that she likes people. It is not a place to which to promote, even in today's push, the demanding girls who want to get away from the secretary syndrome or from being the official white-collar drudge. Just because women are yelling about being promoted, don't foist them on the personnel department—not unless they are well qualified and have the education and experience necessary for this difficult job.

Not so many years ago it was almost possible to count on the fingers of both hands the vice presidents of personnel. Now there are many who have reached that status. Their counsel is requested and received when top management decisions are made on new sites, on new benefit plans, on acquisitions, and on proper utilization of the workforce. If the people planning is done haphazardly, then the best-laid plans on facilities, research, market forecasts, and financial aid will fall apart. Is it easy to take care of today's complicated staffing problems? Not by a long shot. It is even harder to crystal-ball the future.

Are there women in these top management levels who sit with the presidents of their companies and other policy-making officials? There are some, but not as many as you will see in ten years when the crop of young, bright, ambitious women move up the ladder. Just as an example, a recruitment agency, currently engaged in a search for a personnel director of a large firm that employs many women, is looking for a *woman* personnel director—of course with experience and education and with real decision-making powers. The beginning salary is $30,000 plus a year's-end bonus. Naturally, according to the agency, the woman should be in her thirties. The searcher says he is amazed at the qualified women he has found. Most of them have been assistants in their own firms, sometimes really doing the job without having the title or salary. Their own firms have paid them around $20,000 or less. Even in today's times a beginning salary of $30,000 is not to be sneezed at by either a man or a woman. Such an offer would have been extremely rare 10 or 15 years ago. Look for more women in the top personnel job.

The women in the top personnel spots are indeed talented—often maybe more so than men in similar positions. If you look long and hard, you will find a lone man or two who could match these outstanding women.

Store Vice President

One of the most interesting of these women is Mary S. Girard (now retired), former vice president of personnel at Ohrbach's in New York. She had the broad responsibilities for the total personnel function of this department store, which does many million dollars' worth of sales per year and operates ten branch stores. Finding employees for the multitudinous, many-level jobs in a mammoth department store is no easy task. Mrs. Girard did more in really coping with the rough problems of getting and keeping good employees than anyone else in the complex, multilingual New York City market. She also knew where to find executives for every management function—from recruitment on college campuses for trainee jobs to the more sophisticated ways of finding executives for hard-to-fill jobs. More important, she knew the people, and their skills, at Ohrbach's and helped capable employees up the ladder.

After quite a number of years in the field, Mrs. Girard still is searching for better ways of management and deeper understanding of what makes people tick. She is steadily working for a doctorate in psychology and with her capabilities she will earn it.

Mrs. Girard decided to take early retirement so that she can begin another exciting career. When Mrs. Girard obtains her doctorate, she plans to continue the group dynamics she has used so successfully at Ohrbach's. A comparatively new field, it offers guidance and counseling for groups, such as church, hospital, and youth groups or for couples whose marriages otherwise might fall apart. With her years of fine personnel work behind her, Mrs. Girard will do an excellent job.

Soft-spoken, smart Mary Garzoni is well known as a leader in personnel circles in Chicago. As corporate vice president of Charles A. Stevens & Co., a high-class specialty store, she has responsibility for the overall personnel function in eight stores—training, wage and salary administration, and executive development. In addition to these duties, she is in charge of all food services in the company. She is concerned about doing a good job and making Stevens a place that both employees and customers know as a fine store. Such a position is a far cry from the old version of the hand-holding, non-profit-oriented, old-fashioned personnel director who too often was on the way down instead of on the way up the management ladder.

Mrs. Garzoni has come up the ladder step by step, starting as a secretary and next training to be a pension and profit-sharing specialist. Maybe in the future some of these steps can be skipped, but many of the women who have made it to the top have had to come up by the slower route. Will the next generation of young women who will probably travel the shorter route have—or even need—the same hard-nosed perseverance as the women who have done it the hard way? Who knows? But if young hopefuls can perhaps learn a little about the successful combination of compassion, employee relations skills, and determination that have unlocked these jobs for those who have gone ahead of them, the climb may be easier.

By "hard-nosed perseverance" and "determination" we do not mean to say that women have not added a welcome "feminine" touch to the stores in which they are VP's. Their offices, for example, are not the cold, barren, metallic offices of so many male executives. You are more likely to find fresh flowers on a side table, softer colors on the walls, and even more comfortable seats for visitors. Employees, especially women employees, usually are particularly well groomed, and there are occasional touches of what is considered feminine in some personnel circles —like giving an employee flowers in recognition of a special event.

Bank Vice President

It is said that banks and retailers probably have more top-level jobs for women than other industries. If so, then hurrah for these two far-sighted industries. Perhaps the rest of the world will eventually catch up. Margaret Bowes, vice president of Kings Lafayette Bank in Brooklyn, is in complete charge of personnel and the payroll function at her bank. How did she get there? Her entire career was spent in banking, but she, too, came to her present position step by step—starting as a bookkeeper and moving up to head bookkeeper, to junior officer, to assistant vice president, and finally to her present spot. She speaks with appreciation of the men who have helped her attain her position, but she, too, has the magic combination of understanding, patience, and appreciation of people.

Store Personnel Manager

Many good women personnel managers are on the way up to top spots. One young woman on her way is Carol Ivansheck, personnel manager for Frederick Atkins, buying office, in New York City. Young and pretty, Mrs. Ivansheck keeps tabs on what is happening in the world. She alerts other personnel directors in 47 stores scattered throughout the country of meetings they should know about, what is happening in legislatures, and what is going on in union relations. She carefully screens seminars, investigates tests, checks on who is who in personnel training, and knows where to find the personnel tools her stores need. A bit offbeat from the usual personnel function, her job illustrates one of the sidetracks that one can find in this field.

Personnel Manager, International

Dorothy D. Chappel, director of personnel plans and programs of IBM World Trade Corporation, is the first woman to hold this position. She is responsible for personnel planning, developing programs related to personnel policies, personnel development and employee services, and providing guidance to World Trade groups, areas, and countries in these operations. There are IBM facilities in 117 countries around the world employing more than 200,000 people. These figures reflect the importance of her job. In an interview with Mrs. Chappel, we were impressed with the breadth of her vision and understanding in working with the executives of different countries. Her concern and her respect for management with different backgrounds are probably keys to her success. Her job is to help provide equity to employees wherever they are, while still being sensitive to the laws and customs of the countries involved. She evidently is doing a good job of that.

Mrs. Chappel's path up the management ladder started when she was reminded by her boss that being a secretary isn't necessarily the greatest position in the world and that there are other paths to follow. As she says, "I consider myself lucky to have had the opportunity to work into a position such as this. I have to be competitive with men, and I find the whole thing a fantastically interesting experience."

If you have had experience in trying to understand and justify personnel practices in our country, you probably have an idea as to how much more difficult it is to do so for 117 countries, where customs and practices vary greatly from our own and from each other. It takes understanding, patience, and character. Mrs. Chappel's continuous success speaks well for her capabilities and finesse in handling delicate situations.

Leila L. Colmen, personnel director of the Institute of International Education, has found it exciting to work for an organization that has offices in Hong Kong, Lima, Nairobi, Paris, and Tokyo. The Institute is a nonprofit organization devoted to bettering international relationships in education, a lofty purpose that gives a somewhat different flavor to the job of personnel director. This job requires abandonment of all provincial thinking. It is difficult to understand local problems in the United States, but to ever venture understanding all the nations represented by the Institute is even a more difficult task. Yet the very existence of the Institute proves that in this world where geographical distances no longer mean much, gallant efforts are being made for better understanding among people. Part of Mrs. Colmen's job is to advise management on all personnel issues, including human resources utilization, economic benefits, and wages and salaries. Sounds like an interesting job.

Do these women in personnel have easy jobs? No. They take their lumps like men executives, work long hours, and spend time away from their families. They are not complaining. They honestly seem to be enjoying their work and are finding more exciting challenges ahead. Selecting, training, placing, and checking accomplishments of other people bring job satisfaction, particularly when these women see how much their efforts contribute to the overall success of the company, store, or bank.

Management positions are not easy to fill. Today's complicated world demands executives and professionals who have many special skills and who can do a myriad of different jobs well. Growth in the job no longer can be a haphazard operation that is left to chance. How, for example, can you, a manager, pick managers with potential—can you pick them at random from a workforce of thousands of people? How do you keep track of the talents of your people, and how do you help them reach their potential? While paying attention to individuals you must also keep track not only of the short-range jobs that need to be filled in your firm but also of the long-range organizational changes and growth that will demand managers with different skills in the future.

Women in Management Development
and Organization Planning

Management development and organization planning have finally come into their own in today's competitive climate. Many companies have five-, ten-, and twenty-year plans. The person responsible for planning usually has the title director of manpower planning and organization or director of management development and executive training or combinations of these terms. Besides being clairvoyant, such a person must be well educated, must know the latest and best thinking in the management of human resources, and must be flexible, intelligent, and enthusiastic about other people's talents. The planning director must be able to develop the skills and capabilities of the current workforce, make plans for them to expand their duties and attain higher-level jobs, and when necessary supplement this workforce by looking outside the company for managers who can meet the qualifications. Are executives who have the imagination and foresight to fill these jobs easy to find? Not by a long shot.

Are women suited to this specialized job of selecting, training, and managing high-caliber talents? Do they have the critical analytical skills it takes to nurture management's current and future crop of executives? There are many good men in the field, but two exceptional women illustrate the point that women can handle the job, too.

Consultant, Management Development

Long before I met Marion Kellogg of General Electric I had heard about her from at least ten men whose potential she had helped them realize. I was prepared to meet some shrewd, overambitious female and just couldn't really believe that she could be as competent as these men claimed. Not only is Miss Kellogg as good as the men said, she is better. She, too, mixes brains and attractiveness and is much admired and liked by all who come in contact with her. What is the secret of her charisma? She has a thorough appreciation for other people's talents and finds where they can best be used. She also knows General Electric and its needs and has helped many people advance. Her job now at GE is consultant—marketing, management, and development. (One could write a book just about job titles.)

Miss Kellogg's background includes degrees in mathematics and physics—perhaps that helps her in her analysis of people's talents. Not only has Miss Kellogg done much for GE; she has inspired many other executives who have heard her at the American Management Association's Management Course, at talks before the American Society for Training and Development, and the Silver Bay Association.

A word in passing about American industry's willingness to share ideas with others. By appearing at seminars around the world, Miss Kellogg has brought her fine philosophy and advice to thousands of other people from different industries and from many companies and institutions. Perhaps this sharing of know-how was always a part of American tradition, but the extent to which it has been done in the past 20 years is a marvel to behold. Miss Kellogg is eminently qualified to further management knowledge.

Perhaps it is because Miss Kellogg had full responsibility as manager of employee relations of GE's Flight Propulsion Laboratory Department that her current teachings are practical as well as inspirational. Her five books, *What To Do About Performance Appraisal*, *Closing the Performance Gap*, *Career Management*, *Putting Management Theories to Work*, and *When Man and Manager Talk*, have become management bibles.[1] These books have been frequently used in college courses, either as texts or as supplementary reading. On a recent term paper a supervisory trainee (who, like many of the successful women before her, attends night school), said of one of Miss Kellogg's books, "Everything is so practical. I can really use her ideas in my own courses at the company. She has done much to broaden my perspective." And that is what Marion Kellogg has done for many.

Manager, Personnel Development

Betty Ann Duval, manager of personnel development at General Foods Corporation, also has her coterie of ardent admirers—those she has helped reach their potential. Both men and women discuss in glowing terms how Miss Duval recognized their talents before they themselves did. This is how she describes her job at this mammoth corporation: "Responsible for providing consultation and guidance on all matters relating to individual and organizational development throughout the corporation."

Did she reach her current job easily? She started by training hourly workers in a plant, went on to training supervisors in a manufacturing plant, then became training assistant at the divisional level, and then moved on to corporate headquarters at RCA. When her boss, Albert S. Waters, moved from RCA, she went with him to General Foods, where she has done much to help keep that company well staffed in a highly competitive field. Even though Mr. Waters is now vice president at Allied Chemical, Miss Duval has carried on at General Foods. She, too, has led many seminars at AMA and has lectured at many universities and community groups. She has the extra empathy needed to detect and direct the talents of other people. She is practical and knows the plans of her company, both short term and long term. In other words, both she and Miss Kellogg gear their planning and development to the needs of their firms. Both have done extremely fine jobs and are highly respected for doing these jobs well.

Training Director

Margaret Carter, training director at Gimbel Bros., New York City, says that her greatest assets include "a sense of humor, an ability to organize work, which came from secretarial experience, and an involuntary need to finish what I start." With a staff of four full-time people and two part-time people, she coordinates all staff and executive training at the New York store and gives guidance to the branch stores. Before joining Gimbel's Miss Carter was personnel coordinator for the National Alliance of Businessmen, which was established for hiring the underprivileged and unemployed. She brings to her job a zest that is contagious. She worries about women becoming so concerned about not being appreciated and the fact that too many women feel that really buckling down and competing is unfeminine.

Women as Communicators—
Writers and Editors

Women, historically, have been known to write well. Back in the Greek days there was Sappho, who wrote beautiful verse; in the Victorian days there was George Eliot (Mary Ann Evans), who knew that a man's byline would gain better acceptance for her books. There were Jane Austen and Louisa May Alcott, who wrote under their own names. Elizabeth Barrett Browning's love poems may no longer be avidly read, but their beauty equals or surpasses much of today's love poetry. But what did women write about? Primarily, they wrote about the trials and tribulations of the lovelorn, great sorrowful tales of lost loves and bleeding hearts. There was, of course, Harriet Beecher Stowe and her *Uncle Tom's Cabin*. Some say she almost started the Civil War with her impassioned literature. On a calmer side, there was Mary Baker Eddy and the great newspaper *The Christian Science Monitor*, which is still one of the great newspapers of the world.

Today there are many women writers, many of them involved in writing about women in the world of work. What about women writers at the management level?

Management Development and Communications

Very few people can communicate well and even fewer can teach others how to develop their writing skills. Mary S. McMahon excels in a field that offers great possibilities for women and suggests to men who are responsible for filling management jobs not to overlook the talented female writers on their staffs.

In addition to her many responsibilities at The Equitable Life Assurance Society of the United States—again no small outfit—Miss McMahon is in charge of management development and communications. Her job is to help management develop individuals and teams competent to carry on the Society's business now and in the future; to help the organization create and maintain a climate where problem solving, organizational effectiveness, and individual development are maximized.

Her management development functions are similar to those of Marion Kellogg and Betty Ann Duval. On the communications side of the picture she is to develop new ways of improving the communications climate within the Society in order to increase motivation, involvement, and commitment to the objectives of the organization. Miss McMahon is responsible for outside communications and also designs and carries out programs to improve the Society's relations with the people with whom its employees correspond. Programs include formal courses, quality maintenance through analysis of correspondence, and form letter review and revision. She also communicates the Society's programs through press releases, handbooks, and other formal channels.

Executives often are called on to make speeches, write articles, and communicate their special knowledge to other staff members. Many of them are great in their own field, but don't know how to make themselves clear. Many executives, too, find it difficult to make a speech—if they write it themselves it can be, and too often is, as dry as dust. Who is the catalyst? It is the staff person with special skills who gives these executives either a finished or a working paper, sometimes adding ideas of his own. Mary McMahon is well recognized for this talent both at Equitable and in international personnel circles.

Miss McMahon now devotes 20 percent of her time to communications. She qualified for this important function serving as director of consulting services at Equitable, on the professional consulting staff at

Rogers, Slade and Hill, and as editor and community relations assistant at Hyatt Bearings Division of General Motors. Speech writer, editor, teacher, and now management developer are all big responsibilities, but Miss McMahon can do them all with tremendous capability.

Magazine Editor

An editing job at the management level demands the ability to recognize good material and to coordinate it so that the readers will keep buying. The job requires supervisory and other management skills as well as writing talent.

Coline Covington, editorial coordinator of *Glamour*, is responsible for coordinating various departments, for continuity, for tightening—day-to-day management and supervision—and often for working out the timetables and budgeting and seeing that they are carried out. Mrs. Covington's job reflects the elements of good management thinking—the coordination and the follow-through too often are neglected in the management field, which is too often dominated by prima donnas, male and female.

In America today probably one of the most talented but relatively untapped pools of management skill is the married woman whose children have grown up. Mrs. Covington is an excellent example of how such dormant talent can be utilized. She recognized the importance of staying close to her children in their early years, but after 17 years away from newspaper work she returned to the exciting field of journalism in a management spot. This speaks well for both her and the company she represents.

Her background includes newspaper reporting and editing women's pages. Mrs. Covington's completed questionnaire is extremely interesting because she, like many of the others, brings an enthusiasm to her work that is exhilarating.

Grace Bechtold, executive editor, Bantam Books, Incorporated, is another editor with an interesting management job. Her job is to develop new publishing projects in all fields, both fiction and nonfiction. She works with authors in perfecting their work and reads many hardcover books to determine whether they qualify as suitable paperback offerings. Because of the wide range of the subject matter she deals with and the variety of authors she works with, she finds her job interesting and exciting.

It takes imagination to construct and edit programmed learning material that will be useful and that will save thousands of hours of learning time. Judy Wilson, young and bright, is the editor of the new series at John Wiley & Sons, New York. It's a relatively new field for a woman. Because she is Wiley's first woman editor the high quality of her work will pave the way for other women.

The so-called women's jobs of today (which even the most chauvinistic male concedes they handle well) are a far cry from the simplified versions that preceded them. Now the personnel vice president, the top communications experts, and the management developers and organization planners sit at the decision-making level of management. Their ideas are doing much to shape the policies of the companies for which they work. Other women can be proud of these women who have made it to this level—they are capable, well-respected individuals who have lost none of their femininity on the upward management journey.

The women discussed in this chapter are only representative of the women who participated in the study. The ideas and quotes from many others are also included.

6
TRADITIONAL JOBS FOR WOMEN:
With Major Variations

The rapidly changing times have brought into existence new jobs. Many of these seem to fit the more realistic view of women but do not upset the traditional concept of where women excel. Historically women are expected to know more about the jobs that are tied in with human relations and with the "people" end of the business. They are supposed to be more aware of the outside influences that shape man's existence. For example, it has traditionally been the woman's place to ward off the outside influences of evil while her boss has been out mixing with the more "masculine" duties of competition and production.

Perhaps women do have special talents for these new jobs—at least they don't have to cope with the prejudice they encounter in other jobs that men claim as male territory. Perhaps this is partially true because these positions have arisen at just the right time, when there has been no time to build up prejudice and when women are being considered for more professional jobs.

Consumer Relations

It is high time that consumerism came into its own. There is a growing concern as to whether or not quality is being built into American products. Ralph Nader and his crew have done much to uncover some myths about American excellence of production. His methods and his thinking may not be to your liking, or to industry's, but the old adage of "where there's smoke, there's fire" is unfortunately too often true of our American way of life and of today's whirlwind production and consumption. Now the buyer has been assured that he has the right to inquire as to the veracity of advertising claims.

Consumer Affairs Adviser

Probably no one is more qualified for the job of consumer affairs adviser than Esther Peterson, now consumer adviser to the president of Giant Food in Washington, D.C. An outstanding woman with a special verve that has made every job she has done a successful one, Mrs. Peterson brings a wealth of experience to her job. Well known in labor circles early in her life, she was later assistant secretary of labor in the Johnson Administration, advising the president on consumer affairs.

Giant Food Inc. is no small, backwoods operation. It is primarily a food chain with 94 outlets including pharmacies and general merchandise. Mrs. Peterson advises top management on consumer programs and also initiates programs. She sits on the company's policy-making group, composed of vice presidents.

She says, "Mine is a new profession—I'd call it consumer advocate 'on the inside.' All my previous jobs helped, though one does not see them as steps in a career ladder."

Mrs. Peterson makes an interesting observation: Many of the women who have been working for several years have developed mature judgment through holding many important jobs. This experience has made them capable of holding a variety of decision-making positions. Instead of becoming set in their ways, they have become more versatile and more flexible. Although there may not be too many women like this, there are several, and management might well use their talents in filling special positions. These women are not easy to find, but an honest search will uncover much talent, some of it lying dormant. Don't look for it only in the traditional places. There are many women who have excellent experience in several fields, and the next time you need a very special person to head up a new job look carefully at their backgrounds.

Another young woman in consumer relations is Mary-Jane Raphael, who has a threefold job at PepsiCo. She is the director of consumer affairs, manager of women's activities, and coordinator of Joan Crawford's business and publicity schedule.

She represents the legitimate concerns of consumer to the management and on the other side tries hard to work out reasonable solutions and reflects, not only in individual correspondence with consumers but also in general public relations programs, the image that PepsiCo is a company that cares and is very interested in the needs and concerns of its consumers. Mrs. Raphael works hard in the other two facets of her job, too. She leads a busy life—a great deal of it spent in travel. She brings a wealth of work background and good solid education to her job.

Her attitude toward her job epitomizes so well the attitude of many of the women in the study. "At the risk of sounding overconfident, I believe the only thing that could hold me back personally from future achievements would be if I didn't set my goals high enough. With a lot of hard work on my part I believe my position could become one of the best for women in the public relations field.

Consultants

In order to utilize mature talents, many companies retain some of their retired employees as "consultants." Instead of losing the cumulative knowledge of years of experience, the retirees are on call for advice or come in several days a week. This process differs greatly from the callous dumping at 65 of some of the nation's most talented people. True, some people are old at retirement age—probably haven't had a new idea since they were 30. The "live" ones, however, should be cherished by management, no matter how young that management may be. And smart firms are waking up to that fact.

A prime example in this survey is Harriet Wilinsky, a retail consultant who was sales promotion manager and vice president of Filene's of Boston until her "retirement." Miss Wilinsky reached the vice presidency step by step, starting with copywriter and advertising manager; she gradually moved up to fashion director and combined the duties of that job with managing Filene's advertising. Some stores have only a local reputation, but Filene's has been well known over the years in even out-of-the-way places in America. Much of the credit for the store's excellent image surely belongs to Miss Wilinsky, and she is often called on by Filene's alert management.

Women's Rights and Urban Affairs Executives

The widespread attention given to minorities during the 1960s was no accident. Despite the great demand for competent people to fill jobs in industry, the talent pool of minorities has been largely neglected. On the other hand, even though minority groups have gained some of their educational goals, there still is a long way to go in helping them acquire the tools they need to meet today's challenges. Individuals have managed, but as a group minorities still need plenty of help to catch up. Women, usually excluded from management careers until lately, have long been a forgotten minority and the accomplishments of which they are capable have been largely overlooked.

It is said that the black minority held the spotlight in the 1960s; the 1970s will be the era of the realization of women's rights. The push for equal pay and equal recognition in the management field may not be to everyone's liking, but the time is *now*, not 20 years in the future! The momentum for women's rights is gaining force.

When the National Organization for Women (NOW) was founded in October 1966 it was a fairly weak organization with only a dream behind it—that of bringing women into the mainstream of American life, truly equal in partnership with men. In a few short years this organization has become nationally known for bringing women closer to that goal. It has its detractors because of its aggressiveness, but perhaps it may still be one impressive approach for getting done what is hoped to be done by this book—to prove that there are capable women around and that they deserve a place in management's sun. Both methods may be needed.

Past President of NOW

Even though there may be some justification for questioning the techniques of NOW, the women involved have awakened many executives and officeholders to the fact that there are capable women around. No one underestimates the qualifications of Aileen Hernandez, a very capable and charming leader. Her work as an Equal Employment Opportunity Commission (EEOC) commissioner was outstanding. Her appointment by President Johnson was confirmed by the Senate in June 1965 for a full five-year term. She was the only woman member of the Commission, but stayed with it only a year because she became impatient with the lack of progress exhibited by the then-ponderous government agency. She is a past president of NOW and is currently chairone of the board.

Mrs. Hernandez operates her own freelance consulting firm specializing in urban affairs. She advises labor, government, and private industry on programs for utilizing minority groups and women and insuring that these groups have full access to education, housing, and employment opportunities. The victim of discrimination too often, Mrs. Hernandez firmly believes that a democratic government requires full participation by all citizens in decision making. She also believes in actively pushing a just cause—and maintains that the fight for women's rights is such a cause.

Again, the work of NOW is one way of trying to obtain equalization and as long as women like Mrs. Hernandez champion the cause, it surely has a great chance of succeeding.

It is interesting to note that Mrs. (or should we say Ms.) Hernandez is listed as chairone instead of chairman. Many women are serious about having this designation put in front of their names. Will the *Ms.* become universal? Who knows! Perhaps the desexing of titles for women will aid the movement but how much is anyone's guess.

Incidentally, or not so incidentally, many men with foresight recognized Mrs. Hernandez's talents early in the game. One nationally known vice president said, "If you want an outstanding speaker and one who knows what she is talking about on women's talents, get Aileen. She's smart." There is no question that she qualifies on all points.

Equal Opportunity Executives

Several companies have recognized that equal opportunity must be considered seriously. Like many important functions it often gets lost in the shuffle. Equal opportunity does not flourish under neglect. Unless carefully nurtured, it dies an early death. Consequently, the comparatively new job of equal opportunity coordinator, administrator, or director has been created. The firms that have decided to install such a person in a responsible job are not just paying lip service to an idea; they are actively doing something about discrimination in employment and in promotion.

There is some disagreement in management circles about what you should call a woman in charge of women's jobs. You can't say "Manager of Women"—nor can you say "In Charge of Sex Discrimination" or any variation of these titles. So you settle for "Special Projects," which isn't bad because in the 1970s the utilization of women in management is really a very special project. One could argue long into the night that women should not be singled out as requiring a special project, and to me this sounds logical. But there probably is justification to the argument that because of long neglect in this area there must be some crash reaction.

Too often, however, some firms are eager to publicize the fact that they are really going all out for their women—at long last. An example is the firm that has no management development program of any kind for *anyone*. Yet its somewhat flamboyant management now wants a woman to take care of all of its restless womanpower. This seems especially important to the firm because it is engaged in consumer goods and has had a skeptical eye focused on it by its women customers. The starting salary its executives are willing to pay for a woman to take charge of getting the program rolling ranges from $30,000 to $40,000. It seems to an outsider that qualified men in the organization would have a case for yelling loud and long.

Wouldn't it be more advisable to hire a topflight management director, man or woman, who would set up a solid management development program with some special publicity, if necessary, to let the women in the firm and the consumers know that women will be included in the race for good jobs? Are women to be given preferential treatment? That is what many of them are insisting on. Basically, this seems to be a terribly unsound premise whether it be for women or for blacks. A woman worth her salt and who is willing to take her chances on her own capabilities should feel insulted by such condescension.

Equal Opportunity Coordinator

There are firms that have hired or promoted well-qualified women to do the job. Both IBM and Atlantic Richfield have long had solid management development programs and now have women in charge of equal opportunity.

A well-liked, capable woman, Jean M. Moore is manager of equal opportunity affairs at Atlantic Richfield Company. This is how she describes her job: "Responsible for the development of corporate equal opportunity policies and programs leading to the employment and upgrading of minorities and women." (Note that she has responsibility for both minority groups and women.)

Atlantic Richfield is well known for its efforts in moving women from secretarial and stenographic positions to more responsible jobs. It is looking for methods of finding and motivating those women among these groups who want to move up.

Special Projects Coordinator

IBM has long been a leader in practicing good personnel policies. "Whoever leaves IBM?" is a well-known expression. It is not unexpected, then, that when the national limelight is focused on the "woman issue," IBM should be one of the companies that conscientiously undertake to examine themselves on the issue, and appropriately select a woman to fill the spot.

As corporate manager of special programs at IBM, Barbara Boyle was responsible for policy and development of equal opportunity for women within the entire corporation.

It was a big job, but Ms. Boyle was well suited to it and handled it extraordinarily well.

Probably one of the points about the young people of today that troubles older workers is that they want to jump into top jobs immediately. Perhaps in the future this will become more feasible through improved preparatory education that will allow them to do so. Perhaps, too, in the newer, more technical jobs, they will be able to accomplish this sooner and better than they can in the management jobs described in this book.

Like most of the others, Ms. Boyle came to IBM through a series of other jobs at IBM. As with many others, too, the early jobs bore only a slight resemblance to the present one. She started as a systems analyst and at one time held the position of systems engineering manager of Eastern and Central Europe. A smart executive in charge of management development recognized her talent. Even though she had been with the company for ten years, he forced her to sit down and seriously consider where she was going. He helped her set realistic goals and objectives outside the realm of traditional women-type positions. Barbara Boyle's story points up one of the key elements of success shared by most of the women in this book—the quality of hanging loose— being flexible and willing to listen, to take direction, and to shift gears in order to move ahead.

After leaving this headquarters position, she became marketing manager and assistant branch manager for one of IBM's largest branch offices in the United States. However, this prior experience in developing equal opportunity programs was sought after by many major corporations suddenly faced with the dilemma of federal compliance. In answer to this need for assistance, Ms. Boyle resigned after 14 years with IBM to become president of Boyle, Kirkman Associates Inc., a management consulting firm specializing in affirmative action programs for women.

Urban Affairs Director

Other jobs symptomatic of our times are those found in urban affairs. The problems of today's cities are almost overwhelming, especially in the major ones like New York and Chicago. What is the real responsibility of a company for hiring from the ghettos, for day care for children of working mothers, for employment and education of the dropouts? A job for a woman? "Yes," says Guin Hall, an urban affairs supervisor at New York Telephone Company. She describes her job as a middle-management position in personnel concerned with equal employment opportunity and affirmative action. She and the three people who report to her are responsible for initiating programs that will speed the career development and advancement of women and minority employees in all levels and job categories in the company.

Counselors

If the right kind of job isn't available, there are women who have created positions for themselves that in turn have helped other women. The bright graduates of the Seven Sisters Colleges of the East (Wellesley, Bryn Mawr, Pembroke, Radcliffe, Barnard, Vassar, Sarah Lawrence) too often were misdirected. Alice Gore King established the Alumnae Advisory Center to help graduates obtain jobs commensurate with their abilities. She brought to her own work both a business background as a supervisor at Pratt and Whitney Aircraft and her experience in the educational field. She did educational and counseling work at the Brearley School in New York and was a vocational advisor at Bryn Mawr. (An interesting sidelight is that the Ivy League, which has gone coeducational, is hoping to use the services of the Advisory Center.)

There is the perennial question whether a good liberal arts education can be really useful in industry. Many of the young women from the Seven Sisters have the best of such education and there are many with specialized skills, too. Miss King has done an excellent placement job for these young women (both the liberal arts and specialized graduates). Both the women and the firms where they were placed are pleased.

Data Processing

Computer Consultant

Data processing opened up a whole new world for bright young women as well as bright young men. Mathematics, a subject once thought "too complicated for little girls," is handled with considerable ease by many women. Sharyn Yanoshak, technical consultant at Cyphernetics, headquartered at Ann Arbor, Michigan, is bright and responsible. Pretty enough to be an asset to any team, she backs up her charm with a fast mind, knowledge of her job, and good solid hard work. Her work habits are exemplary. Her future in the computer field is indeed bright.

Here is how she describes her demanding job: "My main function is to help people in various professions use data processing tools in the most effective manner. My duties include pre-sales support, account management, and technical support (conducting seminars and classes; analyzing, designing, and programming data processing applications and individual instruction)." Not bad for a youngster whose skills enable her to deal with top and middle management across the country.

As a systems engineer at IBM, Pamela Duncan consults with customers and advises them on the installation of EDP equipment and software. Is this job within the definition of "management"? If management jobs are considered "think" jobs, this job qualifies well. Ms. Duncan's professional skill plus her ability to deal with people qualifies her as a member of management. Her position is indicative of the variety of jobs now open to women in the exciting world of electronics and computers.

Hospital Technicians

There have always been many women employees in hospitals. They have been the nurses, the aides, and the clerical help. Now, the pressure for better health care and the advances in medical science have opened a whole new field of jobs for bright women. Barbara Carstensen, less than 30 years of age, is an inhalation specialist at Mercy Hospital in Toledo, Ohio. Technically skilled, she also has supervisory responsibility for 30 people. Many lives owe their continuance to her skill. Her managerial skills are built on a deep understanding and respect for others' talents. When there are young women like Barbara Carstensen moving into management jobs by the same route of brains plus hard work, one wonders about some women, fortunately a small minority, who often talk equal rights but are unwilling to take the responsibilities that go with a good management job.

Psychologists

There are several women psychologists working in management positions in developing tests, in counseling, and in personnel advisory spots. Because of the concern about their work in the sensitive area of fair employment practices (especially under the EEOC guidelines) they prefer not to be identified. They are doing fine work. Psychology does offer an interesting and rewarding career for young people.

Researchers

A number of qualified women are performing all types of research —jobs that used to fall only to men. Dr. Joan B. Berkowitz is a project director at A. D. Little, Inc., Cambridge, Massachusetts. She is responsible for selling research contracts, putting together a team to do the work, doing the job within budget, and reporting to the client. She has been at A. D. Little since 1957 and continues to do a fine job in highly skilled research. She lives and works in a man's world, but her knowledge and finesse have earned her the respect of her associates and clients.

Other women are engaged in various types of research that affect management decisions. Among them are jobs in collective bargaining preparation, grievance handling, and other union matters. Still other women are involved in site location for new plants or stores, and in personnel practices such as vacations, holidays, pensions, and other employee benefits. Several are found in the compensation area, holding such positions as wage analyst or director of compensation.

Lawyers

The professions have long held opportunities for women, but the usual openings for women have traditionally been in the academic and medical fields—and here, too, men have usually held the choice spots. Now the field of law is opening up to more and more women. You will note that there have been other lawyers mentioned previously— Jacqueline Delafuente and Judith Vladeck. Still another fine lawyer is

Shirley O'Neill, attorney at Sullivan and Cromwell, one of the country's best-known law firms. Time was when a woman lawyer dressed and acted as much like her male counterparts as she could. Now women are maintaining their femininity but equaling men in the handling of their responsibilities.

Miss O'Neill is a senior associate in the trusts and estates department, where she does all the drafting, estate planning, and administration of decedents' estates. Managing these large estates is an exacting, demanding job that she handles competently and efficiently.

The rapid growth of corporations has brought about the need for an executive who can determine where plants should be located as well as deal with all the legal ramifications of owning valuable real estate. Claire Carlson has been a project engineer, a project manager, and the manager for real estate at Wetvaco. Now she has her own professional practice. Both a professional engineer and an attorney, she acts as a consultant to corporations in real estate projects. Her work is unusual for a woman. Call her job a happy union of having the right talents at the right time.

Educators

The field of education has been filled with women teachers—mostly on an elementary or high school level. Now there are more women pressuring for professorships at colleges and universities across the country. Rather than striving only for being heads of women's physical education departments, they are becoming professors of other disciplines. There is still a long way to go in this field, but times are changing.

A school situation with a new twist in the 1970s is the two-year accredited college that offers an associate degree and often provides a stepping-stone to a good job or entrance to a four-year school.

One of the most exciting of these schools is the Fashion Institute of Design and Merchandising in Los Angeles. Graduates of this school are requested by the retail industry, numerous manufacturing firms, banks, and insurance companies. The school has the active cooperation of more than four hundred companies. Graduates have degrees in design and/or merchandising.

In three and one-half years the number of students has increased to seven hundred students. Tony Thomas, president, and Donna Smith, a member of the board of directors, both no more than thirty, built up the Institute with a dream, with imagination, and with a solid selling job. These two young women are representative of a growing group of young women who have the guts to start a business and make it successful.

At the opposite side of the country is Webber College at Lake Wales, Florida, another two-year retailing college whose graduates are eagerly sought. There Jean Lang, chairman of the department of retailing, a well-informed professor of retailing, combines theory with practical training. Thoroughly familiar with the markets of New York and Paris as well as the mercantile industry all along the East Coast, each January Professor Lang takes 30 or 40 of her students on a behind-the-scenes "buying" tour in New York. The opportunity to meld education on a practical yet exciting level has been her ambition. As discussed elsewhere in this book, she is well known in yachting circles as well as in education. Like so many of the other women in this study, she leads an interesting life both on and off the job.

Margaret Green, who is dean of students at the Borough of Manhattan Community College of the City University of New York, is a counselor par excellence. She performs such diversified duties as counseling, arranging financial aid, and directing the College Discovery Program. In addition, she is chairwoman of the personnel and budget committees of the school. She deals with many of the discipline problems, which can be pretty rough in a city like New York. Dr. Green's qualifications for the job are solid, and the way she obtained her job shows ingenuity and courage. Her letter-writing campaign to the heads of New York colleges, and her persistence in following through on all the leads she turned up, got her what she went after.

Combining medicine and college teaching is a rewarding career for Dr. Hilda Pedersen, who holds many degrees. Trained at medical schools in Canada, Scotland, and the United States, Dr. Pedersen is now assistant professor of anesthesiology at Columbia University. Her job is half academic, half clinical. It involves clinical medicine and some administrative duties, plus the instruction of resident doctors and medical students. Traditionally, this was hardly considered a job for a woman, but this woman handles it extremely well.

Another educator who has combined her outstanding educational background with management skills is Carolyne K. Davis, who as chairman of the baccalaureate nursing program at Syracuse University, is responsible for planning and supervising the nursing program for more than 300 students. This means careful coordination with other departments as well as counseling the students involved. She must have a knowledge of her field and the students involved. It's a different kind of management job, but it takes a highly skilled manager to keep everything going smoothly.

Placement Work

Placement work in a personnel or executive search agency bears some resemblance to corporate personnel work. A good number of women have found success in this field.

Patricia Leonard is personnel manager for Hal-Ba Personnel Associates, a prestigious New York City agency. Her job entails counseling the applicant, filling vacancies for the client, and really working eyeball to eyeball, as she puts it, until everyone is satisfied.

Constance W. Klages, vice president of Battalia, Lotz & Associates, Inc., New York City, conducts executive search assignments, heads the research department, and performs general administrative functions. Her background includes research in the personnel field and wage and salary administration. Because of her in-depth knowledge of industry and its needs, she brings a very practical approach to her search assignments. In addition to her realistic approach, however, she calls on her creativity to match the right applicants to hard-to-fill positions.

Husband-and-Wife Teams

Many women have used their skills to help their husbands in their professions. There are many doctor–nurse or doctor teams and husband–wife teams in other fields, too.

One team that has proved eminently successful, one that is based on imagination and foresight, is that of Bette and Al Heydrick, management trainers. From their home–office houseboat in Ft. Lauderdale, Florida, they accept management assignments and travel the country to conduct management training courses. Formerly a highly skilled secretary, Mrs. Heydrick realized the importance of that job, but also recognized how few management skills were passed along to secretaries.

With her husband she conducts secretarial seminars on management know-how around the country. The Heydricks have helped many managers by returning their secretaries to them better trained and better able to handle their jobs in a professional manner. In addition, Mrs. Heydrick efficiently manages their office and keeps the firm's business records. This team of entrepreneurs really enjoys life and helps others to do so, too. This success should be a lesson to the critics who maintain that women cannot combine marriage with a career.

There is much propaganda about the discontent of young suburbanites—about the loss of the great American dream, as one television program described it. Is this picture the true one? Or are young women still getting married and finding joy in raising a family—while making sure their educational know-how does not go to waste? There are many women who belie the idea that marrage has to be a humdrum affair with no management responsibilities. Working with their husbands or holding down a job of their own, many women are happy, interesting, exciting people in their own right.

Homemaker—Professional

Tax Expert

A few examples of well-educated women who have taken the path of staying home—at least until their children are grown—follow. Maryellen Schwarz, wife of the well-known labor attorney Carl Schwarz, left tax accounting and estate administration at Kelley, Drye, Warren, Clark, Carr, and Ellis in New York to be a full-time housewife and mother. To keep her hand in business, however, she takes tax jobs at home and during the tax season has as many accounts to handle as she wants.

Farm Manager

Betsy Carstensen has five children, three of whom attend Ohio State University. She helps her husband manage a 500-acre farm in northern Ohio. Farming is big business, and a well-organized, resourceful woman does much to make the operation successful. Perhaps her master's in chemistry from Oregon State could be considered better training for a chemist's job, but undoubtedly her broad educational background has made her so eager to see that her children are well educated. (Her homemade "still" for making fine wines may have been helped along, too, by her chemistry education.)

Community Activities

Mrs. Jean Friend, wife of the plant manager of the Saginaw Steering Gear Division of General Motors in Saginaw, Michigan, has four children, one attending The University of Michigan. Mrs. Friend, too, has her master's—this one in home economics. She currently is involved in enough community activities (which really need doing but which offer little remuneration) to fill her spare time and manages a fine, happy household. Is she eager to change? Does she have enough to do? She says the days are not long enough to do all she wants to get done. Is she bored, as suburbanites are reputed to be? Not this busy, well-respected individual. Is her education wasted? "No, never," says she. She uses it every day—not only the technical part but also the human relations part.

Doctor

Dr. Elizabeth Coryllos Lardi had been chief of pediatric surgery at Flower Hospital in Manhattan, where she had much management responsibility. Dr. Coryllos is now married to a fine lawyer and has three children. She runs her home, has a private practice in pediatric surgery, and is in charge of pediatric surgery at Nassau County Medical Center, now part of Stony Brook University. She is happily married but still hasn't deserted her profession. A busy life? When I interviewed her, she was on a 6:30 A.M. train to attend a medical seminar in Philadelphia. Does she do a good management job both at home and at work? Absolutely yes.

Editor

Janet Thomas, educated at Ohio State, a teacher for about four years, and happily married to Thomas L. Thomas of Cyphernetics, is too busy to be bored. She thoroughly enjoys her young child and understands her husband's highly technical data processing work. She, too, is the opposite of the unhappy suburban mother who is becoming a major topic of concern in the 1970s. She continues to do freelance editing—mainly on dissertations and technical articles for magazines.

A common sorrow of many young families is that they never can settle down anyplace for very long. The newer crop of young executives and their wives fortunately does not seem to have this hangup. The Thomases, who left a home in Dearborn for suburban life in Scotch Plains, New Jersey, figure that it wouldn't be bad to pick up and live in other parts of the country. Perhaps the solid family background in Ohio offers them the security that so many other young people miss. For one born with wanderlust it sounds exciting and as long as some positions are dependent on a person's staying flexible, such changes won't be too bad. It is encouraging that so many newer young executives and their wives don't have to be tied to their mothers' apron strings.

Assistant-to

Michaelyn Robison has crossed over from supersecretary and teacher to being assistant to the president of Cyphernetics. This fast-moving computer time-sharing company has room for bright women, and Mrs. Robison is learning and moving fast up the ladder. She typifies some of the young assistants who have the world by the tail and are going to make good use of their knowledge. Assistants-to can be the water boys or they can be thinking professionals. Mrs. Robison is on her way to being one of the latter.

Service Adviser

A position requiring plenty of tact, for which women are supposedly noted, is that of service adviser for telephone companies. Lorle Guntsch not only advises firms on what service is best for them according to their needs but also follows up on service. She comes to this position with a wealth of supervisory experience. Her position represents many of the jobs that can be done by women—perhaps better than if these same jobs were done by men.

Usual Jobs with a Special Twist

Librarians used to be one of the most scoffed-at professional people, yet their jobs are very worthwhile, particularly if those jobs have a very special purpose. Virginia Varnum, who comes to the American Management Association with a good, solid industrial background and a fine education from Bates and the Sorbonne, does a fine job in the Information Center of AMA. This Center is widely known in the business community. From it an executive can obtain information on management development programs, behavioral sciences, labor relations, fringe benefits, and personnel practices throughout the world. Much of this information can be pinpointed by individual companies that are leaders in the fields of management. As a highly skilled researcher, Mrs. Varnum is well respected both in educational and business circles.

7

WHAT IS THE SUCCESSFUL WOMAN REALLY LIKE?

Vive la différence has long been the slogan of men who like being men and women who like being women. Is this attitude so different on the job? Are we management women out to desex the workplace? There is much talk about desexing jobs, and most women, whether they are members of the feminist movement or not, wholeheartedly support that proposition. They want an equal chance to get the job that best matches their background and their talents.

Desex the Job, Not the People

"It will be a sad day, however," says one high-level woman executive, "when . . . we are no longer aware that we are women—when the extra zip provided by sparring on a male–female basis is lost.

"The ratio of males to females is way out of whack in executive positions and I'll welcome the time when there is a more equitable distribution, but heaven help us if the men lose their virility just because there are some more of us smart women around running things."

Women's Inherent Talents

What talents are the women claiming as peculiarly their own? "Women are better at detail," says one woman executive, although others say they are trying to change this attitude. She continues, "I will stick to a job with greater persistence than most men. I would say, however, that in addition to ability to do a good job, a female executive must be extremely flexible, have a sense of humor (or how could we stand men), be completely unabashed by male ego, and not take herself too seriously."

A woman president says, "She must carry her load of work and then some. She must be a female female. She must be patient, polite, sympathetic, and understanding, and at the same time be very decisive. She must always maintain a coolness, dignity, and aloofness, while still being warm and friendly."

Another woman says, "A woman executive who is stable is able to balance an impersonal approach with measured warmth. She must manage well. She must be totally committed to her job. She must be talented, have brains, and be able to produce."

According to another executive, "I have a harder time delegating to other women in my department. They still resist taking direction from another woman."

And one more woman says, "I try harder to be considerate because I know that women bosses are supposed to be bitches. I know about human relations and I try to practice what I preach. I have my own personal problems—my only trouble is that I know when I make a mistake. Most men I know can't quite put themselves in the other person's spot."

The women in the survey are sure of their talents on the job. They believe that they have earned the recognition they now have. They have had plenty of hard knocks on the way up but in the process fortunately have not become hardened.

On the whole they picture themselves as talented, hardworking, enthusiastic, flexible, persevering, and more understanding of behavior than their fellow male executives. They are perhaps a bit more eager to do a good job—they want to prove that a woman *can* do a good job. They are, for the most part, confident that they are doing a good job. They are willing to take a chance on their talents paying off and will change jobs at the age of 50 or 55, or will leave a good job to start a new business at an age when men might be more cautious.

Perhaps this is because they are versatile—they have learned many things on the way to the top. They can write, teach, arbitrate, run a business, as well as their traditional jobs of selling, researching, or being a secretary. They are more willing to take chances than their male counterparts.

Some women, it is true, have the extra security of being married to a man with a good job. They do not have to take the guff that some men do and can afford to walk out and look for a new job. They are supported emotionally by strong men at home, which may not be the case with an insecure male who has a weak wife and the full weight of family responsibility on his shoulders—not that some men don't rely heavily on their wives for emotional support.

Younger women, with their talents, their drives, their fresh good looks, have much going for them and should make the world realize that giving the women equal job rights has not been a mistake. A caveat: they should not let their ambitions run away with them and make them forget the pleasures of being a woman.

Alice Rohloff, treasurer of Rohloff Bros., lists the necessary talents for successful women as follows:

1. A head for business.
2. Reasonably good health.
3. An extra amount of energy—almost more important than intelligence. This is what set men like John Kennedy apart from ordinary men.
4. Attention to details.
5. Ability to plan and organize.
6. Enough push to see that the job gets done. I really light a firecracker under people.
7. Being flexible and willing to change as change becomes necessary.
8. A certain inner toughness.
9. The presence of command. If you are running the show, you are running the show and you leave no question about that in anyone's mind.

Men's Opinions of Management Women

Men's opinions cover a wide range.

I hate to admit it but I want my wife to be home. I don't want her out in the rat race. I need comfort when I get home.

My wife doesn't dare make any extra money. She can do anything she wants to do as long as she doesn't push us up into the next tax bracket. There are many jobs left undone—like really

*seeing that the school board is run right and the church is func-
tioning. The world is crying for capable women to handle these
jobs and my wife does them beautifully. I am proud of what she
has done.*

*Yes, we'd like as a company to do right and we have promoted
quite a few secretaries to management spots. We're worried about
how we'll take care of the restless horde of clericals and secretaries who are anxious to move up.*

Does this man understand today's problems? We're not so sure.
Are the secretaries and women clerical workers willing to take all the
extra time, effort, and study it takes to shoulder a management job? If
they are willing, then they should be given a chance. If not, then perhaps they should be more content where they now are and let others
take the risks and the responsibilities.

Another man says, "Women have a tendency to nag even when
they are close to the top. Guess it's their unwillingness to get a broad
perspective. They hang on like bulldogs if they think someone is taking
over their pet project."

"My woman assistant (and this is one of the bright young technical
workers) is the best of the lot. She's pretty, she's pleasant, and she's
smart. She really gets the job done."

"It all depends on the woman," says another executive. "My personnel vice president does as good as or better than any man in the
field. She really understands what makes people tick."

And here, as a specific example, is what John W. Sheldon, president of Chas. A. Stevens & Co. (and supervisor of Mary Garzoni, vice
president), says about women in business. His statement is the way an
enlightened management looks at the picture.

> More and more women will succeed to top executive positions in
> the future. This will be the natural result of many things, foremost of
> which is the feminine desire to achieve success in the business world,
> and male acceptance (begrudging at times) of this fact. Education and
> leadership training are bringing more and more capable and qualified fe-
> males into all fields of business each year.
>
> It is my hope that female desire for success, in what has been up
> until now a "man's world," will not lead to a gradual breakdown or elim-
> ination of those feminine qualities which have been so admired and im-
> portant in the past: desire for family life, motherhood, the ability to give
> love and affection, gentleness, beauty of appearance, and so on. In the
> battle for equality in the business world, it would also be unfortunate if
> the male lost his qualities of chivalry and the accompanying respect for
> the female as the more "dependent" sex. . . . But perhaps women, with
> their desire for equality in all things . . . , will no longer be willing to
> accept or acknowledge that there is a difference between the sexes.

Women in top executive positions have long been a way of life in the retail field. There have been several store presidents, many merchandise managers, and perhaps more female buyers than male. In our store, we have long accepted equality of the sexes—the only criterion used is who is qualified to do the job. I believe in a store dealing mainly with women (such as Stevens) it is logical that a well-trained female executive should someday take over the top position of management.

A bank executive says that he likes the bright, younger women coming along because they don't seem to have the feminine hangups that some of the older women executives had. They are willing to pitch in and work hard. He also claims that women are more eager to get credit for their work—no matter how trivial.

In summary, men do respect the capable women they know. They still have a tendency to speak of isolated cases—examples of either perfection or gross incompetence. Many of them claim that women are best in jobs dealing with personnel, with urban problems, and environmental and consumer affairs. They grant that if a woman is good she is apt to be better at her job than a male counterpart. They also say this will change because of the equality of hiring and promotion practices among younger management. From now on women will probably be as good as but no better than their male co-workers.

They still like their all-male hangouts, and are often reluctant to let women in on their important planning projects. Many of the less enlightened ones still think that women are more apt to talk too much. If there is an isolated case where one woman makes a mistake or is a domineering, hard-to-live-with boss, they are quick to castigate all women managers. On the whole, however, the men who work with top-flight women executives treat them as equals, give credit where credit is due, and brag that their companies have been ahead of the game in recognizing that women can do the job.

Are men afraid of being overwhelmed by the rising female horde? They joke a little about the women's liberation movement, but because of the pressures from that group and from all sides, they are concerned about their own jobs, about what will happen if too many women executives are forced on them before the men have figured out ways to safeguard themselves. In 50 years it may not be a man's world—in 1972 their bastions in executive suites are still strong, but they are cracking.

Steps Toward the Management Job

When confronted with envious younger workers, the successful older management woman often hears this remark, "How can you understand us? You are a vice president and what do you know about our grievances and our struggles?" Unless time and position have acted as memory clouders, nothing can be further from the truth for a majority of the older management women mentioned in the study. (A definition of the term *older* is 35 and over.) Most started from humble job beginnings and advanced slowly toward the executive suite. Like many men in similar spots several had to change jobs four or five times to reach their current level.

Did they all start as secretaries? No. Only four of the women in the study started as secretaries. The most popular starting spot was teaching—elementary, high school, and college. Five of the respondents started in education and usually became disenchanted with the salaries and the lack of opportunity to use their management talents. The variety of starting points is illuminating. A listing of them includes systems analysts, newspaper reporters, music teachers, ad managers, copywriters, communication specialist, college-level physics teachers, tax accountant, cost and formula analyst for a baking company, benefits manager, rehabilitation counselor, workshop supervisor for women returning to the field of work, medical general practitioner, lawyer, supervisor of arts and crafts, postdoctoral fellow, and assistant fashion editor.

Probably the future women executives of department stores will come up through the executive training programs, but those in good management jobs now usually started in a different place. Some of the women presidents started as assistant buyers, as salesclerks, as assistants to merchandising managers, and as assistant ad managers and copywriters. The vice presidents of personnel or those who reached the top through personnel started as interviewers, editors of the company newspapers, assistant training directors, or assistant personnel directors.

Did the women reach the top in one fell swoop? The average number of jobs before "making it" was four. Most moved at least three times, and one person took eight moves to reach her present spot. Perhaps women coming into the field won't have to move up step by step, but the current picture, at least in our study, shows that the progress to the top, with a few exceptions, was not an overnight miraculous happening. Today's women who are looking for a top job will have to face the tough competiton of the women who are on the move within companies —those who have plenty of experience and know-how. Their advice, admittedly easy to give and often hard to take, is to get as much knowledge and job skill as you can before you begin shouting for your rights.

Did the women work while they were in college or before? Many of them talk of part-time sales jobs, a few of waiting tables at the national parks or at dormitories. Several used special talents in part-time jobs like tutoring while in college. There is no clear-cut pattern that early slaving in the salt mines leads to special achievement afterward.

Young women in college now seem to have more unique ways of earning extra money—giving birthday parties for youngsters, helping the local art museums, writing other people's term papers, and performing laboratory experiments. (Using these talents early certainly indicates that these young women will be successful.) These nondrudgery jobs sound more exciting than the old-fashioned table-waiting, baby-sitting, chore jobs that helped some management women struggle through college.

Significant Factors in Advancement

Many women tell of chance encounters that have turned the course of their lives. One told of starting to work for the U.S. Department of Labor. Because of a last-minute change in plans, the personnel director assigned her to the Wage Analysis Division as a statistical clerk, which eventually led to a career in labor and industrial relations outside the Department. Initially she was to be assigned to the Cost of Living Branch, where employees are more likely to remain statisticians.

Another woman tells of trying to interest an employer in one of her friends. Impressed with the plea, the employer decided to hire the woman herself instead of her friend.

A luncheon meeting and a chance conversation helped another woman get her job.

One woman said, "It is being in the right spot at the right time and not being afraid to take a chance."

Esther Peterson, then assistant to the president, tells of meeting Paul S. Forbes, president of Giant Food at the Inaugural Ball in 1965 when she was White House Consumer Adviser. Mr. Forbes offered assistance from Giant Food and asked that she visit him. In 1970 she became consumer adviser to Giant.

Help from Men Executives

Here is what the women answered to the query, "Do you believe that men higher in the organization really hate to hire or promote a woman? If so, why?"

If such a man is convinced of the qualifications of the woman, he believes sometimes that other men may not accept her. In other words, he knows it would be the thing to do, but will others approve of his choice? It can be a tough decision. Hiring is not as difficult, I believe, as promoting since the competition is rough among the male prospects.

I'm not sure. If they won't do it, it is because they have bought the myths. The man whose wife, mother, or sister believes that a woman's place is in the home frequently carries their beliefs into his working life. It tends to eliminate friction at home. There used to be, and probably still is, great influence on male executives whose wives resent or disapprove of women executives.

The higher men are in the organization the less threatened they feel by women and the more apt they are to encourage equal opportunity for women.

If males wouldn't promote good women, I wouldn't be where I am. Open-minded, appreciative men promoted women based on talent long before it was the popular thing to do.

It depends on the climate in the organization. This is likely to reflect cultural attitudes in the society, but it certainly varies in different types of organizations.

Yes. Feel threatened. This depends a lot on cultural background. Worse in Japanese and Latin–American men, but many Americans are very afraid of women.

Quite possibly. The hunt-culture puts the men together, while the women toil over the stove and the young children—mere details in their important life. Who will mind these details if they release the women? Worse, won't the unglamorous side of their hunt and their mistakes get into the wrong hands if a woman is allowed to chase with them? Maybe she'd be on the animals' side. If only one or two women should rise higher, they'd be lonely, wouldn't they? Anyway, they'd be divisive as hell, adding a whole new element to what was supposed to be a manly venture.

The men who say they would hate to work for a woman are generally men who have never had the experience. Many men who have worked under women supervisors report that it makes no difference to them one way or another. Of those that do hate to work for women, and have actually had the experience, some may feel that their masculinity is threatened. If the woman is not a good supervisor, however, neither men nor women like to work for her. Personally, the worst supervisor I ever had happened to be a woman.

Hate is too strong a word. I think men feel uncomfortable— particularly if the woman will be the first to "invade" what has been an exclusive male area. This will require evolving some new ground rules.

Yes. Ego-bruising.

Yes and except for government intervention I don't think that they would promote women. They think they'll get married and pregnant and leave.

Men won't forget the former job you had. Once you have been a secretary, you are always a secretary in their eyes.

Men don't always hate to promote women. Sometimes women are a threat unless you work hard at building up trust with charm, wisdom, and talent. Men will tend to generalize.

College Education as a Key

Analysis of the overall backgrounds of the women in the study shows that a college education has helped. A few of the respondents answered only that they had attended college but did not indicate either their schools or their degrees. The following list shows the degrees held (sometimes more than one) by the 60 women who did answer this question.

Degree	Women Holding Degree
BA	26
BS	20
MA	17
MS	3
MBA	3
PhD	5
LLB	7
MD	2

In addition, there is one graduate of a nursing school and one graduate of the ILGWU Training Institute who holds more than one college degree. Six women graduated cum laude, and three magna cum laude.

In the past, education has helped on the long haul. Note the advanced degrees listed—often taken at night or on personal time. This study certainly indicates a high correlation between success and education. The successful women in this study should emphasize the importance of education to the young people now in school. They also should indicate to the male manager that if he wants to promote or hire women in executive row he should be able to expect a better-than-fair education. How many of the "girls" in secretary's row or of the young members of the feminist movement have taken the time to get an education? One of the prominent women interviewed said, "Time in class will probably help more than time on the protest march." This statement doesn't mean to indict all secretaries or protesters. Has anyone taken the time or effort to analyze the educational background of the vast number of women pushing for promotions? If not, perhaps it is time to do so.

Is attendance at one or two special colleges and universities a main asset? Somewhat weighted to the Eastern and Midwestern schools, the sample probably didn't contain enough successful Western and Southern school graduates. The variety of schools represented, however, indicates that what is more important than attendance at a special college or university is how avidly a student studies and makes a success of her college years.

Were the women satisfied with their colleges? No direct question was asked, but some women wrote in comments. Here are a few:

> My college was academically very poor. Thank God I went on to a university which was better.

> I went to_____College when it was all female. A horrid school but free.

> [It was] terrible academically and socially. Besides lack of prestige I think that I studied as an isolated embryo for four years.

There is no question that many of the women involved, some of whom were born during the Great Depression or came from large families, attended free universities not because they were the best schools but because they were nearby and the tuition was free. Several who are second- or third-generation Americans heard about education as the key to success practically from babyhood. The study shows that many of the women involved received their advanced degrees on money they earned themselves.

Women Executives' Salaries

Telephone and interview questions indicated that the salaries run from approximately $18,000 to well over $50,000 per year, with the biggest cluster in the $22,000 to $30,000 bracket. How does this compare with men with similar educational and training background? There is no way of knowing, but the hunch is that it is somewhat low on the lower end of the scale without much difference at the top end.

Did these women always make as much as their male equals? Most of them admit it was hard to get a toehold. "My boss said, 'I hired you because I could get you cheaper than a man and you had more brains at the price I could pay.'" Discrimination, maybe, but it gave this woman the start she was looking for.

I had a hard time convincing my boss that I should get the same $35,000 he had paid the man ahead of me.

I had to move three times before I found someone who would pay me the same as he pays a man.

I'll never get the same as a man for the same job. I get good pay and I've almost given up the male–female battle.

These are what the older women are saying. Will the young ones have the same trouble? It is doubtful because the times are different and many managers are aware of the management talents of young women and are starting them at the higher salary levels that took years for some of the women in the study to make.

How Old Is the Successful Woman Manager?

At what age can a woman expect to be successful? The approximate average age of the successful woman in the study is in the early 40s although the range is from 23 to the early 60s. There are the exceptions, like Jane Evans Sheer, who became president of I. Miller at 25. It is possible, too, that at the top of the age scale the salaries at the lower end of the scale can be found.

Average tenure in management jobs comes out to about 24 years. Some of the older women talk about working for 40 years without blinking an eye and they are still going strong, too. "Seems like a long time to envision when one is young, but short from the vantage point of age," says one successful entrepreneur.

The length of one's working life should give young women entering the field pause for thought. The women in the study expressed satisfaction with their current jobs but indicated that their final selection was more hit-and-miss than they would have liked. Steering people into the right spot is a big responsibility for a management counselor. The surface of really matching job talents with work to be performed has just been scratched and hopefully will be better handled in the future.

"Twenty years more or less wasted before I found my niche," is too often the cry of the older worker (man or woman). It is hoped that this will not be true in the future.

The length of service of these successful women should also silence the management man who is afraid to take a chance on promoting or hiring a woman for a tough management spot because he is afraid she will leave. Women do stay in challenging jobs just as long as or longer than men. It is unjust not to give them a chance.

Who Set the Spark?

Let's backtrack just a bit to find out who lit the fire under these successful women to make them want to achieve. Again, this is not a deep psychological study although some of the longhairs could probably find meat in the answers. There are almost as many variances as there are women in the survey.

When asked who helped them the most, professionally, the women were generous in their praise of peers, bosses, and the inspirational work of professors who have contributed much toward human relations studies. The granting of responsibilities, the giving of credit where credit was due, the encouragement, and the lack of sex discrimination that were instrumental in the careers of these women all were applauded.

A few of the quotes will suffice.

Chief of surgery—he gave me my position and a completely free hand in running my department. He also gave me much encouragement.

There has been invaluable support from my general director and the assistant general director for whom I work directly—as manifested in confidence in my decisions, a willingness to rely on my judgment, and maximum support.

General manager and chief executive officer—gave me my head. Inspired and encouraged me.

My father, by encouraging but not forcing me to major in business and economics—to learn and work in a variety of aspects of the store.

Bob Blake [Blake-Mouton Managerial Grid®]—by encouraging me to learn more about group dynamics, human relations, and so on, both through personal Grid® experiences and from his books.

A very able statistician. He trained me to thoroughness, accuracy, and tenacity, and he trusted me to follow through, giving credit where credit was due. Another man—who threw me in the water and let me swim and at the same time took the time to educate me from day to day.

Middle and upper management (the people I've worked directly for and their management) have allowed me to shoulder as much responsibility as I chose. Other people I've worked with are intelligent and secure enough to help, and subsequently recommended me.

The senior partner of the first law firm for which I worked. He encouraged me to work even after my children were born (causing him inconvenience in staffing and so on).

My immediate supervisor in each job.

My former boss for 16 years. He was extremely capable, intelligent and quite generous to those whose work pleased him. He was critical in a constructive way, quite sure of his own capacities so not hung up in any relationship with his staff. He would never allow you to present a problem to him without some suggestions as to its solution. He would never belittle you but you knew he wouldn't tolerate an untruth, coverup, or sloppy work. He made you stretch and then made you proud that you had.

There are some who surprisingly enough take the credit themselves, and no one underestimates the push that has been necessary for them to get where they are. Here are their opinions:

No one—I got my own first job and every one after that.

No one really helped me; I took advantage of certain opportunities to show others that the work can be done on the same level as a male counterpart.

In our company, I as vice president knew more about my work than the president and he trusts my judgment in my field.

No one individual—I prefer to think I did it on my own.

Who has helped these women on a personal basis? Not all of them said their fathers or their brothers, although this often was the case. The ones who are married invariably gave their husbands much of the credit. The enormous support, emotionally and often professionally, of husbands makes this study most revealing. The equalitarian marriage of today, which often bogs down in details about sharing household chores and baby sitting, hardly compares with the marriages of these successful women, who give such glowing tributes to their husbands.

Mothers, fathers, sisters, brothers, and even an uncle or two came in for much credit, especially the parents who recognized early in the game that girls were to be encouraged to succeed as well as the boys in the family.

Women like Eleanor Roosevelt and Lillian Gilbreth, Frieda Miller, and Frances Perkins were most inspiring to many of the women in the study.

Here are a few of the answers to the question, "Who has or had the most influence, on a personal basis, in shaping your career?"

Husband. I probably never would have made a job change upward without his encouragement.

My father and my husband.

My husband—he is intellectually and completely sympathetic with my work.

My parents managed to instill in me a respect for hard work and for all people (no matter how much "below" you they are). They expect me to do well, be honest, and respect myself.

My husband, who encouraged me to get my PhD and encouraged me to take and do various jobs.

My mother, through example more than anything else. I always thought she was doing an important job and enjoying it.

My father talked freely about business at home—gave me much encouragement.

My parents. They had little education and maybe overemphasized its importance. They also recognized that I had wits even if I was a girl and so encouraged me to use them.

Enormous support from my husband—professionally and emotionally.

As Eileen Ahern of Continental Can Company sums it up, "I was very fortunate in having throughout my early life wonderful 'models' or 'examples' of family members and others doing interesting work."

Outside Activities

Are the women so company-oriented that they are interested only in their jobs? Just as most all of them are energetic at their work their off-job activities are fantastic. What do they do for fun?

Jean Lang, professor at Webber College in Florida, piloted her 24½-foot Trojan powerboat from Tampa to the southern shores of Lake Erie alone. Jean says she is no feminist, but because she has done so well in nautical circles, she states, "Perhaps in my own small way, I'll make it easier for women to be accepted in boating circles."

Some are gourmet cooks. Helen Bentley is interested in antiques and dogs. Rita Perna prefers metaphysics, home decorating, antiques, and travel. Judith Vladeck has been interested in the New York Civil Liberties Union but was also active in PTA's when her children were young.

Most say they are not joiners and several get impatient with women's clubs. One woman, who now teaches religion in a parochial school, said: "Nothing gets done—even my alumnae activities get me frustrated. I find non-businesswomen hard to work with."

Many, whose husbands are also prominent, do a good deal of home entertaining over the weekend. And a person like Jean Head Sisco, wife of Joseph Sisco of the U.S. State Department, has accompanied her husband on several overseas journeys. Africa and the Far East have both been on Mrs. Sisco's itinerary. She received the National Retail Merchants' Association award for meritorious service to the industry. One of the proudest in the audience was Mr. Sisco.

Arneta Dow's main outside interest is her riding stables.

Coline Covington is active in charity groups and serves on a county committee of the Republican Party.

Others find time to teach a college course or two at night, superintend Sunday schools or help the Girl Scouts and Boy Scouts and local community projects. Most of them have an itchy foot and have traveled almost everywhere in the world.

Some can quote baseball, basketball, and football scores and know which horse is expected to win the Derby.

Dr. Joan Berkowitz admits to being an opera buff. She is a member of NOW.

Aileen Hernandez, past president of NOW, is interested in fishing, dogs, and reading.

Mary McMahon of Equitable says she tries to keep some outside activities going—community and professional organizations, cultural education (from MA to yoga).

Esther Peterson says her home is her greatest "outside" interest. This is also true of many of the other women, especially those with small children, who curtail their own outside activities so they can spend time at home and learn to know and cherish their families. From observation it seems that many of these women spend more time with their families than stay-at-homes who shoo their children out as soon as the husband departs for work. Such a study would be interesting.

Another is a member of a hiking club and is very much interested in the stock market. Mary Girard is interested in sports, church, volunteer work, good friends, and continuing her formal education.

If all the outside activities the women mentioned were listed, they would probably fill a chapter. But there is no question that the off-hour lives of the working women are as diverse and interesting as their jobs are. They don't sit home at night and think only about work.

This doesn't mean that briefcases of work don't go home when the job gets ahead of them—when the days are not long enough to get the job done. They talk, just as male executives do, of a 50- to 60-hour week.

Most however, seem to be able to unwind better than some of their male counterparts who can never leave the office behind.

Position in Family

Do you really have to be the seventh child of a seventh child to succeed? Does being an only child help? Unlike some studies that have found the most successful women to be either the oldest or to come from a family of all girls, there seems to be no set pattern among the women studied.

Those that came from big families of seven or eight are either the oldest or close to being the oldest. Perhaps the drive to succeed was fostered more by necessity than by the spot in the family lineup.

Where the girl happened to be the "sandwich" child between two brothers she seems to have tried to emulate their success.

Young, well-educated women came from families who have been able and willing to give them a good start in life.

Habits of success seem to run in families—two sisters in the study are both successful. One executive talks fondly of her two brothers—one a doctor, the other a professor.

There may be some truth to the belief that a second daughter may have an unconscious ambition to succeed because she has always thought she should have been born a boy.

In one big family, all have turned out to be successful—two professors (one woman, one man), a woman vice president, a woman treasurer, a male engineer, a male scientific farmer, and two successful homemakers.

Other, more psychologically inclined surveyors may be able to read a pattern in the data on family size or place in the family as predictors of success. This study negates such findings.

Additional Education and Skills

Additonal education and additional skills have also been factors in advancement. The steady progress toward the top has been a building experience. Women have been able to switch gears to take on more assignments than were included in the job when they first took it. They have moved with the times. Often their jobs have been enlarged because they have been willing to learn new approaches, to find solutions to company problems.

Managers Who Have Returned to the Workforce

Three women have come back into the management field after a 15- to 20-year absence.

Beatrice F. M. Wilson is now the manager of employment services for Allied Chemical Corporation in Morristown, New Jersey. Her job (a new one) involves development and training for flexibility of interviewers in recruiting from new sources, placement and promotional placement, exit interviewing, school and college recruiting from lower-level positions, counseling for preparation training for advancement, and so on. Her plans for the future, hopefully, will include counseling for retirement and utilization of benefits. It is interesting that Mrs. Wilson is another businesswoman whose talents have been recognized by vice president Albert F. Waters, who has done much over the years in helping women in management progress.

Even though Mrs. Wilson has come back to work she, like so many of the women in the study, keeps busy with volunteer work. She is presently the vice president of Homecrafters, Inc., a private, non-profit-making organization to provide low- and middle-income housing by redoing existing houses and coverting them into apartments.

It is also interesting to note that Mrs. Wilson was the first woman personnel director in the Macy corporation.

Another admirable woman back in the labor market is Hermine Levine, now a writer and an editor at Prentice-Hall. With solid working experience behind her in the field of industrial relations, Mrs. Levine will soon become as well known in the field as she was when she left it to raise her children.

Another back-to-work officer is Evelyn G. Enteman, who is trust officer in financial planning at the American National Bank and Trust of New Jersey, Morristown, New Jersey. In a steady rise from an administrative assistant to a trust administrator, she describes her job as a "financial planning officer selling trust service including current money management and estate planning services to a prospect's objective and to solve prospect's personal and financial problems." She develops leads and also addresses community groups regarding trust services.

Mrs. Enteman was out of the workforce for 15 years. She says that the interlude "enriched my understanding of human beings because I personally was involved with family responsibilities and extracurricular activities (primarily educational)."

These three women are representative of the growing number of women who come back into the workforce when their children are self-sufficient.

It is especially worth noting that these women have come back to better spots than those they left. Their lives, in the interim, were busy ones, spent in managing necessary volunteer activities. Their skills did not become rusty, and alert management recognized this fact.

In summary, women have progressed in their jobs because they have been alert, have built toward their next positions on a solid base of a present job well done, have taken further education when the job demanded it, and perhaps most important of all have had men supervisors who have been willing to promote them.

Some have not advanced because they have not been sure they would be given the top spot. They have only *assumed* that the boss *knew* they wanted the top spot but wouldn't advance them. Lack of communication has blocked more than one promotion.

The chief roadblock to their advancement has been, until now, management's reluctance to "take a chance" on them. Many have moved out in order to move up. The women's liberation members talk of male chauvinism. Whatever name this prejudice has, it has been slow to disappear from industry. The climate is getting better—right now many firms are eager to find good executives.

The second biggest handicap, for whatever reason, is the woman herself. Too many have been reluctant to prepare for management jobs. Too many will not assume the responsibilities, and too many will not spend the long hours necessary to do the executive job. They have been unsure of their talents and reluctant to test them.

Again, the younger women intent on careers don't seem to have these hangups. But if they think their brains alone will assure them of a spot, they need to readjust their thinking. The competition is tough. The "jungle," the "rat race," the "shop," the "office," whatever the label, is a demanding place and no spot for weaklings. The rewards are great but the pace is fast and rough.

Are the women satisfied with their present spots? Most are pleased that they have succeeded, but just wave a new, interesting job with an advance in pay and position before their noses and, to a woman, they will take a chance in newer, greener fields. In this respect they are no different from men.

The myth of a person's being too old to change jobs doesn't seem to bother them. More confident of their talents at 40 than at 30 and even more confident at 50 or even close to or over 60, they talk of new worlds to conquer—a professorship at retirement, writing a book, going into private practice, founding a school, and so on. The fact that many have changed jobs four or five times indicates a willingness to take on new and bigger jobs. Perhaps it is because they are more secure than many of their male counterparts who are worried by heavy family responsibilities they are not hampered by the fear of changing jobs to better themselves.

Do women want the top spot in the company or the university or the store? No one said so outright, but the time is over when women are willing to report to and make incompetent males look good. Women will go far to see that they get spots where their own talents are recognized and respected. They will not be content with mediocre, second-class jobs and any management that does not wake up to this fact is not long for this world. Sad as it is for some men to face, the traditionally all-male management world is finally opening up to all talented people —as evidenced by the attainments of the women in this study.

A composite picture of today's woman executive shows her to be well-educated, experienced, involved most of the time in a normal, happy home life, interested in outside fun and constructive activities. She is concerned about her own and her company's success and is well aware of the rough problems of the world. She has attained success between 35 and 40 years of age and has moved two or three times before attaining it. She has been battered by some rough experiences on the way up but has reached an "inner calmness" and sureness that are hard to beat.

Today's management woman earns over $20,000 a year and a very few go up to $100,000. There are more men in the highest brackets, but the women are moving up.

Is this whole picture different from that of male executives? We'd have to make a study to determine that. We assume that as of now the men reach their higher earnings sooner and perhaps don't have to move so often to do so.

As discussed in earlier chapters, women are found in almost every facet of working life. In the past they have leaned toward the "people" positions, but there seems to be no limit to the positions they will hold in the future.

Are there unique contributions that women can make? They have been remarkably good in personnel—they will probably continue to flourish in this field. The new fields of urban development, community relations, environmental concerns, and consumerism are all close to the interests of women. They have been concerned with and responsible for these facets of the home and perhaps will carry over special talents to these new fields. The technical fields, especially those tied in with the computer, also seem to have special appeal, and women are doing well here. Architects, lawyers, and doctors all are finding women eager and willing to enter and share in these almost exclusively male worlds. Can they contribute anything special to top management jobs? Perhaps so, but they will have to compete for these jobs.

Are women naturally sweeter, kinder, and less tough than men, and do these attributes shine through so that women will settle the world's problems when they assume more power? It is doubtful. Wars didn't stop when women received the vote and it is doubtful if corporations will run a whole lot differently when women do have more voice in management. But who knows?

The Black Woman Manager

An effort was made to include black women's opinions in this book, but unfortunately few replied to the questionnaire. Those who did reply made no comments on racial issues. An interview with one woman manager and informal conversations with several others gave a wide scope of answers ranging from some bitterness on the part of capable black women who had been bypassed on promotions, to militancy on the part of some young blacks, to disregard of color by others. These last women do not forget that they are black and are more than willing to help their black sisters. By disregarding color, they chose to concentrate intensely on doing a good job to answer the critics who say that blacks do not measure up. As one of the women put it, "As to the black question, I'm not a good candidate on this topic. With the female and black issues I pretend they don't exist. As to the resentment I have encountered, I feel they are more female than black in origin."

It is hoped that black women, because of their efforts and talent, will be recognized—and moved up—for what they can offer.

8
THE WOMAN EXECUTIVE
COPES WITH
BEING FEMALE

The implication still remains that if you have an important job with heavy responsibilities you are somewhat different from your "more feminine" sisters who stay home in the traditional role of mother and wife. You are different, too, from your less ambitious and, sometimes, less able sisters who are willing to take a job as a secondary wage earner so they can devote more time to the home. Both these myths are a long time dying.

If you mean that by being feminine a woman is lighthearted, light-headed, and frivolous, and cares more for her clothes and chitchat than she does for handling big responsibilities with adeptness equal to that of a man, then women in management jobs might be considered less feminine. Ambitious and hardworking, they want to do their jobs well. It is true that the job takes on more importance than it does for the others in less responsible jobs. Many of them handle projects with agility, skill, and grace—and in addition manage their homes well.

Grooming

Sitting behind an executive desk in no way dampens a woman's interest in good grooming. Like her male counterpart, the modern woman executive is well dressed and impeccably groomed. Often the men rely on their wives to do their shopping, but the woman executive has to do her own. Rather than making frequent trips to the stores like her friends in less responsible, lower-paid jobs, she usually plans her wardrobe carefully and, to conserve her very limited time, may buy several outfits on one trip.

Management women are impatient with their female colleagues who play the little girl role by wearing too many buttons and bows. Such frills just don't jibe with the management woman's thinking. But the old-time mannish dress of the woman manager is no longer the order of the day. Women are not trying to look like their male counterparts. Sometimes, in fact, the trend seems to be in the other direction—with the frilly, colorful shirts some men wear to their executive dress affairs.

The women included in this survey prove that women can be feminine without detracting from their keen wits or ability to handle their jobs. Esther Peterson is as ladylike as any woman you can find; there is G. G. Michelson, well groomed and well dressed; Eileen Casey, with her special dash; and Jane Sisco, beautifully dressed in smart outfits.

Most women executives keep their "clothes thinking" in perspective. While some women spend hours at cocktail parties talking only about clothes, the management woman usually participates in meaningful conversation and is usually popular at these functions because of her ease in discussing so-called men's affairs. Some, however, score extra points by being unique in their dress. Aileen Hernandez has always been known for her hats as well as for her ability. There are also some men who are distinctive because of their ties or their offbeat, sharp clothes.

The main point here is that women dress well, just as their male counterparts do, because good grooming is an asset to any executive.

Swearing

Do women imitate some of the men they work with and lapse into occasional swearwords and temper displays? Many of us do have fairly colorful vocabularies that will match any man's. But does swearing make a woman less feminine, or does it just show that she is human?

Although some women have taken on the traditionally male attribute of swearing, most women, even the ones who sometimes express themselves in strong language, for the most part rely on using good grammar, a soft voice, and other effective communication tools. As Jane Evans Sheer puts it, "She must *act* like a woman. Her uniqueness as a woman is destroyed if she starts slamming her fist on the desk, using obscenities, and so forth. And it is precisely this *uniqueness* that is one of the foremost attributes of a female executive."

The Menstrual Cycle and Menopause

Not one woman in the study mentioned these as special problems. It is assumed that women who shoulder as many responsible duties as they do know when to seek competent medical advice.

The menopause is probably a more pertinent subject, although working women executives do not seem to be bothered tremendously. Again, women seek medical help, if necessary, to ease them through when they have difficulty. Again, it's like having babies; menopause has to be considered in the scheme of things for women executives, but from the survey notes there is no indication that either menstruation or menopause presents major problems. Nuisances, yes, but not major obstacles to a woman's on-the-job performance.

Interpersonal Relations

In today's world extra effort is needed on the part of management to halt the dehumanizing trend of business life so that the finer qualities of interpersonal relations can again flourish. Such effort is also good business: evidence shows that the management that pays attention to its human resources is the one that will pull ahead.

Some people believe that women by nature are more compassionate and kinder than men and that that is why women have been so successful in human relations jobs. Some also fear that when a woman reaches executive status she will lose her "natural" feminine concern about social problems. But there are people in business, both men and women, who are overly ambitious, cruel cutthroats. It is unfair to say that most women managers are "good" and most men "bad." Either the individual executive is concerned about and sensitive to the needs of people, or the executive is unconcerned and insensitive. Sex has little to do with human relations. Reaching the top does not mean that a woman —or a man—will automatically become unconcerned about people.

The Married Woman Executive

A working wife, whatever her level of responsibility, usually has to do some fancy balancing of time, effort, and talent to be sure that she has a happy home. Over three-quarters of the women surveyed are married. Perhaps this is a lopsided sample, but the individual opinions are interesting.

The most evident conclusion is that the women have happy, successful marriages. Such remarks as "My husband is a saint," "My husband is a beautiful man," and "Man, he's the greatest" wouldn't really be expected from sophisticated working women. Maybe because they usually work with high-caliber male executives most of the day, these women have nearly always selected, or been selected by, men who are wonderful helpmates and inspirations, and almost always are in an equal or better position than the wife–executive. Although there were three divorcées in the sample, not one of the women said she was disillusioned with marriage.

It is evident that marriage adds one more important facet to a very busy schedule. As one woman put it, "My biggest hangup is my schizophrenic responsibility to home."

The Equalitarian Marriage

Some of the younger women in the study are married, too, but their marriages are based on a more rigid agreement with their husbands to share household duties. The "equalitarian marriage" or a version thereof is their answer. Their arrangements are what so many working women executives have had informally for a long time. It may be the answer for the next generation of working women executives. Here is how one woman executive, who did not want to be identified, describes it, "An equalitarian marriage means that marriage is a partnership rather than a dictatorship where one decides and the other follows.

"An equalitarian marriage is founded on mutual respect for the identities, views, and careers of both participants. Both share in the household duties involved, either by performing them together or dividing them up; and both discuss matters which affect the family unit and come to a mutual decision as to how to handle such matters. Both contribute to family income and both decide on such matters as attending social functions, spending money, changing jobs, moving, and so on, with the standard being: what is best for both parties involved, what is best for the husband—wife unit."

This same executive goes on to say, "I have found it impossible physically for a woman to work full time and carry on the responsibilities of a home full time. I fear many married women attempt this and some, perhaps, manage it. But I consider it inequitable, physically impossible, and also impossible timewise. Women's rights is meaningless if all it means is that a woman has the opportunity to work at an outside job, but then also comes home and carries on full-time household activities. The change in the women's work situation requires a corresponding change in her home duties; and equal participation by her husband in the performance of such duties."

To that, all the women would add a hearty "Amen."

Most of the women in the study have the old-fashioned kind of marriage, but are willing to concede and are happy that the young women of today have found a way they think may make their marriages work. Many of them do remember some of the early days of their careers when it was rough to face some of the household chores alone— just because that is the way things had always been done in a home relationship. Most, however, remember thoughtful husbands who did share the early struggle. At that time their husbands weren't always so successful either. Most had a way of evening out the chores; the woman supplemented the husband's income, and he in turn helped with the household responsibilities.

One young woman professor, not sure she wants marriage on a long-term basis but sure of her career plans, has set it up this way. She and her husband review their marriage every five years to see if they want to continue the relationship. So far they are in the seventh year of marriage and are happy both at work and at home.

What do men executives think of the equalitarian marriage? Probably the same as their less sophisticated friends. "Sign a contract like that? I'd tell her to leave first or I'd get out of town." Or, "What is this world coming to? A real man would be crazy to sign something like that." Another: "What would it be worth after a month? My old lady and I had some real downright battles before we settled down in an armed truce. I don't think a piece of paper would have helped us."

One man comments, "A contract is a sacred thing with me. I'd hate like everything to sign where the human factors are so variable. It takes a lot of adjusting to stay married and I don't think the rigidity of a contract—if I understand this 'equalitarian' marriage deal—will work any better than the old-fashioned kind if two people don't work at it. And for that you don't need this new kind of deal."

The Traditional Way, with Variations

Perhaps the answer to the question of how to work and still live happily with your husband depends much on the individual. Many women, and particularly those in management jobs, maintain that such an arrangement as spelled out in the equalitarian marriage is not for them. Even at home, they like to maintain their own identities and have worked out their own rules of home living—from one extreme to the other. One woman, while maintaining that her husband was a prince, admitted that he never helped with details like shopping, dishwashing, or planning wardrobes for the children. He became deeply involved in the major issues affecting the home, such as school planning, and what was going on in the neighborhood that would affect his family, served on the school board, and so on. His word was still final, and everyone agreed it wasn't such a bad way of life.

There is the old story going the rounds that the husband is allowed to form all the major opinions around the house—on ending the war or the state of the nation—while his wife makes all the other decisions, such as how to spend the family's money or where they should go on vacation. The decision making in any household may level out on such a plane, but in most households where husband and wife work in management jobs, it's more of a problem to plan their personal time together than to decide what to do with it. Vacations must be planned early to jibe with two management timetables. Sudden management meetings—and what company doesn't have some—mean last-minute alterations in family plans.

In two-management-member households everybody has to learn to play it loose, to be ready if you want to, to pick up on fairly sudden notice and go along on business trips, to alter dinner plans, to go to the theater with someone else.

Sharing Responsibilities for
Participating in Family Occasions

Most married management men try to plan their business lives as carefully as possible around the family life. Women try, or so it seems, to plan more carefully around the family. Often it is considered a cardinal sin if at least one parent is not around for graduations, family occasions, important parties, and parent–teacher meetings. Women executives work at keeping those important family dates, and plan carefully with their husbands to see that the occasions are covered. Do women deal with this aspect of their home lives better than men or their stay-at-home sisters? It seems that they take it on as their responsibility. They are more likely to recognize the importance of these occasions than those who often have more time to attend to these functions and tend to take them for granted.

Do You Have to Be Married to Be Happy on the Job?

The women who aren't married seem content without husbands— they have many other activities to keep them busy and happy. Do they lead a sexless life? "Not by a long shot," says one of them. "There are plenty of unhappy married men to escort you when you want them around and plenty of eligible nonmarrieds to live with for a time without the permanence of marriage." This setup would shock some of our mothers, but in the day of the pill, some management women as well as their younger counterparts are not demanding or requiring marriage as the only way to having a sex life. Does this mean that they think less of marriage? Not necessarily. They just don't want to be dried-up old prunes, and as one of them so aptly says, "Marriage is an individual decision which neither makes nor breaks a woman in a management job."

So, if you are contemplating a management job and will listen to the advice of the happily married, you'll not bypass marriage, but life won't fall apart if you decide to go it alone.

Husbands of Management Women

The women's husbands usually have positions equal to or better than those of their working wives. Perhaps this won't always be true when more and more women attain management jobs. One personnel vice president is taking a second look—is concerned about whether she really has as full a family relationship with her president husband as possible. Most of the husbands, or so say the working women executives, are proud of their wives. Both seem sure enough of their own abilities not to wince when one or the other gets extra kudos.

It's true, however, that there are still embarrassing moments, especially if the woman or her company insists she use her maiden name. Nothing is worse than to have a successful husband referred to as Mr. Smith when his name is Mr. Jones, or to attend a wife's management function and be introduced as: "And here is Mr. Black—he's Mary's husband." The introduction can be handled more gracefully by finding out in advance what he does and introducing him in his own right, and then mentioning that he is Mary's husband. Most husbands prefer to stay in the background at such affairs, and the host who drags them from behind the post is not very popular in executive households. It is still a delicate position.

Change of Location—A Marital Decision

When it comes to changes in job location, the husband's job usually takes precedence, although it's a mutually made decision. There are a few long-distance setups where the man works in one city and his wife and children stay in another. Usually this is a temporary situation, because weekend setups are hard to maintain financially and emotionally for long periods, especially when children are involved.

Although there are many stay-at-home wives who will pick up on a week's notice and settle elsewhere when their husband's job demands it, there are many who want to stay close to their mothers or who just couldn't stand living in another part of the country. This is not true of the woman executive. Many times she has worked long and hard to get to her management spot. She is, even so, less likely to panic and is more flexible when a family move is necessary. Most women in the study, admitting to numerous changes of home addresses while their husbands were moving up, have now settled in one location. Younger executives may find relocating more of a problem when women start nearer the top and have equal to or better jobs than their husbands—it may be tougher to decide whose job takes precedence. This will be a family decision.

Here's the advice of one management woman: "Find a loving husband who believes in your career having as much importance as his. Limit your family size. Keep them well informed about what you do, what your problems are so they feel they are, and *are,* a part of your life."

Working Women as Mothers

With her busy life and her 12 children, Lillian Gilbreth proved that women could work in high-level jobs outside the home and still provide love and affection for and inspire achievement in her family. Again, it isn't easy. To do a job well and at the same time manage your own home means juggling your time.

Some interesting statistics in the *Monthly Labor Review* indicate that highly educated women are more likely to be working than less-educated women.[1] About half the married women with four years of college education are working, while one-third of the married women with 11 years of schooling or less are working. Women in top management positions have fewer children, according to the statistics.

Way over half the women in the study have children—one or two or even three; the woman with more than three is the exception. Do these women have special problems? Yes. A clerk or a factory worker can keep regular hours. She can close the door on her job, plan a regular schedule, and not "take her job home with her." Loaded briefcases, unexpected last-minute projects, and unscheduled trips are part of the work of a successful management woman. Is she is not entitled to ask for special privileges because she is a woman?

Competent child care is the biggest source of concern for the working wife whether she is a top or middle manager or holds a job lower in the hierarchy.

A few women included in the study solved the issue by waiting until the youngest child was six years old before going back to work. Some have been able to carry on part of their old jobs at home. Tax work, real estate, architecture, writing, law, and medicine offer one solution to this problem.

The upper management woman who does decide to work outside the home has very special child-care problems. If she wants to make sure her children are well cared for, she must make an extra effort. Her advantage is that she probably has more money to spend to hire someone to care for her children. Usually she tries to get someone to live in and does not, as so many working mothers are forced to do, deposit the children with neighbors, relatives, or "hired mothers" who keep other people's children in their own homes.

This is not easy for the woman executive. Like so many women everywhere, she still is concerned, and sometimes even in the middle of a management meeting she copes with the nagging question: Is my child really being well cared for?

Here is what the women in the study say about the problem and how they have dealt with it.

Some, like Esther Peterson, have been fortunate in having competent housekeepers for many years. She says, "My husband and children are very cooperative. I've always had good household help. Essentially two housekeepers (one at a time) over about 30 years of active participation. My present housekeeper has been with us over 25 years. . . ."

Some of the mothers have worked by necessity.

"I was divorced when my children were growing up. Work for me was a necessity and the children knew it. Travel for a time was a problem because of getting household help, and the expenses."

"We would now be considered the 'working poor' when we first got married. I worked because we really wanted our children to have the best in education. I believe it has paid off."

On looking back, some say, "I probably worked too hard for what was achieved by my working—except for self-gratification and identification. I have raised six wonderful children."

One working executive relates how she didn't learn until long afterward how her little girl got over a cold that hung on persistently. The old remedy of hot gin seems hardly appropriate today, but that's how one "nurse" broke the cold. Would the mother have done the same thing? Hardly, but the child survived and still laughs about the high old time she had with this carefree young woman who watched over her while her mother was gone. Mistakes have been made, but some of these probably could have happened even while the mother was home.

When both father and mother work long hours during the week, they often bypass many adult social affairs to be with their children because they are concerned about them. If the hours spent with their children were added up, they might well exceed the time spent with children by some nonworking women who kick them out early in the morning and never see them until nightfall. Such women may know less about their children than the executive who double-checks by phone during the day to see where her children are and what they are doing.

I believe Barbara Boyle summarizes the working executive's home situation well. She says, "It is essential that a husband and wife discuss things out together. They need to respect each other's personalities as well as family needs. I think that children can enjoy a home environment that is truly a happy one because each person in the family is a self-fulfilled individual. While they might lose sometimes during the week, weekends are full of family happenings and togetherness.

"It is a joy to be able to help one another with people-type situations or general decisions. Talking things out with an objective person who *really understands* is tremendously helpful to all parties."

Approaches to the Problems of Child Care

If the worry that all working women have could be eased, they probably could concentrate even better on their jobs; most management women have tried to partition off their minds from such problems, but the nagging concern is still there.

Although fathers are cooperative, child care usually remains the responsiblity of the mother. It is difficult to find people to take good care of your child. Are day care centers the answer? Not until they are better staffed and do not serve just as child-watching services. If this were the case, then responsible mothers would not be so worried about leaving their offspring. There seem to be many good nursery schools where working mothers are willing to leave their children. But often the schools' hours do not correlate with those of the mother's job, so a friend or neighbor has to take the child to school, pick him up, and watch him until his mother comes home. Summer camps provide part of the answer, and there seem to be plenty of camps. Improved public schools, a national problem, would help the working mother, too.

Finding a reliable person to manage your home is difficult. Anyone who has ever tried to get a full-time housekeeper could write a book on the trials and tribulations involved. If a person is good at child care, she is sometimes neglectful of housekeeping; if she gets married while she is working for you, then her husband helps her second-guess your wishes; some people seem responsible during the interview, but they leave the gas on, let the baby fall down the stairs, or go out without telling you they are taking the baby with them.

Relatives can be a big help to working mothers. One widow in her sixties says she just couldn't have brought up her three children without the help of her mother.

It is regrettable that housekeeping has too often been termed a menial job and has had the accompanying low pay. Perhaps if society would emphasize the dignity of doing work for which one is equipped and if the pay were higher, a better quality of household employees would be available. Incidentally, if people would appreciate and respect domestic employees, there might be better results. Too often people who treat their office staff well treat their household employees abominably.

The *Monthly Labor Review* gives these remedies for upgrading child care:

> Upgrading household employment.
> More efficient home management. (Important for management women.) Planning and organizing housework, utilizing laborsaving devices and convenience products, *determining priorities,* and *taking a relaxed attitude toward chores of lesser importance.*
> Adaptable work rules. (This is the most difficult one for working management women, but some as discussed above, are managing.)
> Recognition of life-cycle patterns—the problems of working women can be eased if employers come to accept and make provision for interrupted education and employment patterns.
> Fuller sharing of family responsibilities. [Again discussed above—

if husbands and wives haven't worked this out, then certainly it is important to do so.] [2]

Women in management are usually good mothers. They may have had to figure different approaches to child rearing, but again by nature, by desire, and by need, they have dealt very well with this very important function.

The Shorter Workweek as an Answer to Concern for Home Responsibilities

Would shorter workweeks help? The experiments so far have proved that most women enjoy the extra day at home. The executive workweek is harder to plan. It is difficult to see how executives will be able to reschedule their weeks, but if it can be done, it will be a boon to the working management woman.

More Time Off

The trend toward more time off (regrettably it doesn't happen very often) is most helpful. Unfortunately longer vacations come after longer years of service; by then the children usually are out of school. The growing trend toward longer vacations based on job content and responsibility will be a real help to the working woman executive because although most of them are happy with their jobs, they still would like more time with their families.

A sympathetic management is probably the most important help to a working mother, whether she is the girl on the assembly line or the vice president. A woman should be able to give full effort to the job and should not ask for special favors. However, an understanding boss who recognizes that it's almost impossible for a woman to come to work when her child has a real emergency can be a great help. Women's attendance records are usually as good as men's, but many employers are reluctant to hire or advance mothers with young children. They will often find, though, that these women are more responsible because they really need the job to help support their children in a world where prices keep skyrocketing. Abuse of the privileges of special dispensation during emergencies should not be permitted.

Will the new legal regulations help the working mother who is an executive? The new sex guidelines under the Equal Employment Opportunity Commission (EEOC) supposedly spell out special benefits for

pregnancy and maternity leave (see Chapter 10). Right now these regulations have most management men vowing they will try to find ways
around hiring too many potential mothers, or holding their heads and
saying, "I have two thousand potential mothers! This new set of regulations will cost me millions." A word or two to this troubled executive:
Look at the record. Your women executives have usually taken short
maternity leaves. Weigh their contributions against the short time you
pay them while they are away. You'll miss a lot if you don't hire them
just because they *may* get pregnant and desert you for a short time.

Working Mothers Speak Out

Here is what working mothers say are the advantages of working.

Doing your own thing. Meeting your own potential. Leading an exciting life.

I'd hate to stay home every day. It's nice on the weekends, but I'm not really a very good housekeeper. I do my outside work much better.

My children—I love them dearly—but I'm afraid if I'd be around them all the time I just wouldn't do as good a job as I do [when I am] working.

It means the difference, financially, of sending our three children to the best schools in the country. Unfortunately, the public schools in our city have become discipline chambers, overcrowded, under-staffed, and poorly managed. I'm glad that my children, and both their dad and I check often, are getting what we hope is the best education in the country. They seem to be healthy, happy, smart kids with only the usual number of trials and tribulations.

Management Women Who Stay Home

There is the other side of the picture—the women who leave their
jobs when they marry. Here is what one well-educated, talented young
woman who is happily married to a fast-paced young executive says: "I
guess I was brought up thinking that a woman's place was at home, at
least while children are small and when a husband needs her at home.
However, it was always in the light that this place could be very interesting and fulfilling. I have found it to be so and I believe that I intend
to bring up my daughters in the same way—through example rather
than instruction. I could not in good conscience leave my son with

someone while I worked. Some people can. I couldn't. This is so vital a time for him (two years old) and I want to be the one there to do the shaping and molding if there is any to be done. . . . Plus being home with him is a lot of fun! I'm not saying it is wrong for other people to want to work, but it's just not for me."

And still another comment, in a very serious vein, from a former teacher:

"My biggest argument is that there is a place for the girl with high potential in the home. I know that female executives are not the type of females I know who work—but I worry so about the little things kids are no longer taught—like not littering, decent work habits, the work of their hands, caring deeply for other members of the family, and their poor nutritional habits."

And one more:

"I was irritated in college when my female instructor said, 'I have to leave early because my pre-schooler is in the hospital.' Instead of sympathy I felt only irritation. This is one of the reasons I didn't work —to cover situations like this. I wouldn't penalize others. . . . I never could imagine taking a job without the expectation of giving completely of my talents and concern. . . . We crack up at least a dozen times a day over something said by any one of my wise offspring. . . . My husband and my kids are my good friends."

Any one of these three are potentially high-caliber executives, but have chosen a different management job. Will they go back into the workforce? They may and perhaps, even though they have missed ten work years, will be better than or as good as those who have kept their noses to the grindstone.

Education for Daughters

What would working mothers ask of education for their daughters?

A black executive replies: "It will be easier for her—it was a terrible struggle for me to get a good education."

Other comments:

My daughter goes to Princeton and I hope she gets a more serious education than I did.

When I went to the city system 20 years ago it was good, but not now. I'd want my daughter to go to a smaller school.

I hope they receive a broader education. Many fields I'd like to pursue, but never had time.

I want my daughter to have the college education of her choice.

I would send my child to the school which provided the best courses he or she wanted to choose.

I definitely want my daughter to attend a coed college and would encourage either a technical degree with an MBA or else a professional course.

All these women assume that their daughters naturally will go to college, but the women are more willing than their own mothers to let them make their own choices. It is difficult for older women to cope with a young person's desire to leave college or to delay college for a year when they themselves found it so hard to get enough money or support to attend a good college or university. (See Chapter 14 for a discussion of the generation gap and what the children of working mothers are saying.)

Miss, Mrs., or Ms.?

One of today's dilemmas, which we touched on briefly earlier, is whether to address a woman as *Mrs., Miss,* or *Ms.* Many of today's women insist on being called *Ms.* If it is important to them, then their wishes should be respected. *Ms.* is also handy when you don't know if a woman is married. Few women in the study were terribly concerned about this issue. Most of them are so busy that they consider it a minor issue, and one of them went so far as to say: "In their desire to be known as *Ms.* and in attempting to gain the dominance associated with manhood, they may sacrifice attributes of special womanly charm and attractiveness possessed by many highly respected women executives."

Conclusions

1. Management women are just as "feminine" as women at home or in jobs lower in the hierarchy.
2. Most topflight management women are married to men who are their peers or who hold higher-level positions. Those who aren't married remain so by choice.
3. A management woman with children has rough problems, but they are not insurmountable.

All in all, the working management woman seems to have the best of all worlds—a good job, a fine husband, and hopefully happy and successful children. She has kept her femininity and her independence as an individual even though she has become deeply involved in the "man's world."

9
SOME OF THE THINGS YOU DON'T PUT INTO BOOKS

Today's work world is complex. There are many side issues that are almost as important as what shows on the surface. Work and social life are often interrelated. How does this complexity affect women executives? Here are some of the problems that you won't find in job descriptions.

On the Road

Going on the road sounds glamorous until you have sat in O'Hare Airport for a day while the snow beats across the vast air terminal—or until you have had ice from nearby cornices nearly fall on your head as you walk along Michigan Avenue.

There are dust storms above Dallas that force your plane to land in Tulsa. A long midnight bus ride gets you into Dallas early in the morning; the only saving grace is that the moon looks mighty pretty over the changing landscape.

The wives' and children's pictures you have been asked to look at could stretch around the world. Try flashing a picture of *your* husband and children and watch the men's bored reactions. It just doesn't seem to work both ways.

One director gave his departing female manager this advice: "Do you have everything? Have you checked? I do want you to have a good time, but don't get pregnant. If you do, I'll really have to work." It almost reminds you of a mother trying to tell her daughter what this big, bad, male world is all about.

If you haven't been chased around the room four or five times by a "charming" male (either co-worker or other lonesome male) on the road or if you haven't practically fled to your room alone, then there may be doubt about your veracity or your charm.

True, few admit it and most say you learn early to cope with sex on the road, but most women managers admit to some problems. Some, of course, are very proper and claim to have always had everything under control. Perhaps it is because their current position awes the males they meet on the road, or perhaps the years have helped dim their views of such antics.

Because executive women, just like men, are often out late and alone in a strange city or airport it is a rare one who sometime in her career hasn't had a scare or two—a drunk insisting you need his tender loving care or, even more scary, a direct, nasty encounter on a subway. Most women have learned to use cabs instead of subways and have learned more than one trick to avoid the most obnoxious of men. To say that there is no danger is foolish. "If you are going to travel alone," says one woman, "be careful. Don't think you can go anywhere without some protection. Don't roam strange cities alone at night even if it means staying in a hotel room alone. Stay at recommended hotels even if the boss screams the first time at the size of your expense voucher."

It is still amazing to many men that when you are away from home, you don't kick up your heels and fall into the arms of the most attractive male around—each of them meaning himself. Men brag about their escapades; women don't, at least not in a book. It is also true that one soon learns the art of the gentle rebuff that sticks, and then everyone can relax and go dining or dancing.

How many women fall in and out of bed easily and often when they are on the road is a moot question. If there are some, they aren't talking.

Or as one young, pretty executive said, "Frequently I've found men I deal with for PR purposes feel that sex should be part of the program. I don't agree and I tell them so. It has nothing to do with business. I wouldn't expect or accept business favors—to me that's paramount to prostitution. I'm most against it and find it degrading. I keep business and pleasure separate."

There is no question, however, that you are usually given somewhat special attention. Some attention ranges from concern that you don't spend lonesome evenings alone to all kinds of unusual experiences, like being asked to accompany a group of your co-workers to an elegant striptease joint in Dallas. Seems there had been a controversy the night before about whether a certain dancer's mammary equipment was real or false. Imagine arbitrating such a discussion! In a similar situation another admits lending her glasses to a male working companion so that he wouldn't miss the slightest twist or wiggle.

All fun on the road? Like her male companions, the woman on the road is there to get a job done. If she stays out until 5 A.M. or so and has to be on the work scene at 8 A.M., it gets pretty rough going. The cold morning light and the work ahead are sobering factors indeed. But like her male companions, she will let loose once in a while and probably has to go to bed early the next night. She's learned to pace herself —usually knows when and where she should go and with whom she can have fun.

Again, the slightest bit of gossip gets blown sky-high, so even a girl who plays it fast and loose at home has to watch her step away from home. She is conspicuous, and men are still suspicious about the job she, as a woman, can do.

If one woman makes a fool of herself or gets drunk or goes to bed with someone and everybody knows what's happening, the story gets around the home office awfully fast. It can happen to a man a few times and it is laughed at as a good joke. Some men are recognized as Don Juans on the road or even at home, but women just can't do it and get away with it. The word "tramp" is soon assigned to a woman who isn't circumspect on the road or at the home base.

The road is really fun, for a while. It means you'll probably see Underground Atlanta, Bourbon Street in New Orleans, Mount Royale in Montreal, Myrtle Beach in South Carolina, and Market Street in San Francisco along with State and Rush Streets in Chicago. Some of the women in the study know Paris, London, Rome, and other cities around the world. Now several of them are off to the Orient. Margaret Scarbrough Wilson talks of her travels to Japan and Australia. Esther Peterson, who knows Europe well, talks of a trip to China, and Dorothy Chappel talks of South America and other parts of the world. Mrs. Vescia, too, talks with understanding of the ways of the South and Central Americas.

If you are around long enough, you'll also probably see Piqua,

Ohio; Oshkosh, Wisconsin; and "Nellies Elbow" in Oklahoma. Not that there is anything wrong with the small towns of this country, but try to find something to do in some of them in the evening or try to get in and out in a hurry. Sometimes it seems you can't get there from here. So the road is not as glamorous as some people imagine it to be.

Many women don't want to bother the boss about their family problems when they have to be on the road. Women managers with small children find it difficult to be too far from home, especially if there is sickness or trouble. This is a situation that upsets many a woman manager. Lucky are those whose children are healthy. Otherwise, travel might be an impossibility. That is why it is so important to know the travel requirements before taking the job. As one executive says, "Excessive travel requirements are hard on everyone, especially if families are involved. They should be pointed out beforehand and figured in an individual's decision to take the job."

"Traveling alone can be a very lonely business," is the opinion of another woman, "particularly when it comes to dining in the evening. Like most women, I do not feel comfortable entering a restaurant or a bar by myself, so sometimes I just stay in my hotel room and get caught up on my reading."

This young lady is not the first who has done that. Most women are still reluctant to ask men out to dinner—perhaps eventually we'll get over this hurdle, but most of us do not want to intrude. We figure if the men want us along, they will ask us; most of the time they do.

Sex on the Job

Here are the women's comments on this subject.

I am honest but tactful. I like compliments on my sexuality, but that's as far as it should go if a woman hopes to maintain self-respect.

Whenever sales techniques are discussed in our company, one of the men invariably comments on the importance of getting into bed with the client. As the only woman in the room, I always snicker inwardly. Actually, I think it is to a woman's advantage to keep sex out of the office. Plenty of satisfactory bed partners can be found among men who are not in any way business associates.

I doubt sincerely if I could function independently and objectively with a romantic attachment. Maybe because I lead a very full and nonsubjugated life, I have never desired a romantic involvement other than my marriage.

Frankly, I've encountered no problems traveling alone or with men. I think a great deal depends on the woman and how she controls the situation and presents herself to the public.

It's a rough deal on the road, especially if you are attractive. The minute you hit a hotel alone, or the firm knows you are coming out alone, get ready for flowers, phone calls, and pressure. It's not easy to resist always, but I am sent out as a representative of my company and I'm not about to destroy myself. I think men are just pulling your leg, so to speak, when they suggest "bed" on the road. The plea, "Nobody will know—you're a long way from there," goes over like a lead balloon with me.

Two married women commented on leaving their husbands behind while traveling.

Travel is no problem. My husband loves my trips and usually tries to join me for a weekend.

I'd have seen the world if I didn't think I'd better get home for the weekend. I wasn't too sure of my husband—figured he would soon find someone else to be nice to him if I didn't give him his TLC.

In summary, women who travel alone learn what the scene is early in their careers. They learn to cope with oversexed, lonesome men and have a fair assortment of techniques for getting rid of the drunks and the "lovers." They do, however, enjoy spending the evening out dancing instead of reading alone in the room or seeing the sights of the cities. Traveling on the job, until it gets burdensome, for either a man or a woman can be fun and interesting.

Sleeping with the Boss

Should you sleep with or get romantically involved with the boss or some colleague you think can help you on the way up? A resounding "No!" comes from the distaff side of the office. Some of the women in the study did meet and marry their husbands while on the job, but these were aboveboard romances. And while one situation reached the point where it was "Give in or get out" and the woman quit, most women in this survey say it doesn't pay, careerwise, to sleep with the boss or co-workers.

I find my boss very attractive, that is, as a boss. I'm afraid that if I slept with him we'd lose our boss–subordinate relationship, and neither of us would like to be around the other in the office.

Sleep with the boss—it's putting your job as well as lots of other things on the line. I surely don't advise it.

The boss chased me around one night while we were on the road. The next morning, I continued the trip alone. I worried that I would get fired for refusing him. After a month on the road, when I got back to the office, he greeted me as if nothing had happened. Neither of us has ever mentioned it. I find that one "joins the club" when she has literally been chased by the boss. Did the other girls succumb? If so, no one ever admitted it.

Office sexual relationships, especially with the boss, can be messy business—usually ends up as bad sex and bad business.

I worked with a company once where a co-worker decided to have an affair with the boss. She immediately got extra spending money and seemingly had a great, easy job. She didn't work much but took credit for everything. At the same time, she wasn't learning or gaining in her abilities. Today the affair is over and she's working as a secretary somewhere else—never having gained the true ability for the executive job she supposedly wanted.

Keep in mind you may still have to work with the guy when the romance is dead. Can you?

On the other side, here's what two executives say:

I met my husband at the office. He happened to be my boss at that time. We kept our romance quiet and I don't think anyone knew that we were having a fine romance.

Sex—it's great. With the boss? Sometimes, and he's great too. Do I worry? Why should I? I take the pill and he knows it. It surely takes the tension out of the office.

(Judging by the tension in some offices, perhaps sex should sometimes be advocated as a cure—but it's pretty dangerous medicine according to most of the women.)

If I were in a position to become romantically involved, I certainly would not let the fact that someone is my colleague or my boss stand in the way. Of necessity, however, they should be of a certain caliber, someone who would not discuss it or cause gossip among other colleagues. Nor would I expect to be told things about work situations which were none of my business. Each individual should know herself and the other person well enough to decide whether or not she can handle any situation which would occur.

In sum, perhaps sleeping with the boss is either a curse or a privilege best reserved for the nonmanagement women in the office.

Although not related to the question of sleeping with the boss, the following quote on sex in the office pretty well sums up a sensible approach: "It is my honest feeling that men enjoy working with a woman who is conscious of being a woman and who does some mild flirting. I kiss many of my colleagues when we meet. Only a few have tried to get more involved and I've been able to put them off lightly and continue being friends. A little sex interest adds spice to men and women working together."

Credit for Work

Failure to be given credit where it is due irks women to no end. If you are a male executive who sins in this respect, just realize that you have an unhappy executive working for you. In today's market it might be wise to rectify your ways. Here's what the women are saying.

> *I'll bide my time and I'll get even. It was my work that he claimed as his own. I'd have raised hell with a woman but I didn't want to embarrass him in front of his and my colleagues. It may take a while but I'll remember.*
>
> *I've had people take credit for my ideas for years. Somehow that never bothers me as long as the idea is a good one and I can still see it working years later. I get my satisfaction from creating, not from pats on the back. As the only female officer of the company, I am sometimes treated like the mascot and this can be a problem.*
>
> *I have been most fortunate in that my "bosses" have usually gone out of their way to give me credit for my work. This, I would say, is one of the keys to upward movement. If you work for a man who doesn't—find another job.*
>
> *I have sometimes found that my male bosses like to take credit for some of the work I do, but I have usually found that the best way to countermand this is by sending memos on really important developments to the president, just to keep him posted, and send a copy to my boss.*
>
> *Other people always take credit for your work. I can't honestly say it's because I'm a woman. I prepare a policy and my boss takes the credit. That's life.*
>
> *I don't dare take too much credit for the success of our business*

unless my husband allows it. Otherwise our personal relationship suffers.

My husband still makes the decisions without letting me know about them, and it bothers me.

I've deliberately shared ideas and tried to make them belong to other people. That's a formula for success in the business of selling ideas.

On taking credit for my work, they used to try it but I started to put my foot down and let them know that nobody was going to take credit for something I did. I never boasted about what I did, but I made it clear that nobody else did the work. Anybody who has to talk continuously about what he or she does is not a very capable person.

On the other side of the picture there is the true story of the woman boss who wouldn't give credit to her male subordinates. When times got tough for her, they all deserted her. What it all adds up to is that giving credit where credit is due is one of the fundamentals of good management. If you abuse women to this point, you'll get even more resentment than from a man. Women just won't take it, and either move away or get even with male bosses who are stingy in their praises and dishonest in their actions. There are macabre stories of "getting even," but usually this is a waste of time on everyone's part and often both boss and subordinate lose face and position. These histories are not often written, but all too often the facts are there.

What If the Boss Is Dull?

What does a woman manager do when her boss is dull and unresponsive? Can she tell him about it? It's a difficult spot to be in. If a manager wants to keep his turnover down, he should not put a really bright female (or male) under the supervision of a dope. Some mothers push their daughters into marriages on this basis. It doesn't work at home and it won't work at the office. Here is what two women say.

It's very tough for anyone of my temperament to work under a lazy or less intelligent man—and it happened as a secretary (my first job during the depression). I definitely had trouble effacing myself.

I have had many bosses. When I find I'm working for one who is too dull, I give up and change jobs. I've found I can't correct the situation internally.

Potpourri

Here are a few other "little" things that, although not loudly proclaimed, irritate women.

One big problem is that a woman's always having to prove herself and her work in a new situation. For example, being in a one-time group with managers from other areas in the company or other companies and having one's ideas completely ignored. Having new superiors who assume at first that you are a glorified clerk and need to be closely supervised. A second problem is the reluctance of top management to deal directly with a lower-level woman manager; they must necessarily always go to a woman's manager with a question in her area—this is not the case with men.

Male executives tend to see women as their fathers saw their mothers—as wives and homemakers—possessing and lovable but not with necessarily practical qualities. They, of course, also tend to see women as people to handle their chores like homemakers do.

I don't like it when men say they can't tell a joke because "she" is here. I don't like it either when I'm told I can be promoted but that I won't be vice president because I'm a woman.

I resent the fact that men feel they can ride over me because I'm a woman and won't fight back.

Male executives will recognize women as top-notch assistants but won't let them into the mainstream of an established organization. They regard competent females as "special."

I've been annoyed by decisions made in the men's room, by business meetings being held at a club that doesn't admit women, and so on. I have sometimes protested these, but they are passing parts of an older order.

Embarrassing or Humorous Incidents

Life at work can have its lighter moments, too. Here is what the women responded when asked to comment on the question: "On your job you probably have had some embarrassing, humorous, or irritating situations with respect to being a female executive in a male-dominated world."

When I was pregnant I worked until the day before my oldest child was born. At that time I negotiated a contract which I took to the board for approval and there were some obvious comments from the chairman as to whether anyone present could deliver a baby, and subsequent tittering was heard throughout the boardroom. I didn't take offense at the remark at all, and, in fact, felt that the situation called for a remark concerning my pregnancy. On the other hand, the unions with which I was negotiating at the time, on their own, asked for the date I was due to be delivered so that they could conveniently schedule negotiating sessions and suspend meetings while I was in the hospital. It was perfectly friendly, agreeable, and cooperative.

They made book at the office on whether or not I'd have the baby there or at home. I never found out who won the bet.

One of my most amusing episodes was interviewing at Harvard Business School around 1950. I was the only female recruiter. When we left for lunch, I was asked if I would mind entering the restaurant by the back door since only men could go in the front door.

I recall attending a cocktail party—about five years ago—and being met by the thoroughly smashed husband of a friend of mine, who said, "They tell me that you are a vice president." I answered, "That's what they tell me, too!" To which he slurred, "You don't look smart enough to be a vice president." While I held my husband back from hitting him in the nose, I secretly cherished that as one of my nicest compliments. I still do.

Such a reaction comes from the old idea that you can't be smart and pretty, too, or that if you are a vice president you are expected to wear unattractive shoes and no makeup and look like yesterday's warmed-over mess.

Only once in my professional life did I have a client who refused to follow my [legal] advice. He was a physician and he vigorously disagreed with everything I told him. I had to fire him as a client —later I married him.

One of my chief lieutenants has seven children. At the dinner table one evening it came out that his boss is a woman. The children wouldn't believe it. They had to be brought to the office and shown the lady in question.

Since I always use my initials, most business people assume I'm a man. When I get on the phone, they always assume it's the secretary.

When I attended staff meetings at the Harvard Club, they had to take me in via the ladies' entrance, whisk me quickly through the library, hoping no comfortable, dozing male would wake up, and tell me they had posted a "Ladies" sign on a certain room near where we met.

An Arab was in my group when I worked in Europe—he always thought I should walk three paces behind and wear a veil. I've experienced the usual shock at appearing before audiences, the men's business clubs, the selection of joint hotel rooms assuming all-male groups.

I was having a drink with my boss and another person. The third person left, and we waited a few more minutes before my boss caught his train. In the meantime we were seen by one of his neighbors, who didn't come over to say hello because he assumed I was a female friend and not an employee.

Often the "boys" come out with some very humorous dirty jokes. Usually the men are more embarrassed than I am, so I tend to regard such situations as a compliment since the men obviously feel relaxed enough in my presence to tell off-color jokes in the first place.

Most women have received apologies from men for not telling off-color jokes in their presence, for excluding them from the fun. Nine times out of ten, though, the story wasn't new enough or funny enough to be told.

One of the most interesting experiences I have had in this connection was when I made my first stop in Peru many years ago. Peruvian females from good families do not work. Our distributor took me out to dinner (all males). The men were seated at a table not too far away. They kept looking over and laughing and finally sent him a note. He blushed when he read it. I can imagine what it said. In any event, he must have decided I was fit to bring home. The next night I was invited into his home and met all his children and from then on I spent every evening with him and his family.

I always get a kick out of impressing a "male chauvinist" with my brains. Upon first meeting me these men think "Another dumb broad—oh, well, maybe I can get something out of this!" I love to see the wow-she-really-knows-what-she's-talking-about look to replace it.

One traumatic experience—my boss shook his fist at me in anger when a job wasn't completed as soon as he expected—he apologized later.

How to get in and out of the ladies room in time not to be left out of luncheon groups. All women executives face this problem. You surely have to get your makeup freshened quickly. Men like to have you look pretty, but in business they don't like women who putter around.

My first trip to New York as a buyer gave me a once-in-a-lifetime experience. Invited by a couple of major executives to a cocktail party at the St. Moritz, I arrived on time (I was new in the game) and found myself as the only female guest present. The senior vice president of a nationally known store crashed the party stone drunk and in his alcoholic state mistook me for a call girl. A massive man (he once played pro football), it took all the hosts present to keep him from tearing my clothes off before others arrived and helped get him out!

And so it goes on and on—embarrassments because of "no ladies allowed" signs, comments over pregnancy, and social customs that separate men from women. All in all, most of the escapades discussed above still echo a world of male chauvinism, which is fast changing.

Patience and Progress

Patience is hard to come by. Considering how much longer women have to wait to get to the top, they have shown plenty of patience, whether they have wanted to or not. When a woman has brains and competence it's a hard wait. Until recently only the most aggressive women talked out loud about this issue. It is one you'll hear more about in the future.

"I'm only a department head," says one woman. "The men with the same experience and less brains are all vice presidents. Do I like it? Of course I don't, but I know I'll have to wait and scheme around the situation so that eventually I'll get there."

Another woman says, "When I took my first job the only way I got it was that I decided to concede and take the required typing test. Men in the same position were able to dictate their words of wisdom. I had my degree in industrial relations and the firms did want me. Looking back, I don't regret the decision but, believe me, I've stewed a long time about the procedures that made it necessary."

The inevitable insinuation by many men that the only way into a management job for a woman is through the secretarial route is slowly but definitely dying down. Call it patience on the part of the women—it's been a long hard job to break down that barrier.

"It took seven bosses—each of whom left the company on a fast turnover—before I was finally offered the top spot," says another. "It was with some glee that I told the president that I had just accepted a top job elsewhere." But imagine seven turnovers before this woman's worth was discovered.

"I waited a long time to get my spot, but now it's worth it," says another gray-haired executive.

Men often have to exercise patience, too, in dealing with day-to-day management problems, but not to the extent that women do. "She's an emotionl woman, so what do you expect?" is the condemnation that has upset many a good plan. Patience to wait to accomplish what you wish is one thing but fighting against the odds is sometimes too much. For example:

"My story for our monthly newsletter was a good one, but the editor laughed and said it was unrealistic. Three weeks later he came in with a brilliant idea, all his own. You guessed it—my story. Could I tell him so? I needed my job, so I held my tongue. Call it patience if you want. Maybe I was foolish, but I did need my job."

Will the young women from today's campuses be as patient? All signs point to the negative: "What, work on Saturdays—not I!" "I don't intend to wait as long as you did to get a good salary." "I believe my talents are greater than yours at your age—or should I say I have been trained more specifically for a good-paying job than you were." "What do you mean I'd have to do the secretarial work when a man doesn't? Are you crazy?"

Management recruiters say now, "I'm conscious of our lack of women in management spots. I've been given a quota to fill and I intend to do it." And, "We're really looking at our management inventory so that no one gets overlooked. Before this, I'll admit we often bypassed women because we assumed they didn't want to travel, change locations, or uproot their families. We're on the spot, if we want to keep on getting government contracts, to find some competent women and find them fast. It's been a surprise to us at how many of our women can accept the responsibilities of management jobs. We just needed to ask them."

Although patience is never easy for anyone, the women of the study have exercised it to an astonishing degree. It's taken hard work, excellence on the job, some scheming, and help from the outside to bring women more or less into their own in management. In the 1970s, they seem to be well on their way.

Women and Their Subordinates

All of us like to think our subordinates love us. Here are some of the remarks heard about women bosses. Some of them come from subordinates who are a bit envious. You can take them with a grain of salt, but as a woman executive you may get a hint or two from them. Contrast them with the remarks quoted earlier indicating all was sweetness and light between woman boss and subordinate.

> *She's a nut—mean as dirt and won't listen to reason. She thinks she's God almighty. Getting a management job has gone to her head. I'm asking for a transfer.*
>
> *Since she became a vice president, she thinks she deserves a key to the executive's john. She doesn't talk to us common folks any more.*
>
> *You can't get in to see her unless you have an appointment these days. It's a long, roundabout way into her office. You'd think we'd never been friends.*
>
> *She knows what she wants and wants it fast. Because she drives herself she drives the rest of us, too. She doesn't know when to stop and take a break or to give in once in a while to her subordinates.*

One woman was given top advice by her man boss, "Just remember, your subordinates, even the lowest among them, can wreck your job faster than anybody. Any manager who forgets this is in for real trouble —poor secretarial help, poor print jobs, fouled-up meeting rooms and supplemental material, late project necessities, and untold nuisances."

These remarks indicate that when women are rough bosses they are even worse than bad men bosses. On the other hand, when women are good bosses, they are often more understanding of talents than the best of men, and most of them have the respect of their subordinates.

The Help of Good Men Is Not
Often Publicized

More than once a woman owes her management job to the help of a farsighted man. Often they have been remiss in telling him, but here is how they really feel about that one special boss. These are quotes you don't often find in books.

Can I repay what Mr. B did for me? He shook the whole company up when he said I should be promoted to a vice presidency. "We've never had one before" was a slogan he had to overcome, but he did.

My boss was essentially lazy, so he worked my tail off. One thing to his credit, however, was that he never took credit for my work and saw that I was promoted. He said that I deserved better than himself. In looking back, I know that this was unselfish and decent.

"I'll teach you all I know because I think you have both the guts and the brains to be successful." Can I repay that kind of help? Never. He meant it when he said he'd teach me. He was just great, and I am grateful even after many years. He was ahead of his time.

It all goes back to my home, where there was no different standard for sending boys and girls to college. I feel sorry for some of the women who resent the fact that way back when someone thought it was fine to send a dull boy to college but his brilliant sister had to be contented with high school. . . . . It wasn't easy because there were eight of us and we had little money. Sure, all five girls and three boys did get more degrees than you would think possible. Sentimental feeling towards the old folks? It's more than that —it's a great respect.

"I've got no time to train you—just follow me around." Or, "Quit your crying; I've got no time for tears." "Grow up, will you?" These are the admonitions of one high-caliber boss to his flailing, wailing assistant. She learned and looking back blesses the boss who was so generous in both his help and advice.

One could go on and on about the escapades, the slights, the plots, the nastiness, and the intrigues that are never discussed in public or written about in books or company policy manuals. Every executive knows that there are informal chains of command—that what meets the eye is only half of the management story. Only a few of the hush-hush episodes were discussed in this chapter. Perhaps they are only the tamer ones. No doubt if you look at your own company you can match the behind-the-scenes maneuverings and happenings that are never publicized.

The management world is no bed of roses. It's a fast-moving world where yesterday's policies and practices become outmoded in a fraction of the time that it used to take. There are overambitious, negligent, thoughtless people intent on their own success who won't take the time to help *any* subordinates, let alone women. The chip-on-the-shoulder, belligerent women of today may cut off the help of those enlightened men who do wish to see talented women succeed and have in the past offered their assistance. It's something to guard against because in the management world, just like the outside world, you can't do it all by yourself, be you man or woman.

On the other hand, because today's women have a better start and because they are reaching the top faster, they may not have to depend on a man to fight their battles for them. It was harder to crack the barrier before and the men who helped certainly deserve and get the thanks of the management women they so gallantly assisted.

This doesn't mean that the women didn't have to live up to their side of the bargain. These same men point with pride to the successful women they helped. Conversely, practically every woman in the study can point with affection and pride to the men who helped her on the way up. Because these women know what getting such help means, most of them are interested in giving others the same kind of help, usually on request only.

The future looks bright for women today. With brains and fortitude they will reach the top management spots much sooner and at much younger ages than their predecessors who reached good management positions only through years of patience, hard work, and hard knocks. It is hoped that when they arrive they will have the *joie de vivre* and the broad perspective exhibited by the women in this study and that they won't be afraid to praise the people who helped them on the way up.

10
SIGNS OF THE TIMES: The Women's Liberation Movement

The women's liberation movement must be considered in any discussion of women in business. "Are you for it or against it?" is a question frequently asked by male executives. "Are you one of us?" is the query from women's groups when they learn about your management job.

You'll find all kinds of ill-informed women in the movement as well as many who have really studied the situation and found it very bleak. Is the women's liberation movement really necessary? Is it accomplishing anything? Is it causing more harm than good in many instances? These are some of the questions asked by executive women. Most of those included in the study are reluctant to get involved in the movement. They have made it mostly on their own, are doing an excellent job in their current spots, and literally detest the methods and the words used by some women associated with the movement. Others, many of whom have been really scarred, are involved and hold no love for what they call the smugness of many successful women. It is a time of trouble. Has anyone come up with viable approaches to deal with the grievances voiced by some of the more belligerent women in the liberation front?

The top management women included in the study no longer need anyone to fight their battles for them. They are not smug about their attainments and know that they have not reached their current status easily.

What Management Women Are Saying

"Scratch any woman and deep down you'll find a feminist." It's true that discrimination based on sex gets even a self-made woman executive upset. She hates to see anyone else have to go through some of the rigors she has had to undergo to get ahead.

Here is the way one of the executives puts it, "In my opinion, women's liberation only underscores how many women want to have special treatment because they are women, and they make a target for men to revive all the old stories about the instability of the eternal female. As for legislation, after about 50 years of trying to protect women from exploitation, now the big thinkers want to dismantle it to soothe their own egos—I'm talking about the so-called executive woman who wants to rid the books of protective laws about weight lifting, hours, rest periods, and so on, which were created for the factory woman. At a meeting of our personnel club, I heard such a woman get up and compare the lifting of a baby to the lifting of a crate on a paid job." Pretty strong statement, but fairly typical.

"There is a direct correlation between their looks and their involvement in women's liberation," says a bright, young potential executive. "They seem so messy in their bra-less, unkempt fashion." Seems unfair to group them all together, but isn't it true that sometimes such organizations are an escape from the hard reality that no men are interested in them?

"Do-gooders give me a pain and I count the feminists as do-gooders," says still another executive.

A Day at Women's Liberation Headquarters

What happens at a women's liberation headquarters during a typical day? Here are just some of the things that happened during a day at

New York City headquarters (Women's Liberation Center of New York). The members received more than 200 calls from women needing information about the women's liberation movement, doctors, lawyers, gynecologists, dentists, money, a place to sleep, child care, demonstrations and activities, therapy, someone to talk to, and sisterhood. During the week the women's abortion project may schedule more than 150 abortions and answer countless medical and health questions. What will happen if New York's controversial abortion law is repealed? No one has the answer.

The organization also has been known to receive obscene, threatening, and hate phone calls from men.

It seems that society with primarily men leaders has not been able to meet the special needs of women. If "do-gooding" is a label you want to put on the activities listed above, then you are welcome to do so. The movement does serve a purpose—especially in a big city like New York, where many girls from far away cities do need help.

Incidentally, no men are allowed except repairmen and an occasional man who helps on women's problems.

The literature of the New York Center states:

> All women have been oppressed at one time or another—the movement represents the collective efforts of all women to see the nature of oppression from the general point of view—fundamental to the movement is the belief that women have not realized their potential.

"If the movement really helps in uncovering problems and helps in solving them, we'll try to help," says an executive. "My experience with it is that it is terribly self-centered. I just don't have time to waste in group joining. I'd rather pick my own candidate to help jobwise."

Still another says, "If the young girls involved in the movement—the demonstrators and the name callers—would spend time at school or trying to do their jobs better, I believe they would get further ahead."

A Closer Look at the Movement—
Common Taboos and Prejudices
Against Women

Undoubtedly many women feel they have been wronged, socially and intellectually, and thus believe they should act drastically to correct these wrongs on a worldwide scale. Ancient taboos and prejudices still exert considerable pressure in modern society, and sometimes scar the female consciousness very deeply. Many intelligent and gifted women resent keenly the fact that their brothers, regardless of their comparative intelligence (which is sometimes inferior to theirs), are automatically sent off to good colleges whereas no plans are made for the women.

Since the beginning of civilization this sort of thinking has produced primarily male leaders. Cleopatra, Queens Victoria and Elizabeth, and Empress Catherine of Russia are notable if outnumbered exceptions. Today, Indira Gandhi of India and Mrs. Nguyen Thi Binh of the Vietcong's Paris delegation have made a place for themselves in diplomatic and political history. In the military, Colonel Norma E. Brown became the first woman to command a mixed air force unit upon her appointment to head the 6970 Air Base Group in Maryland. Domestically, some of the states have honored their women with tradition. For example, New Mexico has for decades reserved the office of secretary of state for a female representative.

Despite these exceptions, men have obviously always had special privileges. In the Jewish family, it was the tradition for the sons to learn Hebrew, the language of the scholars. Religious as well as intellectual rituals are often closed to women in many cultures. For example, the cliff dwellers of Mesa Verde forbade women to enter the kivas, or sacred gathering place. (It is somewhat revealing to discover that dice were found in some of the kivas, indicating that they were used for a social gathering place and gossip center. Women have always suspected that gossip was actually a mildly contagious male weakness.)

Women justifiably object to their exclusion from the places of ritual. Until recently, this exclusion ranged from social centers to military bases. McSorley's Ale House in downtown New York, a longtime male stronghold, had a most trying time with the women's liberation groups who loudly demanded admittance. It is now an open pub. The military has always been another stronghold where men have run the show since time immemorial. However, Admiral Elmo R. Zumwalt, Jr., chief of naval operations, has just lifted the ban against women serving aboard warships. Legend has it that, in the days when ships were powered by the winds and protected by the goddesses of the sea, no women were allowed aboard because no one wished to incur the sea deities' jealousy. The admiral was praised by members of various liberation groups who have long believed that women are as fit to serve in the armed forces as men. So far there have been no complaints from Waves or sailors, but a handful of navy wives have made themselves very vocal about their disapproval. One suspects that the air force is proud of its Olympic Gold Medalist, Captain Micki King. Shouldn't the navy have its chance?

In the most outstanding cases of legitimate female complaint, the issue is monetary. Women can operate naval equipment, they can fly planes, and they can command troops with the efficiency and competence of men trained in these lines of work. An interesting protest has been heard from the women of the western states who wish to be able to work in the mines and tunnels of the ore-refining companies because of the high pay. One imagines that the ban against female miners originated in the old West, where women were needed to tend children, work the land, and care for the homestead.

The sorrows and gripes of the women's liberation groups range from concrete professional discrimination prompted by ancient taboos to issues of child care and child rearing. One of these gripes is that girls love to play with dolls instead of, say, erector sets because little girls aren't *supposed* to be interested in that sort of thing. The feminists claim that this dichotomy between what girls are *taught* to do as opposed to what they *can* do is perpetuated by the image of the woman that is forced on society by TV commercials depicting women as useless but beautiful, lovable idiots.

Literature of the Movement

There are many articulate and fast-selling books on the market that set forth and explain the positions of the women's liberation leaders. A review of some of the more noteworthy is enlightening as well as distressing.

The Female Eunuch, by Germaine Greer, centers on several groups. One really nasty cut against women, in Ms. Greer's opinion, is the custom of changing one's name after marriage. She herself is married and has retained her maiden name. To some, this is essential symbolically. In her discussion of Otto Weininger's *Sex and Character*, she is disturbed by the vicarious nature of the female role. For this reason, women need take no moral responsibility for their behavior because they are not instrumental in determining that behavior and consequently have no egos. "Because of their lack of ego and the variety of roles that women manipulate, they have no identity and no one grieves at having to relinquish a name that does not signify an identity. . . . A woman is never genuine at any period in her life." [1]

In her book, Ms. Greer also answers some of the more commonly voiced male criticisms of women. For instance, the claim is often made that women cannot argue logically. Her reply is straightforward:

> It is true that women often refuse to argue logically. In many cases they simply do not know how to, and men may dazzle them with a little pompous sophistry.[2]

She continues on this line, saying:

Female hardheadedness regrets the misguided masculine notion that men (only) are natural animals—women are more aware of their complexity.[3]

It's not hard for management women to agree with her conclusions. Almost all of them, at some point, have been involved in the kinds of situations that Ms. Greer examines.

Another question raised in the book is whether bright women can disagree:

> Women have been charged with divisiveness and duplicity since the dawn of civilization, so they have never been able to pretend that their masks were anything but masks. It is a slender case, but perhaps it does mean that women have always been in closer contact with reality than men; it would seem to be just recompense for being deprived of idealism.[4]

Ms. Greer does not believe that this position or ethic is just, and goes on to present an alternative for liberated women.

> Woman must have the room and scope to devise a morality which does not disqualify her from excellence and a psychology which does not condemn her to the status of a spiritual cripple.[5]

Ms. Greer's views are general, and seem to lack somewhat in concrete examples and programs of the way to liberation. However, she occasionally ties her thoughts together in such a way that any woman can see her point:

> It seems that woman has more likelihood of success the higher she pitches her sights, and the more uncommon she is in her chosen environment. . . . The onus is on women, who must not only equal men in the race for employment, but outstrip them. Such an incentive must ultimately be an advantage.[6]

For an alternative to Ms. Greer's views and limitations, an excellent anthology of the movement is available. *Sisterhood Is Powerful*, edited by Robin Morgan, affords a comprehensive introduction to the writings of some of today's leading feminists.[7] The book is composed of many sections treating different aspects and causes of the movement. One is a series of sexist quotes, which do their utmost to infuriate women. A quick look at some of them reveals the violent resentment of some feminists, and would seem to indicate that they really mean business. There are a few that are unfamiliar to us. "Women executives are castrating bitches" was one that rocked the boat a bit.

One might exclaim, "Shades of Germaine Greer," in reading: "In childhood a woman must be subject to her father; in youth, to her husband; when her husband is dead, to her sons. A woman must never be free of subjugation." That is a quotation from the Hindu Code of Manu the Fifth. To reiterate her point that sexism has its roots in history and has been an eternal problem for women, Ms. Morgan quotes Napoleon Bonaparte:

> Nature intended women to be our slaves—they are our property; we are not theirs. They belong to us, just as a tree that bears fruit belongs to a gardener. What a mad idea to demand equality for women. Women are nothing but machines for producing children.[8]

That should bring about quite a furor in the hearts of women who claim even an ounce of independence for themselves.

The book airs common complaints, such as disgust with household chores, and has much to say about such controversial issues as lesbianism.

In her article, "Notes of a Radical Lesbian," Martha Shelly says:

> Lesbianism is one road to freedom—freedom from oppression [by] men. The Lesbian, through her ability to obtain love and sexual satisfaction from other women, is freed from dependence on men for love, sex, and money. She does not have to do menial chores for them (at least at home) or cater to their egos, or submit to hasty and inept sexual encounters. She is freed from fear of unwanted pregnancy and pains of childbirth and from the drudgery of child raising. The Lesbian still must compete with men in the job market, facing the same job and salary discrimination as her straight sister.[9]

It becomes clear that the women's liberation movement is many-faceted. One of the least understood and most put down is lesbianism; one of the best understood and best accepted is discrimination in the job market.

This complexity of ideology is due in part to the multitude of sources that feminists see for sexism. In the same book, Kate Millett scathingly attacks sexism in literature. Her article, "Sexual Politics in Literature," scores Henry Miller's *Sexus* and *Black Spring*, Norman Mailer's *An American Dream*, and Jean Genet's *The Thief's Journal*, among others. The sexual scenes starring the dominant, semisadistic male and the abused woman are revolting enough to make Ms. Millett's point several times over. Sadly enough, numerous examples are not difficult to find in modern literature.

To complicate issues still further, feminists claim that sexism and racism are closely linked. The plight of the black woman is indeed regrettable, and the articles by black women in the anthology are most convincing. It is easily understandable that the women's liberation movement has had enthusiastic support from the economic sector that is both black and female. There are no excuses to be made in answer to such an article as Frances M. Bial's "Double Jeopardy; To Be Black and Female." In it she says:

> The entire labor movement in the United States has suffered as a result of the superexploitation of black workers and women. The unions have been historically racist and male-dominated. They have failed to struggle against inequities in the hiring and pay of women workers.[10]

Of a less political nature is the hatred some women have for housework, which is exemplified in "The Politics of Housework," by Pat Mainardi. She sees a passage out of the dark ages for women after years of oppression:

> Then an interesting thing happened. I can only explain it by stating that we women have been brainwashed more than we can imagine. Probably too many years of seeing television women in ecstasy over their shining waxed floors or breaking down over their dirty shirt collars. Men have no such conditioning. They recognize the essential fact of housework right from the beginning. Which is, that it stinks.[11]

She goes on to say:

> In a sense, all men are slightly schizoid—divorced from the reality of maintaining life. This makes it easier for them to play games with it. It is almost a cliché that women feel greater grief at sending a son off to war because they bore him, suckled him, and raised him. The men who foment those wars did none of those things and have a more superficial estimate of the worth of human life.[12]

This upsets the thinking reader mildly, as she seems to infer that only mothers, not women in general, are more conscious than men.

With all movements, it is important to judge them by their consistency and adherence to facts. The editor seems to sense this, as she concludes the anthology with a set of statistics, facts, and quotations. Here are two of the more cogent quotes.

> Twenty-eight million women in America work at more menial jobs, at lower pay, and suffer higher unemployment than men.[13]
> In 1900 the typical woman worker was twenty-six and unmarried, now she is forty-one and married.[14]

Both the above quotes in the anthology were reprinted from a release by the Equal Employment Opportunity Commission.

Another excerpt, reprinted from the 1965 Women's Bureau *Handbook on Women Workers* indicated that nearly one-fifth of the employed women with a bachelor's degree have jobs in such categories as clerks, factory workers, and cooks.[15]

On the more encouraging side is a quotation in the same chapter from Alexis de Tocqueville, who states that if he were asked to what the singular prosperity and growing strength of the people might be attributed, he should reply: to the superiority of their women.

In summary, if you want an overview of what the feminists are saying, this is a very fine book.

Another book worth having a look at is *The Young Woman's Guide to Liberation* by Karen DeCrow.[16] It is, according to the flyleaf, a "cogent analysis of the various sources of brainwash which makes women feel, think, and act like second-class citizens—and a timely handbook on how to break through the established barriers."

This book is best characterized by the adjective "fiery." Its style gives the reader a sense of the spirit of the movement. For this reason, the book is best experienced briefly through some spot passages.

> I have worked for ten years, always for men who are earning three to ten times what I am, and who are often not outstanding. I am married.[17]
> The message is simple. As Simone de Beauvoir expressed it, men are punished for being failures, women are punished for being successes.[18]
> Changing the role of women, apparently, is the most revolutionary kind of restructuring of human society. Male protests echo from all quarters: hardhat, playboy, intellectuals. What we are saying is that sex differences are great fun in bed. But everyplace else they serve to keep women down, to deny us full participation in the world.[19]

Like most feminists, Ms. DeCrow turns to history for verification of the statement that discrimination is age-old. She gives us such facts as:

> The Roman women of the Great Republic had a place on earth, but they were chained to it for lack of abstract rights and economic independence; the Roman woman of the decline was the typical product of false emancipation, having only an empty liberty in a world which men remained in fact the sole master. . . .[20]
> St. Paul ordered women to keep silence in the churches. Tertullian in the second century called us the gate which opened the way to the devil. St. Thomas explained that the birth of a female child can be a generative mistake.[21]

(Somewhere in the history books it says that the Spartans left their female babies—at least the unwanted ones—out on the cliffs to die.)

Ms. DeCrow quarrels with the enslaving idea of romantic love. Here's what she says:

> Indeed probably the reason why marriage as an institution has survived through the years is that women cannot earn a living. But the young girl growing up is not told that. She learns in subtle ways that she is not expected to make a career for herself, to earn her way in the world. What

she is told blatantly is that her whole success is dependent on winning a man. Any female of age twelve who doesn't know this has been living on a desert island.[22]

In past centuries, woman's place was defined by economic necessity—someone had to weave the cloth, grow the food. Today "our slavery is to great extents voluntary, what keeps us in our place is the notion of love." [23]

Pages are devoted to the sorrows and problems of the executive wife.

One biting piece of sarcasm, "It might be noted that the Greek origin of the word 'idiot,' 'idion,' means the life to which the women of Greece were confined." [24]

Her final condemnation of women's place in the work world:

> Our position in the world of employment is, along with black people, that of [being] the last hired, the first fired. We do most of the uninteresting, dirty work. And although no one dares to utter such absurdity today about black people, we are supposed to enjoy giving service.[25]

And finally:

> I have not meant to imply that women's having economic independence will mean utopia. I do mean, however, that an end to the repression of women—economic, political, psychological—will produce perhaps the most humane and far-reaching revolution in history.[26]

Is the book a cry to revolution? Yes!

What an Anthropologist Says

A male anthropologist, Ashley Montagu in his new expanded edition of *The Natural Superiority of Women,* speaks of history, saying:

> Women were the second-class citizens of a patriarchal society. Women, it was alleged, had smaller brains than men, and less intelligence; they were more emotional and unstable; in a crisis you could always depend upon them to swoon or become otherwise helpless; they were weak and sickly creatures; they had little judgment and less sense; they could not be entrusted with the handling of money, and as far as the world outside, they could be employed only at the most menial and routine tasks.[27]

He speaks of the emancipation of women in the world wars and the woman's own inferiority complex.

> Having successfully freed herself from the thralldom of man, woman has now to emancipate herself from the myth of inferiority, and to realize her potential to the fullest.[28]

He feels the myths about women should be put in their proper perspective.

> When myths grow heavy with age they are frequently accepted as truths. The myths about women have been accepted as truths by both sexes from time immemorial, and custom and rationalization have helped keep them alive.[29]

He makes a real plea for a better understanding between men and women.

> Who is to remake the world? It is a proper question to ask in a book of this sort which has been written to throw some light on the relation between the sexes with especial reference to man's injustice to woman, but as a part of the larger task of helping human beings to understand themselves better, to understand more fully how they came to be the way they are now, and what they can do about changing the conditions that make men and women function as unhappily as they frequently do at present.[30]

It's a book worth reading by both management woman and male executives, and most of all by radical feminists.

In other parts of the book are quotes from Betty Friedan's *The Feminine Mystique*. Ms. Friedan is not especially easy on women.

> The reluctance of women in the last 20 years to commit themselves to work, paid or unpaid, requiring initiative, leadership, and responsibility is due to the feminine mystique. . . .[31]
>
> No woman in America today who starts her search for identity can be sure where it will take her. No woman starts that search today without struggle, conflict, and taking her courage in her hands.
>
> Who knows what women can be when they are finally free to become themselves? [32]

Betty Friedan, a leader in the feminist movement, is intelligent and incisive, and worth reading. Management women should know what she is saying.

In its Sunday magazine *The New York Times* has done much to keep pace with the women's movement. It has consistently reported the books to be read and the progress being made. In "A Woman Anthropologist Offers a Solution to the Woman Problem," Sheila K. Johnson, a noted American anthropologist, emphasizes the fact that anthropology has contributed two major insights concerning sex roles. The first is that men and women are different "physiologically, endocrinologically and as a result, perhaps, also psychologically." [33] The second is that all known societies assign certain tasks on the basis of the distinction between the sexes. The big problem is that in America, as well as in some of the countries that technology has not yet reached, some of the reasons for the division of the sexes have been eliminated by science. A third reason besides the advance of technology, is that women have become dissatisfied with their roles. Increased longevity of life and reduced fertility have given women plenty of time to think about a new role in society. Housework and home chores have become less confining and have also given more women more time. Raising children has become easier with today's gadgets. Female roles, so says Ms. Johnson, have been underrated by such noted women as Margaret Mead.

In an interesting point on day nurseries, Ms. Johnson states that even the kibbutzim of Israel ended up assigning the heavier work in the fields and orchards to men and leaving most of the jobs in the laundries and children's houses in the hands of the women. Designed in the first place to liberate women, they have not done so.

Her warnings are worth heeding.

> Even if pluralism in male and female roles becomes an entirely accepted fact, it will not be without its cost. When there are no longer any absolute cultural values to guide men and women in how they should shape their lives it takes a good deal of individualism and strength of character to map a course of one's own.[34]

Educated, well-established women in executive roles should take time out to read what the women in the liberation movement are saying. Not only they but male executives as well will be alarmed but impressed. The overconcentration on unreasoning emotions rather than logic, the lack of interest in job-related activities, and the physical emphasis are overbalanced by the real concern about women and their role. It is not a movement to be lightly considered. Based on some justification it cannot or should not be lightly considered.

As one young writer, Catherine Laskey, a freshman at the University of Michigan puts it,

> Since the beginning of history, women have certainly been discriminated against in many ways. The liberation movement is much more complex than most Americans realize, and it deserves a chance to express itself. In a slow but sure way, females in this country are letting themselves be heard and are achieving their principal aims. Hopefully, women will eventually be socially, politically, and economically equal to men in every way.[35]

Some of the feminist literature doesn't seem to do much to help them move up. The current magazines too often concentrate on such topics as abortions, having or not having babies, equalitarian marriages, the sex roles of children, and lesbianism. There are major exceptions. *The New Woman*, for example, has published a guide to executive jobs and what you should know before accepting the success stories of women executives. It layers these stories between articles on shaping up as a housewife and a ribald one about four in a bed.

Many of the women's liberationist newspapers, too, are full of stories that range from vasectomy as a better method of birth control than the pill to pregnancy testing at home to diatribes against men.

As Liz Carpenter (former press secretary to Mrs. Lyndon Johnson) said in a talk in Albany, "There's a little bit of the liberationist in every woman. Most of us are somewhere between the soft, gentle perception of an Anne Morrow Lindbergh and the brilliance of Germaine Greer." [36]

The woman's movement has had many admirable leaders—the truly dedicated women who, through the tolerance and work of sympathetic men, obtained the vote and special legislation for women in the early days; who helped found the Women's Bureau as a special section of the U.S. Department of Labor; and who, through countless struggles, made women's business lives easier or, at least, tried to prevent women from being exploited in the business world.

The current crop of women agitators (too strong a word in many cases) ranges from those really concerned about the waste of individual talents to the wild-eyed, no-talent castaway who protests that she is a victim of discrimination. The language to a newcomer is somewhat confusing. The terminology talks about feminists, liberationists, Lesbians, sisters and male chauvinists. Even high school students talk about male chauvinists. Books about women range from diatribes to scholarly works like *The Feminine Mystique*, by Betty Friedan,[37] and *Born Female*, by Caroline Bird,[38] to *The Sensuous Woman*.[39] One probably shouldn't mention all three in the same paragraph. In 1972, probably more women read *The Sensuous Woman* and have tried some of the advice to entice that "chauvinistic pig" than have assumed that *The Feminine Mystique* could tell them what being a women is really about.

The Feminine Mystique is a particularly intriguing book because it evidently uncovers a very basic problem—that of the unfulfilled woman. A good deal of the ire is directed toward housekeeping chores and the complete involvement of the woman in homemaking. According to the book, women have just not been able to break the chains of conformity and have been slaves to housework, husbands, children, and suburbia.

Most of the women in the study evidently have reached a stage of fulfillment. They talk about an inner confidence or, as one put it, "I've tried lots of things in my life. I am so busy, I guess I really haven't had time to worry whether I was missing so much."

The women executives in the survey probably always took housekeeping in their stride. Maybe the floors weren't polished so often and maybe the special Sunday brunch was a little lopsided because there had been too many important worldly matters settled in high-class conversations among husband and wife and their friends. To our knowledge there has been no study made whether the working executive keeps a better house than her stay-at-home sister or even whether she is happier in her dual role. It is also questionable that as soon as women leave routine household chores behind or as soon as they can become involved in creative activities they will be happy. Management and creative jobs are hard to come by. Are the women whom the liberationists worry about willing to take all the chances and to do the good, solid work required? There is no question that women should be given an equal chance, that they should be allowed to work to the top of their talents, but most executive women will say, "Please, get out and really deliver."

Are there answers to problems examined in *The Feminine Mystique?* Women as well as men will have to solve them together, but most executive women do not think it can be done by strident, raucous, loud-mouthed exhibitionism, particularly where no talent for work or drive for accomplishment is included.

On the other hand, no woman in her right mind will kick another competent woman on her way up. The current thinking in some of the prestigious secretarial schools that it's rough to work for a woman should be stepped on and stepped on hard. If secretaries really want to get ahead, they should forget the quote in *The New York Times,* which says:

> I just think it would be a lot more stimulating to work for a man. Secretaries are here to help *men* with their work, help *men* move up, and then move up with them. A woman would probably expect a lot more out of me, since she's an executive herself.[40]

Intelligent women in good jobs are eager to help you if you have the guts and brains to deliver on an executive job.

One could go on and on about the women's liberation movement —its ramifications, its numerous splinter groups, its power and its nonsense, its sorrows and its triumphs, but this book is really about women who have made it in the executive ranks. Would they be higher in the management ranks if they had been or would now be interested in women's liberation? It's hard to say. Most all of them are too busy with their current heavy workload to get out to march and shout. They do have an underlying concern that no one is cheated of her rights, but also are just as much concerned that women don't degrade themselves. It's fine, they say, to be a vice president or a president, but without the other facets of living, life could be terribly dull.

The reluctance of most of the women in the study to become involved in the more belligerent of the women's groups does not mean that they have abandoned women's groups altogether. Although most profess that they do not have much time to devote to such outside activities, many have been leaders in all-women's groups like The National Association of Personnel Women or its local chapters, the American Association of University Women, the League of Women Voters, the various task forces appointed by political groups, and the President's Special Task Force on Women's Rights and Responsibilities.

By their active participation in other associations where the membership is split between male and female, they have done much for the woman's role in the United States. For example, Cynthia Wedel is president of the World Council of Churches; G. G. Michelson is on the advisory committee at Cornell University Industrial Relations School; and Marie Vescia, a vice president of Airwick, is the first woman president of the International Executives Association; and Margaret Wilson is president of the American Retail Federation. One could go on and on with the honors many of them have gained for their outstanding performances. For example, along with many other honors, Jean Sisco won the coveted Silver Plaque awarded by the National Retail Merchants Association.

Despite all the high-flown talk, there still remains a long way to go before women will have the same opportunity or the same pay as men in the working world. It is a blind woman who doesn't realize that even though there has been some progress, the world is slow to acknowledge the women's role in today's marketplace.

Circumstances, perhaps, and long historical practices have relegated many working women to second-class citizenship. Many, again perhaps, as second wage earners have not regretted it. But to many the rules of the game have proved terribly harsh.

It would be unfair not to report that a minority opinion among the women surveyed favors more overt action for women rather than the slow progress most have had to endure to get good jobs. Eight of the respondents could probably be counted among those who are in favor of women's liberation as it is usually interpreted. At least one has an equalitarian marriage. Some have participated actively in women's causes and marches. Several said that the questionnaire was behind the times—asked questions that had old-fashioned insinuations—and that they were not happy with the tone of the whole thing. A few black minority women executives did not bother to return the completed questionnaire even though they expressed no resentment when called and asked to return it.

It would be pompous and condescending to say that these women, who also are doing well in their positions, are way off base. If that is their way to fulfillment, the rest of us shouldn't criticize them.

11

SIGNS OF THE TIMES:
Protective Legislation
and Constitutional Rights

It is a strange sight to see a little man next to a strapping woman lifting the 50-pound weights off an assembly line. The same is true when you see a little fellow carrying an oversize bag for his more sturdily built older sister. The first situation probably stems from regulations that protect the female from lifting heavy weights. The second situation is a reflection of tradition and custom. Both custom and regulations are changing in the 1970s.

It is true that there have been many protective laws that have sheltered women from extra long hours and have kept women from doing heavier jobs and working nights.

On the other side of the picture, during World War II women did heavy work in the foundries, and no one seems to worry about women cleaning offices during the lonely night hours in the big cities.

There has been a reverse twist today. Women are after the higher-paying jobs and consequently much of the protective legislation is now in question. In their struggle for equal rights, women want to take their equal responsibilities in every job available. Women are after changes in the regulations that affect them.

Laws That Affect Women

Current laws tend to remove some of the earlier protective legislation and to open the avenues for women attaining and holding all kinds of job without prejudice.

One of the best summaries of national legislation affecting women was given in a speech made by Mrs. Sonia Pressman Fuentes, chief, Legislation Counsel Division, Office of the General Counsel, Equal Employment Opportunity Commission, Washington, D.C., before the MDK Associates Seminar on Affirmative Action (Dallas, Texas, May 16, 1972). The title of her speech, "The Law Against Sex Discrimination in Employment." Mrs. Fuentes has graciously given permission for the inclusion of her summary in this book.

Mrs. Fuentes speaks positively for women. Early in her speech, she states,

> Those of us who were concerned with women's rights back in the mid-sixties couldn't imagine that in a short space of a few years the question of women's liberation would become a significant nationwide issue. Events seemed to move more slowly in the early days.
> Today, however, no one will gainsay that equality for women in America is an idea whose time has come.
> Those of us at the EEOC have noted in particular the rapid pace of recent events in this area. Within the past five months, both the EEOC and the OFCC have issued new guidelines on sex discrimination, and new legislation has been passed giving the EEOC the power to secure enforcement of its decisions.

The Women's Bureau

Mrs. Fuentes discusses the statistics of the Women's Bureau, which were examined in Chapter 1. This agency probably has been the best-documented source of statistics about women in America. The prestigious department was created in 1920 to deal with the special problems of women and to protect their rights. It has had such distinguished heads as Frieda Miller and Esther Peterson. Elizabeth Koontz is now at its head and not only ably compiles statistics about women but also represents American women in the international seminars and meetings throughout the world. The Bureau has done much in sponsoring protective regulations and advocating legislation such as day-care centers for children of working women, upgrading the skills of minorities, and bird dogging state legislation. It is doing much to champion women's rights.

Although the women in the study probably are not directly related to the work of the Women's Bureau now, they are interested in some of the causes advocated and in the facts presented by the Bureau.

Mrs. Fuentes's discussion and careful documentation of federal laws and agencies that prohibit sex discrimination follow.

"1. *The Equal Pay Act,* which became generally effective in 1963, requires the payment of equal salaries and wages for equal work without regard to sex. It is administered by the Wage-Hour Administration in the Labor Department.

"2. *Title VII of the Civil Rights Act of 1964,* which became effective in 1965, prohibits discrimination in all terms, conditions, and privileges of employment by employers, employment agencies, and unions based on race, color, religion, sex, and national origin. It is administered by the Equal Employment Opportunity Commission, the EEOC.

"3. *Executive Order 11246,* as amended by 11375, effective October 1968, prohibits discrimination based on race, religion, sex, and national origin by contractors and subcontractors of the federal government and on federally assisted construction contracts. The Order is administered by the Office of Federal Contract Compliance (OFCC) in the Department of Labor. It obligates government contractors to develop and implement written affirmative action programs to eliminate sex discrimination or they may face the termination or cancellation of existing contracts or debarment from future contracts.

"In 1970, OFCC issued its guidelines on sex discrimination.[1] On December 4, 1971, OFCC issued revised Order No. 4, which obligates government contractors to establish specific goals and timetables for the employment of women just as they have previously been required to establish for the employment of minorities.[2]

"4. *Executive Order 11478,* issued by President Nixon in August 1969, prohibits sex discrimination in covered positions in the federal government, and is administered by the Civil Service Commission. In implementation of the Order, the Civil Service Commission has established the Federal Women's Program.*

* While the statutes and executive orders cited are the principal sources for relief in sex discrimination cases, the National Labor Relations Act, administered by the National Labor Relations Board, also prohibits sex discrimination where it is related to union activity. Furthermore, while the Age Discrimination in Employment Act of

"On the state and municipal levels, state and city fair employment practice commissions and state agencies that administer state equal pay legislation serve as additional sources of relief. Some state and local laws and ordinances go beyond existing federal legislation and prohibit sex discrimination not only in employment but also in housing, education, and places of public accommodation.

"I should now like to focus on the rulings of EEOC and the courts under Title VII. EEOC is *the* federal agency with the longest experience in enforcing a statute that prohibits all forms of employment discrimination. Accordingly, its holdings and those of the courts under Title VII frequently establish the principles that are then followed by other agencies on both the federal and state levels.

"A proceeding commences at EEOC through the filing of a charge with one of our district offices in cities throughout the country. Charges of sex discrimination represent the second largest category of employment discrimination cases filed with EEOC. Of the 86,000 charges of discrimination filed during our first six and a half years, over 20 percent, approximately 18,500 charges, involved sex discrimination.

"While most of these charges are filed by women, a number of significant issues have been raised in charges filed by men. Such charges have included the refusal to employ men because of draft status, employer restrictions on the length and style of hair, and discrimination in retirement and pension plans.

"I should like to review for you the principal issues raised in Title VII charges and the status of the law today.† It has been established that, with few exceptions, all jobs must be open to men and women. The act does provide for an exception "in those certain instances where . . . sex . . . is a bona fide occupational qualification [bfoq] reasonably necessary to the normal operation" of a particular business or enterprise. This exception is narrowly construed. The burden of establishing that the exception is applicable rests with the party making the claim.

"In the two most recent appellate court decisions dealing with bfoq, courts viewed the exception as follows. A determination that sex is a bfoq for a job cannot be made on the basis of general assumptions regarding the physical capabilities of men or women. In order for sex to

1967 does not deal with sex discrimination, it may nonetheless be of particular use to women over 40 who wish to return to the labor market or change jobs. That act, which is administered by the Department of Labor, prohibits age discrimination between the ages of 40 and 65.

† While the principles discussed are phrased in terms of employer violations, similar principles are applicable to conduct by employment agencies and unions. Furthermore, employment agencies and unions are prohibited from discriminating with regard to employment referrals.

be a bfoq for a job, it must be established that the sexual characteristics of the employee are crucial to the successful performance of the job, as they would be for the position of wet-nurse; or that there is a need for authenticity or genuiness, as is the case for the position of actor or actress. In other words, discrimination based on sex is valid only when the essence of the business enterprise would be undermined by not hiring members of one sex exclusively.[3]

"Thus jobs can't be denied to women as a class because of the preferences of the employer, co-workers, clients, or customers; because the job has traditionally been held by men; because the job requires work with, or supervision over, men; because it involves late-night hours or work in isolated locations; or because the job involves heavy lifting or other strenuous physical activity.

"Furthermore, the Commission and the courts have found that state laws that prohibit the employment of women in certain occupations, and that limit their hours after work and the weight they may lift, are invalidated by Title VII, and, accordingly, do not justify the refusal to hire women.[4]

"Since 1969, a number of attorneys general have issued opinions finding that Title VII and/or their state fair employment practices legislation superseded their state legislation restricting the employment of women. Such opinions have been issued by the attorneys general of South Dakota, Pennsylvania, Oklahoma, Michigan, Massachusetts, Missouri, Wisconsin, and Washington and by the corporation counsel of the District of Columbia.

"Many states and the District of Columbia have amended or repealed their restrictive legislation to broaden opportunities for women.

Newspaper Ads

"This Commission has stated that as a general rule an advertiser may not indicate a preference or limitation based on sex in the content of classified advertising nor place ads in sex-segregated columns.‡

"Because of the Commission's position, and similar positions taken by city and state fair employment practice commissions, newspapers across the country, including *The New York Times* and all other major New

‡ In its *amicus curiae* brief in the case of *Brush v. San Francisco Newspaper Printing Co.*, the Commission took the position that a newspaper that maintains classified advertising columns is acting as an employment agency, and, therefore, violates Title VII when it segregates such columns on the basis of sex. That position was not sustained by the District Court, 315 F. Supp. 577 (D.D. Calif., 1970); the case is pending appeal.

York City newspapers and the three major newspapers in the District of Columbia, have discontinued the maintenance of sex-segregated columns. §

Title VII and Marriage

"As a general rule, Title VII requires equal terms, conditions, and privileges of employment without regard to sex. Thus employees are entitled to equality with regard to wages and salaries. Title VII covers both the obvious type of discrimination where men and women in the same job classification are receiving disparate wages or salaries and the more subtle type where only women are employed in a job classification and the wage rate is discriminatorily depressed because, traditionally, only women have been employed in that classification.

"The Commission has said that an employer may not refuse to hire married women or women with children and may not discharge female employees because of marriage or parenthood unless it treats men equally.[5]

Guidelines on Sex Discrimination

"On April 5, 1972, EEOC issued revised guidelines on sex discrimination, some of which had been under consideration since July 1965.[6] The principal rulings established in those guidelines are:

"1. Title VII supersedes state laws that discriminate on the basis of sex with regard to the employment of minors to the extent that such laws are more restrictive for one sex. Accordingly, if a state law provides that boys may be employed in certain occupations at age 14 but girls have to be 16, an employer will be deemed in violation of Title VII if he refused to employ girls at age 14.

"2. State requirements with regard to minimum wage and premium pay for overtime for women are equally applicable to men.

"3. Benefits for women required by state law, such as special rest and meal periods and physical facilities, such as seats, must generally be equally provided for men. If, however, an employer can demonstrate

§ On March 14, 1971, in the first state court decision on the issue, the Pittsburgh Press was found in violation of a Pittsburgh ordinance against maintaining sex-segregated columns, 3 EPD para. 8154 (Pa. Ct. of Common Pleas. Allegheny County, 1971), aff'd as modified, 4 EPD para. 7732 (Pa. Commonwealth Ct., 1972). A similar finding was made by the State of New Jersey Department of Law and Public Safety, Division on Civil Rights, in a case involving three Jew Jersey newspapers, Hinfrey v. The Red Bank Register (Case No. E13Bs-4806 et al., October 27, 1971).

that business necessity precludes providing these benefits to men, then he cannot lawfully provide them to women.

"4. Employers may not discriminate on the basis of sex with regard to any fringe benefits, such as medical, hospital, accident, and life insurance and retirement and pension plans.[7] The fact that the cost of the benefits may be greater for one sex than the other is immaterial.

"5. Employers may not refuse to hire applicants for employment or fire employees simply because they are pregnant.[8]

"6. Disabilities caused by pregnancy should be treated as the employer treats other temporary disabilities under its health or temporary disability insurance or sick leave plan. Thus employees are entitled to the same provisions with regard to leave, pay, accrual of seniority, and so on when they are temporarily disabled due to pregnancy as when they are temporarily disabled for other reasons.[9]

Equal Employment Opportunity Act

"On March 24, 1972, President Nixon signed the Equal Employment Opportunity Act of 1972, which amended Title VII. The principal features of interest to women are:

"1. Charges may now be filed by women's rights organizations and others on behalf of aggrieved persons.

"2. EEOC now has the power to institute lawsuits in the federal district courts, but the aggrieved person retains his power to also institute such suits.

"3. Employees of state and municipal governments are now covered by Title VII. However, where charges are filed with EEOC against city and state agencies, if litigation is necessary it will be conducted by the attorney general rather than EEOC.

"4. Employees in the competitive service in the federal government are now covered by Title VII, and they have the right to institute lawsuits, seeking back pay and other relief, after completing Civil Service Commission procedures.

"5. Teachers and administrative personnel of private as well as public educational institutions are covered by Title VII for the first time.

"Until the extension of Title VII to educational institutions, the only relief available to teachers and other employees of such institutions, other than Constitutional actions, was Executive Order 11246, administered by OFCC and its compliance agency, the Department of Health, Education, and Welfare. Since 1970, women and women's rights organizations have charged 350 colleges and universities throughout the

United States with sex discrimination. However, under the Executive Order, the plaintiffs had no right to go to court. Now, under the amendments to Title VII, women teachers have this right for the first time.

Discrimination Costs Money

"Employers and unions are discovering that it's becoming increasingly expensive to discriminate against women, and this should make them more amenable to resolving charges of discrimination. Last year, EEOC announced the award of the largest settlement ever achieved in a sex discrimination case under Title VII.[10] By terms of that settlement, the Anaconda Aluminum Company agreed to pay $190,000 in back wages and court costs to 276 women who had alleged that the company maintained sex-segregated job classifications. In November 1970, in the case of *Hodgson* v. *Wheaton Glass Co.,* an equal pay case involving discrimination in wages paid to females, the District Court of New Jersey ordered the company to pay over $900,000 in back pay with interest to the 2,000 employees involved.

Reports and Information

"EEOC engages in other activities that affect the employment status of women. These activities include the publication of information received from our employer and union reporting systems, research studies, grants to state fair employment practice commissions, affirmative action efforts, and hearings. Among those activities that revealed evidence of sex discrimination were a hearing on the textile industry in North Carolina and South Carolina, largely involving discrimination against black women; hearings on white-collar employment in New York City; hearings on the aerospace and communications industries in Los Angeles; hearings on employment patterns in Houston, Texas; hearings into the utilities industry; and activities before the Federal Communications Commission and the Interstate Commerce Commission.

"The employer reports focus on the breakdown of the workforce by sex, race, and national origin in different work categories, such as officials and managers, professional employees, sales personnel, and laborers. The union reports contain similar breakdowns with regard to union membership, referrals to jobs, and participation in apprenticeship programs. EEOC has published two compilations analyzing the data received from our employer reports for 1966 and 1967 (Equal Employment Opportunity Reports No. 1 and No. 2). Similar reports have been published by the Civil Service Commission showing the distribution of women in the federal workforce from 1967 through 1970.[11]

"EEOC involvement with the Federal Communications Commission (FFC) occurred as follows. In November 1970, the American Telephone and Telegraph Company filed a notice of a proposed increase in long-distance telephone rates with FCC. In December, EEOC filed a petition with FCC claiming that the Bell companies systematically discriminate against women, blacks, Americans with Spanish surnames, and other minorities. FCC declined to suspend the rate increase but did order an immediate investigation of EEOC's charges, to be followed by a public hearing. In connection with that hearing, EEOC submitted a massive report on AT&T to FCC. Over half the report was devoted to charges of discriminatory employment practices against women. . . . The FCC investigation and hearings . . . [marked] the first major attempt by a federal regulatory agency to examine the employment practices of a regulated industry. [On January 19, 1973, *The New York Times* reported that the government ordered AT&T to award $15 million in back pay to women and minority men and to grant them $23 million in raises. According to the *Times*, this historic settlement should serve as a warning to other companies with discriminatory hiring and promotion practices.]

"In 1971, EEOC took similar action when the trucking industry submitted a statement in connection with a notice of proposed rule making issued by Interstate Commerce Commission (ICC). EEOC charged the trucking industry with a 'disgraceful' record of employment discrimination that excludes women, blacks, and Spanish-surnamed Americans from all but the lowest-paying jobs. EEOC pointed out that 93 percent of all women in industry are relegated to office and clerical jobs and that women represent only 2.2. percent of officials and managers. The EEOC position was supported by the Department of Justice, the Department of Transportation, OFCC, and the U.S. Postal Service.[12]

Affirmative Action

"As you see, from the preceding summary of EEOC activity over the past seven years, there have been a host of developments. The name of the game is no longer 'What is employment discrimination?' but 'What should I do about it?' In other words, how can a company take affirmative action?

"Integration of a company's workforce requires the development of special programs geared to achieving that goal. Studies reveal that when top management is as interested in equal employment as it is in its other organizational goals, and when it manifests that interest by the development and implementation of affirmative action programs, results follow. EEOC hearings have revealed that while some companies with poor records of workforce integration bemoan the fact that they cannot find qualified women, other companies in the same industry with ongoing affirmative action programs have managed to recruit and upgrade significant numbers of women.

"If you want to develop affirmative action programs for your own company, first advise all your employees that the elimination of job discrimination has top priority in your company. Then make certain that your personnel and legal departments keep abreast of the law and that significant rulings are passed on to all employees.

"A good way to begin the development of an affirmative action program is to review the composition of your workforce. Are women represented all the way up the line in proportion to their representation in the workforce in your area? In reviewing the status of your women employees, you would want to pay particular attention to minority group women, those who are black, Spanish-surnamed, Oriental, and American Indian. Such women are frequently the victims of two forms of discrimination: that based on sex and that based on race or national origin. Accordingly, they are often found at the very bottom of the occupational and economic totem poles.

"Once you have reviewed the composition of your workforce, you would want to review the gamut of your personnel policies. In making such an evaluation, you should ask yourself the following questions.

"Do my job qualifications, employment interview techniques, and testing procedures screen out women?

"Am I recruiting at schools where women predominate and do I maintain continuing contacts with women's rights organizations so as to receive their advice and assistance in recruiting?

"Am I advertising in media that reach women? Is the content of my advertising free of discrimination, and is it placed in columns that do not discriminate on the basis of sex? Do my ads project an image that will appeal to women? When I use an employment agency, have I indicated my interest in employing women as well as men for all available positions?

"Do my collective bargaining contracts explicitly or implicitly discriminate on the basis of sex? Are my job classifications, wages and salaries, and seniority systems free of discrimination?

"Once you have reviewed your personnel complement and policies, you would be in a position to develop an affirmative action program designed to correct existing imbalances. Such a program should include the establishment of specific goals and timetables for the recruitment, hiring, and upgrading of women.

"To develop your affirmative action program and to implement it, you would want to make sure that you select individuals who are sensitive to the question of women's rights and that they have the authority to implement the program developed.

"These are some of the things you can do in your own organization to help us at EEOC do our job. We all know that the government working alone cannot achieve the goal of an integrated workforce."

No attempt has been made in this book to list the states and municipal legislation affecting women. Many of the state laws, as stated earlier, are superseded by the national law and are being eliminated or changed to move more closely to comply with national standards. Some of the state and city agencies dealing with discrimination are very active, however, and often management has found them very hard to convince that its company is guiltless. Efforts are made by agencies on a national and local basis to coordinate their efforts, but often a businessman finds himself buried in red tape in dealing with the multiple agencies. Perhaps, in time, as there is less and less discrimination, there will be more clear-cut guidelines under which to manage.

Equal Pay Extended

Since Mrs. Fuentes's speech, there have been other national developments. The Equal Pay Act of 1964 applied to women covered by the Fair Labor Standards Act, meaning those in the nonmanagement jobs. In congressional action in 1971 and 1972, when there was a major effort to revise the minimum wage law, both the House and the Senate included in several bills the extension of the equal pay provisions to professional, executive, and administrative employees. Because so much of industry still does not have clear-cut conceptions and descriptions of jobs covered by earlier equal pay provisions, the extended provisions have been both frustrating and expensive to industry. The application of this provision to higher management echelons has sent shudders up management backs.

In addition to the legislation discussed in previous pages there has been a real effort to broaden the scope of the Equal Pay Act to include more people. Here is how Senator Harrison Williams (D-N.J.) included the provision for the equalization of the pay for executive, professional, and administrative employees in his bill calling for changes in the minimum wage as reported in the January 9, 1972, *Congressional Record:*

There can be no quarrel that there is widespread discrimination against women in hiring, promotion, and pay throughout the country. The situation is making mockery of our efforts at the federal level to mandate the equal opportunity and I believe Congress should move quickly to correct it.

While the minimum wage legislation was moving slowly through Congress, the Education Amendment of 1972, signed into law on June 23, 1972, in a three-sentence provision in the bill, did exactly what several congressmen were trying to do. It broadened the scope of equal pay provisions, so that now there should be no discrimination because of sex in administrative, professional, and executive jobs.

The amendment, which became effective July 1, 1972, extends the Equal Pay Act protection to some 15 million people. The act requires the same pay for men and women doing substantially equal work requiring substantially equal skill, effort, and responsibility in similar working conditions in the same establishment. When discrimination exists, pay rates of the lower-paid employees (usually women) must be raised to equal those of the higher-paid employees.

You can well imagine the furor that will be caused when the Labor Department really cracks down on this provision. Does this mean that all companies have been sinning on this issue, and how does it affect women in management positions? Most of the women in the study say they think they are being paid the same as a man in a similar position, but it has usually taken longer to get there, and too often they are still stopped before attaining the very top positions.

The Dangers of Legislating Equality

There is some danger when such legislation becomes law. There are some women who will demand equal pay without really performing. It is hoped that managements across the country will review their compensation plans at the management level to be sure that differentials in pay are based on factors other than sex in managerial jobs as well as among the rank and file. Mrs. Fuentes's suggested affirmative action is not a bad idea because it will point up good as well as poor performers.

Constitutional Amendment

The feeling that women have been discriminated against is so strong that women's groups, with support from individual men and some men's groups, have been agitating for more than 50 years for a constitutional amendment. Up until the second session of the 92d Congress in the spring of 1972, the pressure was effective in one branch of the legislature, but then either the House or the Senate would balk.

Finally, in March 1972, an amendment was passed: "Equality of rights under the law shall not be abridged by the United States or any state on account of sex." If this is ratified, it will be the 27th amendment to the Constitution.

If the "Ladies' Day" in February 1964 on the establishment of Title VII of the Civil Rights Act brought down the House, it could hardly have equaled the legislative flap on the equal rights amendment. Called a "potentially destructive and self-defeating blunderbuss" in the March 28, 1972, *Congressional Record,* the amendment was adopted nonetheless. Championed by such senators as Bayh of Indiana and Javits of New York, it was denounced by many other senators. At its passage Senator Sam Ervin of North Carolina quoted, "Father, forgive them, for they know not what they do." One of the best of the colorful speakers, Senator Ervin also stated that, "I respectfully submit that resorting to an amendment to the Constitution to nullify state laws of this character would be about as wise as using an atomic bomb to exterminate a few mice."

Before becoming the law of the land, an amendment must be ratified by 38 of the legislative bodies of the 50 states. Hawaii claims the honor of being the first to ratify—only a few hours after Congress passed the amendment.

It looks as though the required number of states will pass the amendment within the seven years allowed. It will be effective two years after that.

What will this mean? Perhaps it will not have a direct effect on the job because of the other regulations discussed. But it will remove many barriers. The one that upset congressmen the most was the drafting of women into the armed services. If you want interesting reading, go back over the *Congressional Records* of late March and early April 1972. Property rights, marriage rights, credit rights all will be equalized legally when the constitutional amendment is ratified. This will have indirect bearing on women in management. It is again a sign of revolution by women in the 1970s.

Management Women and the Law

A few words should be said about how management women are affected in their day-to-day work by the laws passed specifically to protect them from discrimination. Most of them are now operating under the same pay scale as their male counterparts. On promotional opportunities there is still plenty of uncultivated territory as comparatively few women get to the very top jobs. The younger management women will probably have better opportunities to reach the top.

Women of today find themselves in a somewhat peculiar position. Actually in the working world there are far more women than men, but management women still find themselves in the minority. Consequently, it is very distressing to be treated as a minority instead of an executive with plenty on the ball. This is not always true, particularly among the women in the study, but all of them recognize the somewhat condescending air that accompanies the current bragging of staff executives about the number of women they have in middle management and top positions. This, too, in time will probably pass.

Of what interest are all these governmental regulations to the management women in the study? They regret that equalization of working conditions has had to come about through legislation rather than reform from within. They are concerned that in the fast action to get squared away with public opinion that "token" women will be placed in responsible positions. However, equal pay for equal work and equal opportunity to advance when and if capabilities are proved is long overdue. Wasted feminine management talent since time began is a fact of life. With the complicated problems facing management today no such talent should be wasted and, if laws will help them, most women favor them. It is hoped, however, that fair employment practices will make future protective legislation unnecessary.

12
ARE WOMEN STUCK IN DEAD-END JOBS?

If a woman has worked in a job for two or three years and has done a good job, is she likely to be stuck there? Does she or anyone else think it is possible for her to move into the next managerial opening? How many firms have included women on their promotional charts? There are still a good number of companies that have replacement charts, some with pictures of the incumbent and the next two or three backup "men." Have you ever seen a woman's picture on that chart, or does the company you work for actually have women slotted into these promotional spots?

The current situation has led some firms to move women two or three jumps to save face or get a government contract. Many more now have them "in the pipeline," ready to move up in regular steps. The bulk of firms still are slow about putting women in executive training with the objective of eventually promoting them a long way up the line.

Earlier we talked about the woman-behind-the-man cliché and

how today's management women feel about it. It's not hard to find a woman as an assistant or the long-time secretary who when her boss retires finds no place in the management hierarchy. Until recently women have played the helper role at home. Often they transfer this same dependency to the job.

If a woman is at home and wants to go back to work she, too, is often in a dead-end job. The thought of going back to work frightens her or she forgets about any work capabilities she has and is willing to settle for a far more mediocre job than she needs to.

Do women have to stay in these dead-end jobs? Whose fault is it —their own or a stupid management that just doesn't recognize their qualifications and talents?

Men, too, worry about moving up. Most of the time, however, it is because the boss is only a few years older and the line of succession is too long. Young people look ahead at the long, long line and shudder at how many years it will take before anyone recognizes their talents. So women share some of the same problems as men when there is no way up.

A recent graduate class was asked what was the roughest work problem each of them faced. Over half said their bosses were the main stumbling block. The bosses were either "over the hill" as far as keeping up with newer techniques, and were just hanging on until retirement, or were too smart and the students felt inadequate. In both cases the result was the same. They were ready to move out in order to move up.

What about women, since there are so many more places to bury them in the dead-end jobs? There may be circumstances that make it necessary to stay in a job, but most of the employees stay because the rut is more comfortable than facing the outside world. Complaining about your rights won't help much. There are positive steps women can take. One of the most common ways of changing executive jobs is through an executive search firm. Are women using these firms? Are the headhunters aware that women are available and want to move upward and onward?

Inside Information from an
Executive Search Firm

To get a realistic picture from the outside we interviewed James Lotz, partner of Battalia & Lotz Associates, Inc., a recruiting firm well known for its executive search work. The firm has recently placed several women in management jobs and is looking for more. To make the interview more interesting, Mr. Lotz was accompanied by Constance

Klages, vice president of the firm. With the stepped-up emphasis on hiring women for management jobs, they come in constant contact with the big problem of matching job talents with very promising openings. They are eager to fill these positions with competent people because a well-satisfied client often comes back for more business.

First of all, the atmosphere of a search firm is different from that of the typical employment agency. There is a degree of confidentiality here that you do not find in the open marketplace. The client can and does ask for certain qualifications on a confidential basis. He can and does say, "I would like a man for this job, or I just don't think a Jew or a Catholic, a New Yorker, or you-name-it would be happy in this situation."

These clients are now asking for women. According to Mr. Lotz, many of them are saying, "I need more women in my upper echelons and I have none trained. I have many coming up but none is ready right now." Such searches are difficult because not many companies are much better off. It's a rare one that has even half the number of women as it has men in its promotable ranks. As Mr. Lotz says, "There just is not a very big pool for the managerial ranks regardless of the function."

Women's Talents Not Readily Identifiable

The other difficulties he encounters are many. It is most difficult to find women because their talents are not easily identifiable. They just don't do enough outside the job to get visibility. They don't go to seminars, they don't attend graduate classes, they don't make speeches, and they don't write. It may be true, according to Mr. Lotz, that their home situation is such that this, too, holds them back. One personnel manager who is now successful and well known didn't show on the scene until after her divorce. Now everyone knows she is around.

Résumés Not Ready

Women just don't seem ready to move. They don't have their résumés prepared. The management man who doesn't is a rare bird, but it's a rare woman who has taken the time to list her assets in résumé form. Lotz referred to a recent ad run by his firm seeking a vice president of industrial relations for a very large international firm based in New York. The client had said he preferred a qualified woman. Of the 200 replies, 7 had the qualifications. But not one woman applied. A check of the local associations with women members revealed that of the 200 applicants many were members of those associations. Why didn't the women reply? They are more visible than most, but they, too, kept their heads in the sand.

The search, then, really depends on the ingenuity of the recruiter to find likely women candidates. He is flooded with qualified males, but where can he find qualified women? Mr. Lotz wouldn't reveal his techniques, but he did find qualified candidates for this job and for others. It was not a simple task.

Women Botch Up the Interview

Some comments from Mrs. Klages and Mr. Lotz may be helpful to management women seeking relief from dead-end jobs.

"Women have a tendency to undersell themselves. They just haven't sat down and really analyzed their assets. Men have a tendency to exaggerate their talents, but women are not sure enough of themselves to really tell the prospective employer how much they really know.

"They forget to find out about the company to which they are applying. It's a crime of the first order after you know the name of the firm not to find out about its products, its markets, and its financial condition. Many men make it their business to know these vital statistics, but women seldom do. They come into the interview without having done their homework.

"Even the capable ones are apt to undo themselves in an interview. Even though they may be belligerent on the job they try to take on some feminine characteristics of shyness or coyness. Perhaps they deprecate their education. This education may be the bridge by which they can cross over into the management ranks. Men may brag about their college records far too much, but women just don't want to seem too bright."

In the opinion of the interviewers, women are reluctant to ask the searching questions necessary to find out whether the job is what they want or one they will be able to handle well. On the other side of the coin, men are apt to probe more. Perhaps it's because the man is still the one with the monkey on his back as far as having to be the aggressor and the breadwinner for his family.

According to Mr. Lotz, most men are still uneasy when interviewing a woman for a management job. It's an extra hurdle to cross, and it's as much the responsibility of the woman interviewee as for the interviewer. If women are aware of this, perhaps they can do something about it. An example, if the interview is held over lunch, don't embarrass your host about who picks up the check and don't spend half the lunch period talking about high-class eating places you have enjoyed.

You must remember to keep the purpose of the interview in mind.

"Remember, too," he says, "that there are certain personal facts your prospective employer would like to know. Your age—why be so coy about it? Most of us who have had any experience have lived a certain number of years. If you have had 10 years here and 12 years there, don't try to get away with being thirty. Don't make him probe to find out whether you are married, divorced, or single. Most men readily talk about these factors, and they do have a bearing on the job."

If you don't have a résumé, write one and follow the same rules: list all the important facts. Mrs. Klages says, "Don't make it hard for me to find out what you can do, who you are, where and when you have worked and on what jobs, your education, and the years you were born and graduated."

"Men are afraid of their judgment in interviewing women," says Mr. Lotz. "They just haven't interviewed enough of them, are not easy in the situation, and need all the help they can get from the interviewee.

"Women just don't size up a work situation fast enough. Sometimes there's a bit of kidding that goes on that men are used to. Women are often dead serious when they should loosen up a bit.

"Having a woman in the situation changes the whole tone of the meeting—not just at the interview stage but all along the way."

Mr. Lotz does admit that there are exceptions.

At interview time, women have had plenty of hits on the head, but go blithely on. Take, for example, the well-qualified applicant for a management job who reports her recent experience. "I went in to apply for the job, but the personnel manager never looked up. He said, 'I have a branch manager who would like a secretary.' He never even looked at either me or my résumé." Women applying for a management job resent the "leg" or "bust" approach. In a way they like it but know they had better forget it when applying for a management spot. They wish men would, too.

Or take the report of a high-placed government official at a meeting in New York attended by one of New York's leading industrial relations vice presidents. He assumed she was someone's secretary until he sat down to dinner and examined his program.

Mr. Lotz's opinions are reinforced by those of other executive recruiters. Frank Canny, president of Canny, Boven, Howard, Peck, and Associates, in a *Dun's Review* article, says, "I doubt if I have two female résumés on file." [1] In the same article the well-known Manhattan recruiter William H. Clark says, "While I think there is a lot of talent being missed by the companies, I don't know that there is that much dedication on the part of women. I believe a woman can make out very well in

Wall Street today, for instance, but those we've looked at just don't want
to work that hard." [2]

It's not all the woman's fault. As one woman recently said, "I always dreamed of marrying a doctor. I never dreamed of *being* one."

That's the problem that today's woman is trying to overcome!

How to Get Out
of a Dead-End Job

The following summary of the interview should prove helpful to
the woman who wants to move out of a dead-end job.

1. *Don't stay in your shell.* Be like the "angry young men" who are
looking for opportunities. Ask the boss to send you to the next seminar
that looks interesting. You probably see the flyer before he does. Get out
to meet people. Ask to become a member of a professional society. You
may surprise him with your sudden interest and enthusiasm.

2. *Start reading the management literature.* When did you last
read the *Harvard Business Review, Nation's Business,* the trade journals,
the union magazines? There are literally hundreds of good management books.

3. *Watch for opportunities.* A perusal of the ads in *The New York
Times* and *The Wall Street Journal,* for example, gives you a good idea
of what talents are in demand. If you want to get a feel for the market,
try answering an ad. Mrs. Klages reports that her firm gets thousands of
unsolicited résumés. Only one-half of one percent are from women. Note
the example of the 200 résumés for the vice presidential job, which no
women applicants answered.

4. *Write your résumé.* Get professional help if you need it.

5. *Prepare for the interview.* Find out as much as you can about
the companies to which you are applying.

6. *Ask questions to find out the information you need.*

7. *Don't undersell yourself.*

8. *Usually you'll be interviewed more than once for an important
job.* Find out what you can about the second interview ahead of time.
Remember, if you are asked back for a second interview you are on your
way—if you handle it right.

9. *If you don't get the job, analyze why.* Don't try to make the
most common excuse: "I didn't get the job because I'm a woman."

10. *If you don't get the job, start talking to other management
women (and men) about the methods they use in the job.* Some of them
may be able to give you valuable advice.

What Other Media and Companies
Are Doing

What are others in the recruitment business saying about finding capable women executives? An article in *The New York Times* states, "Numerous counselors to big business suddenly find themselves threatened by their inability to respond to their clients' currently urgent need —to place women in executive channels and job slots where they seldom have been seen thus far." [3]

Riding the trend, or as the *Times* calls it "this traditional method of climbing aboard a new business bandwagon," [4] has created some interesting so-called experts in answering the need. There are seminars and courses to help women get away from the old routine job. Any woman or man looking for help from such media should examine them first to see if they will really solve the problem.

The American Management Association has been running seminars for executive secretaries for some time. In May 1971 and November of 1972 it held its Women In Management conferences. AMA also has a course, *Excel,* an in-house multimedia training program designed to inspire people in supportive roles to move upward.

Katherine Gibbs, of secretarial training fame, announced seminars in "Management Training for Today's Woman." If the school attains the success in this area that it has in the secretarial field, there will be a new crop of women ready and eager for managerial duties.

There are prepackaged plans, self-help aids, and legal help where necessary. There are agencies like the Association of Feminist Consultants in Princeton, New Jersey, set up to provide professional consulting services to business, government, and women's groups. Another is MS (Management Services), a placement agency for women. This branch of Newtime, Inc. was established in 1970 by Joan Baeder and Ina Torton in Manhattan to get more married women back into the job market with a 5-day 25-hour week.

It is interesting to note that Mrs. Baeder (according to the *Times* article) agrees with much of what Mr. Lotz said in his interview. She says, "Women have to come up to the same professional measurements as men." [5] She does urge managements to revamp their jobs creatively so that they can comfortably and realistically attract women. For example, she says, "Women may not be geared (psychologically) to relocate in little towns in the South or to traveling 90 percent of the time. So I tell them at first to make the women relocate in a town of 200,000 or make her travel 50 percent of the time.

"The employers, however, invariably take advantage of women. They don't know their rights or have enough confidence." [6]

The words about special concessions do not concur with those of the women included in this book, but perhaps the trend may be to go along with Mrs. Baeder's views.

There are local groups scattered throughout the country that are urging women with college educations to get back into the employment world; the nursing shortage is well known and the plea to get them back is well publicized. Although now there is a teaching surplus, certain positions are still in scarce supply of talent.

What, then, does all this frenzy mean to the woman in a dead-end job, either at work or at home? Should she sit and wait to be rescued? Should she expect extra concessions because she is a woman, as suggested by Mrs. Baeder? The answer, of course, is decidedly no. The climate is right for women to move. How much of the task is up to her and how much help from the outside world can she get?

Do You Really Want to Move Up?

First of all, any woman who wants to move can, but she should decide whether she really wants to. For many reasons many actually do not want to move. They have working husbands and are working only to supplement the family income until the children have finished school. Some are contented with little or no responsibility. There are a lot more, however, who would move if they had the opportunity.

Responsibility Rests with the Individual

There was a time when it was fashionable for management to buy canned training programs or to fashion these programs with management needs in mind but then run everyone through these programs indiscriminately. Now there seems to be a trend away from the management development programs that have been built entirely on the spoon-fed method of training. Programs are being built around specific company needs, and the employee is expected to take his or her fair share of responsibility for career planning. As Marion Kellogg says in *Career Management:*

> The proposed system is *career management,* which preserves the freedom of the individual to direct his [her] own life, to maintain responsibility for his career. . . . When he chooses to affiliate with a particular institution as the best way to meet his personal objectives, he cooperates fully with organization systems; yet he is still free to change his affiliation should his personal targets make this desirable. . . . Under career

management an individual is responsible for directing his [her] own career.[7]

As a practical matter, Miss Kellogg goes on to say:

A career for an employed person is one outcome of the relationship of
the person with the institution. When the goals of the organization and
those of the individual match *reasonably*, the individual's occupational
growth follows the organization's closely. At the same time his career
evolves at a rate and in a direction that are the joint results of efforts by
the managerial hierarchy above him and his own self-determining
actions. [8]

In other words, an employee is the master of his or her own career, and hopefully they coincide with the company's aims. If, as too
often happens, a woman finds that she cannot move until her boss does
but he is young and solidly entrenched; if it's a family concern where no
one but family gets the breaks; or if for some reason the whole promotion path is blocked, then it is up to her to at least look outward.

How to Determine your Assets and Liabilities

If you think you are in a dead-end spot, you are likely to underestimate your own talents. Women, are especially reluctant to take a good
hard look at what they can do. Often a few sheets of paper used well
and honestly can give anyone a more realistic view of what the next
move can be.

"Divide your paper into four columns," say one well-known personnel director. "In one column list the things you like to do and can do
well; in the second column those things you dislike; the third column
what you can do about improving your skills, tied in with what you like
to do; and in the fourth column (hopefully a small one) the things that
will hold you back and that you can't do anything about."

Miss Kellogg's career-launching checklist should be helpful.

1. Do I know the things I do best?
2. Have I found some things I like to do very much?
3. Do I work better by myself or with other people? What sorts of
   other people?
4. Do I know what talents I do not have?
5. Do I know the things I very much dislike doing?
6. Have I gotten professional advice on the fields of work I ought to
   consider for myself?
7. Does my education prepare me for these fields, or do I need fur-

ther education or specialization courses or some sort of internship before making a full-fledged beginning?

8. How hard am I willing to work physically or mentally? Can I work long hours?

9. What are my work habits? Short bursts of very intense efforts? Or a steady pace?

10. Have I talked with people doing jobs I think I might or should be interested in so that I have firsthand information on what they do, how they do it, and what a typical day is like for them? [9]

After this critical examination of talents, what is the next step, especially if you are a woman interested in breaking the logjam? This book is not intended to be a how-to book, but yet it is intended to assist potential managers and to indicate that to move up is not a hopeless task. There is much literature in the field, and any woman eager to make a change should know what is available.

Other Helpful Literature

If a somewhat facetious but penetrating look is asked for, read *Up the Organization,* by Robert Townsend.[10] He'll tell you about budgets, about job descriptions, and about management. The women in the study will vouch for some of the barbs in Townsend's book.

Or if you want to learn about another popular analysis, read *The Peter Principle,* which says that you can get promoted until you finally reach a job you can't do.[11] There's a special no-holds-barred section for women on the move.

A more serious approach, *Executive on the Move* is still good.[12] It tells anyone (male or female) the steps to take when looking for a move up. It discusses a number of very practical ideas.

Many times men or women, but especially women, because of the nature of management life, have to move out to move up. *How to Move in Management* is a practical guide to using every avenue available to get placed in a job where talents can be utilized.[13]

The emphasis is that changing jobs is not easy for anyone, particularly in a management position. On the other hand, rewards can be high not only in monetary but also in job-satisfaction returns.

Examining again the steps taken by the women in the study, one is impressed with the various approaches to their current spots, whether it was the long hard road up the internal ladder, or the meteoric rise when someone in management recognized talent, or the shifting sideward and upward of some who changed companies and even careers to get where they wanted to go.

Tied in, of course, is the whole process of job hunting, examination of opportunities, and the early days on the job.

Résumé Writing

Résumé writing, a process some women are reluctant to indulge in, is an art in itself. Volumes have been written about this process, and anyone looking for a change should read *Why and How to Prepare Effective Résumés*, by Juvenal L. Angel.[14] The book is geared for beginning management jobs but does discuss functional résumés, analytical résumés, and chronological résumés. It gives sample résumés for many jobs.

In reading books on this subject, it is wise to heed the advice of Constance Klages of Battalia, Lotz & Associates:

> Write your own résumé. You know yourself better than anyone else.
> Don't make me work to find out the facts I want to know—jobs you have held, your talents, your personal data necessary for filling the job, like education, vital statistics, and anything that would help or hinder you on the job.

On the other side of the picture, the person who spends half an hour criticizing a résumé seldom has a job to offer.

Again, there are many books on the subject of obtaining a job, from interviewing to final acceptance. Helpful books on this stage of the game are *The Making of a Manager* and *Personnel Interviewing*.[15] Both books are written for managers but with a reverse twist can give many hints to people looking for a change in jobs.

An examination of the current literature, much of it geared to women, can be a great asset. This is especially true for the younger executive who wants to move. It is a lucky management person who is able to move through a management program within a company where talent is observed, where openings are always there, and where the timing is perfect. Even all these favorable omens shouldn't keep anyone from analyzing his talents, preparing a good résumé, keeping watch for opportunities both in the company and outside, and having enough courage to jump when the time comes.

Women in the study know the values of such decision making. It's not a skill impossible to develop.

The Woman at Home

The educated woman who has been staying home can follow the same procedures as the woman at work. She has some strikes against her and some real strong points on her side.

First of all when she goes back to work, she usually has a few years to her credit, which makes her a more stable employee. She usually knows what she wants, is no goof-off, and works hard. She has a definite purpose for working.

The biggest strike against her (most of which she can correct) is her somewhat rusty work habits. This is especially true of those jobs that need constant updating. For example, in personnel there is much new in the behavioral sciences. A course at one of the local colleges or a perusal of the books in this area will help bring her up to date very quickly.

Sometimes the husband can be the chief stumbling block, but again some careful talks and even counseling at this particular time can be helpful.

Women who have stayed home often underestimate their talents. There is no reason under the sun that all of them have to reenter the workforce as typists, secretaries, or salesclerks. It is high time that women who are eager to get back into the workforce examine their talents and make good use of them.

So much has been said by the feminists about the horrors of suburbia and housework that most women have begun to at least analyze where they stand.

Don't miss what both Germaine Greer and Betty Friedan say about it, but on the other hand read Ray Killian's book *The Working Woman* [16] and the other encouraging articles. For example, an article in *McCall's* gives a realistic approach to the whole picture. Keep in mind, as the article concludes, "the employer is having a hard time finding enough dedicated, enthusiastic personnel with growth potential. Though he may not know it yet, you can be the answer." [17]

13
OTHER VIEWPOINTS

History is replete with accounts of individual women who have cursed mankind or helped him through all his trials and tribulations. It would take many pages to discuss the novels and the poems written to and about women. Even Saki takes his crack at women: "Women and elephants never forget an injury."

A lesser-known author, Robert Cates Holliday, in his "Walking-Stick Papers" says, "They [women] are too personal for the high enjoyment of going on a journey. They must be forever thinking about you or themselves; with them everything in the world is somewhere tangled up in these matters; and when you are with them (you cannot help it, or if you could they would not allow it), you must be forever thinking about them or yourself. Nothing on either side can be seen detached. They cannot rise to that philosophical plane of mind which is the very marrow of going on a journey. One reason for this is that they can never escape from the idea of society. You are in their society and they are in yours."

These quotes are given because there are many men and women who still hang onto the same old ideas. Who has written all this nonsense and gobbledygook about women, from time immemorial? The male of the species. Can men really tell you about women and what they are really like? On the other hand, is the women's literature discussed in this book the true voice of women today? Or are there other challenges on a much broader base than those that either the men or the women discuss?

Little has been written about management women. Who takes up the cudgels for them? There are none that we know of in literature, but in real life there are some.

Times are changing and intelligent, articulate men and women are proving that they are willing to help responsible women take a new look at their working lives.

A President's Views

An interview with the president of a large actuarial consulting firm in New York City produced some broad-gauge thinking worth consideration by women as well as men. Notice how different his thinking is from that of some of the management people you know. He takes the modern approach, based on a very thoughtful look at the situation. The next few pages summarize his remarks.

In the working world greater emphasis must be put on the tasks to be done. Too often in describing a woman who is doing a good job the emphasis is on her sweet, ladylike qualities. It is conceded that she is doing a good job, but then the extra tagalong is added, "And she is so ladylike." Do you ever hear these personal, sugarcoated remarks made about a man doing a good job? Women and men assigning them to good jobs are apologetic about women being there at all. Instead of saying that the job takes a tough-minded, smart, fast-moving, versatile person to do it, we get smothered in an apologetic, sociological approach.

Looking critically at the workload of today there is a different picture from even last year and measuring back 20 years provides a different work scene altogether. Up until World War II women usually were the supplemental wage earners. No so today. Americans want a different, more affluent life style and a woman works to help maintain that family style.

The format of the American workforce has changed from a predominance of blue collar to a predominance of white collar jobs. Women can do these jobs as well as, or in some cases better than men. This means that they should no longer be considered for only the menial, low-salaried, routine jobs. Technological skills, scientific skills, and great humanitarian skills are needed now and in the future. Women are needed to do these tasks and there is absolutely no evidence that they can't do them as well as men. Mind work is now the order of the day. Physical labor is almost a thing of the past and women can no longer afford to avoid challenging jobs. The task is the important thing and let's forget and knock down all the barriers that are keeping and have kept women from these tasks for so long.

Does this mean forget the pleas of the women's movement? It does not, but it means that the emphasis must be changed. A good, hard, solid look devoid of much of the high-powered, emotion-packed drive is now needed. Better education, more grants for women's medical colleges, more research, and more women assigned to top jobs all help.

The next very important thought involves progress for America. If our country is to maintain its reputation as a leading nation, it cannot afford to bypass the talents of its women (or any other group). Women are needed here as they are needed in the rest of the countries of the world. Necessity makes it so.

In Israel, for example, young Jewish women fight along with the men warriors. This is a long way from the traditional Jewish idea of motherhood and home.

The Russians, who lost 20 million men in World War II, had to depend on woman power. The world has long heard of Russian women as street cleaners, but also witness the record number of women scientists and doctors.

The Chinese have moved from an agrarian society where women always worked to a new world where the same concept [that women should work] prevails. Mao knows the importance of using all available workers.

If the good things planned for the future—such as a more humanistic approach to the industrial scene, the 30-hour week, better environmental control, and an ecology-minded people—are to happen, then the talents of Americans must be utilized not next year or ten years hence, but now. There is an urgency that cannot be ignored and women must be included in the plans. We cannot afford to waste talents.

In summary, the two major points made by the president make good sense: (1) The *task* is the important item in today's world. (2) If America is to continue to be great, it must utilize the talents of all its people—including women.

A Vice President's Opinion

John D. Staley, vice president of Bullock's in Los Angeles, has somewhat the same message.

"As to the future—industry has always had a voracious appetite, since the onset of World War II, for executive talent. There is more and more demand for *talent*. The impetus is added by acceleration of technology, competition, consumer expectations, and so on, which render the future-shocked executive virtually useless. Demand for feminine exec *talent* will continue to burgeon. I underline *talent*, however, since there's clearly a culture gap, which has to be overcome. Studies clearly demonstrate that females in our culture are not induced to be competitive, decisive, and aggressive, but rather to be reticient, dependent, and to a large degree self-oriented.

"Thus the sweet dingaling who "supervises" today can't run on a fast track—she's never been groomed to it. (Neither can the male dingaling, either, but I'm talking about the big, broad spectrum—boys are trained to be jockstrapping competitors, or else they're regarded as sissies—the girl who is competitive is a tomboy or butch.)

"As more and more women see their cultural roles changing from chattel to *person*, as they're *allowed* to compete, more and more will come to top executive jobs. The ones who are successful in this industry (and there are a *lot*) are intelligent, competitive, outward-directed, results-oriented, and in this industry, as often as not, better than the males at what we need."

Another Executive Looks at Today's Picture

The men who view the whole woman situation realistically are growing in number. Irving Delloff, the author of several books, a college professor, and a thinking executive, took the time to put his thoughts in writing. Since the material he covers is so pertinent and even though it may seem that we are overemphasizing some points, Mr. Delloff's remarks appear verbatim to reemphasize the logical approach to helping women achieve their goals.

"Starting from the late sixties, our country has witnessed a dramatic improvement in the acceptance of women in industry. More and more companies have broadened the need and opportunity for women as policewomen, draftswomen, meat cutters, truck drivers, power crane operators, telephone lineswomen, engineers, steel workers, and so forth.

"Many companies found that women can do any job a man can do, limited only by physical strength. Aptitude tests show that women are just as quick to learn, can learn, and do learn as well as men, although they may require more training in the use of tools, simply because they have had no experience with them. As machinery and equipment become more mechanized and automated, women will be operating these machines, for automation and mechanization will not only reduce the amount of skill required but may also reduce the amount of physical exertion expended.

"Women are also gaining recognition in the professions. They have been involved in biology, chemistry, and physics research for years but are now being involved in electronics, aerospace, environmental sciences, and automotive engineering.

"This recognition has not come about by industry's voluntary actions. In the opinion of many involved it resulted from a combination of legislation and the widespread restiveness among women. Sparked by new federal guidelines, militant young women and their sympathizers carried their fight for what they called women's rights into every facet of our everyday lives. The fury that they have aroused has drawn attention to many problems, the most basic of which is that women be given the same opportunities for jobs as men—and at the same pay.

"Despite these advances and the surrounding publicity, most companies hire women only for low-paying, uninteresting jobs that offer no rewards and no opportunity for advancement. There are very few women, if any, in toolmaking. I have yet to see a woman set up and run a boring mill or a tape-controlled CIMX machine. These highly skilled jobs in the metal trades are not beyond the scope of women; they just don't have the training. Although the great majority of women probably prefer not to undertake the long periods of study and apprenticeship required, the opportunities must be made available so women can participate in apprenticeship programs which historically have been closed to them.

"There are other areas where women are not being given equal opportunities. But I would like to address myself only to the one in which I am involved. The stubborn fact still persists that the ranks of management remain in the domain of the white male. Business as a whole still seems unwilling or unprepared to accept women's demands for equality in management opportunities.

"Most organizations have a large number of women in clerical and low-skilled jobs. Some women in these organizations have been advanced to first-line supervision, but it is usually supervising others doing the same work or same type of work which the new supervisor did before she was promoted. As management jobs increase in responsibility, women become increasingly rare. A recent survey indicates that women make up 5 percent or less of the middle managers' jobs and 2 percent or less of the top management staff.

"In my own experience, I find very few women represented in the management development programs I conduct. In the past year I conducted 42 programs representing 23 different organizations. Of this number, 4 programs represented civil service management employees and 38 programs represented private industry. The programs were given for first-line and middle managers. Of a total of 934 people attending all the programs, only 70, or approximately 7½ percent were women. Of 839 participants in the 38 industry programs, only 39, or approximately 4.6 percent, were women.

"It was also of considerable interest to me that in my initial discussions with management's representatives (when we developed the course content and discussed who would be invited to participate) only three companies had a woman among the management representatives and in only one company was a woman a member of top management.

"These data do not include two programs which I conducted exclusively for women supervisors. But even here, of a total of 60 participants representing 6 companies, only 12 were first-line supervisors and only one was a middle manager. The rest were inspectors, lead ladies, trainees, and potential supervisors.

"Why one rarely sees women in management development programs can probably be explained by considering how the image of a promotable person is created. It is usually men whose day-to-day experience determines who is recommended for promotion and who is to be selected for attendance at a training program. If the proportion of women is low or nonexistent the image of a promotable person tends to be male, and as the process continues it becomes self-perpetuating.

"Attitudes and feelings die hard. We are all the products of our environment, and it is difficult to change a lifetime of training and living. Undoubtedly a man's attitudes and feelings affect his decisions. An executive's attitude toward women in management may reflect his attitude toward his mother or his wife or how he perceived his father's attitude to be. The extent to which a man needs to establish his own sex identity by assuming a dominant role over women may reflect the extent to which he will go to develop the reasons he will give for not promoting a woman to an executive position. The same may hold true for a man who feels henpecked under a manager who is a woman or feels threatened by a woman with higher academic achievements.

"There is evidence that some companies have recently begun to take steps to give women greater opportunities in obtaining management positions. Laws passed in recent years have helped, as have the pressures of the feminists, despite their detractors. But for most women this progress is largely an illusion. The same words and phrases are now used by women as were used by blacks several years ago. 'House female,' 'showcase woman,' and 'tokenism' are among the more familiar. Many women, bogged down in a dead-end job, feel that to most businessmen women in middle and upper management is still an idea whose time has not yet come.

"It may be well to point out that despite the millions of women members of organized labor, union leaders seem to share the business leaders' misgivings about the capabilities of women as executives, for union executives have relatively few women in their top ranks.

"Responding to a recent questionnaire, many top business executives, citing their own experiences with women as managers, as well as their own feelings toward man–woman relationships, replied that women are not as career-minded as men, that many women avoid or refuse promotions to a supervisory level, possibly to sidestep responsibility, that women are ill more [frequently] than male employees, that neither men nor women like to work for women supervisors, that women are too emotional for making hard decisions, that women take criticism personally, that women may quit at any time to get married or have a baby, that women work for pin money (they don't really need the job and will absent themselves to attend a class in flower arrangement), and that women do not have the aggressiveness, judgment, and decision-making ability required for management personnel.

"Not so! There is a relatively small sample in any one person's experience, and most people follow the very human tendency to generalize from very few instances. The fact remains that for every generalization, no matter how large the sample on which it is based, there is an exception which may very well prove the rule.

"A Public Health study shows that in 1971 there was very little difference in absenteeism, with 5.9 days a year for women compared to 5.2 for men. Responding to a questionnaire, the evaluation of women managers by both male and female executive respondents was over 75 percent favorable, with those reacting unfavorably to women as managers showing a traditional cultural bias. The U.S. Department of Labor finds that of the more than 31 million women in the labor force nearly half worked because of pressing economic need. They were either single, widowed, or divorced. Another 6 million were married and were working to supplement their husbands' low income.

"While it is true that women leave work for marriage and children, this absence is temporary and most return when their children are in school. With technology minimizing or eliminating the routine tasks connected with homemaking, that is no longer a full-time job. This fact coupled with more and better child-care centers will permit women to return to work sooner than was heretofore possible.

"We haven't really tried to find out whether women want responsibility on the job and want promotions, because relatively few women have been offered positions of responsibility. When given the opportunity women, like men, do meet their job responsibilities in addition to family and personal responsibilities. Emotional? What should one call the male executives who yell, rant, rave, and drink their business problems and failures away?

"Undoubtedly, woman's biological and social role as the person who bears and rears children presents some very practical problems to a businessman and, in addition, the basic concept of "woman's place" in our culture is going to be difficult to change, even in our rapidly changing society. But change we must. Here is where your ingenuity and management acumen can have full sway. Many women either through choice or as heads of families have worked out a satisfying life, to themselves and their families, by going back to work, even when their children are very young. Not all women are married. Most women have many years of productive work left after the youngest child is in school. Women as well as men want a balanced life—an interesting job, a home, and a family to love. Evaluate each woman as you would a man. What is her potential, her background, what does she expect to be doing with her life by the time she reaches 65? She asks only the same fair evaluation you would give a male management candidate.

"Perhaps it is time for a deep, searching reassessment and a true sharing of the management of our country. Men who are highly competent are not afraid of competition—male or female—and welcome innovation. These men, these business executives, must unfurl the banner and lead others in removing all barriers to equal opportunity. Only then will our country truly be making the maximum utilization of our human resources.

"An excellent opportunity is being given to us by the many young people who are entering the labor force. This new breed will not only want a chance for involvement but will not be impressed by a manager because of his title. Rather, they will judge individuals by the results they are able to achieve. Recognition of a person as a *person* will inevitably place greater emphasis on results and less on traditional relationships. Ability will determine acceptance and it will matter less whether men or women are at decision- and policy-making levels. The very sensitivity and perceptiveness of which women are accused may be just the attributes that will be necessary to cope with the predicted changes.

"Management must understand that basically everyone wants to be recognized for what he can do rather than for what he is. Women also want to be judged as individuals without first being categorized as females.

"A leader sets the tone—do it by destroying once and for all the image of 'a man's job' and 'a woman's job.'

"Open your apprenticeship program to all applicants and encourage the women to participate.

"Encourage women to take management-oriented courses in college and the many management development courses offered by universities and management associations.

"Set equitable performance standards, appraise results fairly, and provide unbiased, equivalent promotional reviews.

"Above all, help to change the business community's perception of women and careers by advancing women to positions of responsibility —a good example is often the best sermon."

A "Male Chauvinist's" View

Dr. Richard L. Whitehead, vice president, personnel and company relations of Berkshire Life, Pittsfield, Massachusetts, a highly acclaimed psychologist, has an extraordinarily fine appreciation for women and their many talents. Here's what he has to say.

"The problems of women in business can be summed up in two words: *men, women.*

"Being a true male chauvinist, let me start out by talking about men and their role in what has become today's hot subject.

"For many years, the male has held sway in the office. At home very few of us really are in a position of control (although the smart wife has always made it appear otherwise), and so the office or the plant has been the place where male superiority has prevailed.

"It was really much simpler all the way around in the days of the caveman. The male hunted, brought home the food, traded it for certain desired things, and presumably everyone was reasonably happy.

"Eventually women began to infiltrate the workforce and, consciously or unconsciously, men began to resist this intrusion. After all, was not woman uneducated, illiterate, and didn't she really belong at home with the children or in the factory? And so, for many years woman's role was truly a menial one—laboring in the plant, on the production line, while the office jobs were held by men.

"Slowly women moved into this reserved area and there were a few female clerks and even a lady secretary here and there. Nothing important, of course—really couldn't trust their judgment.

"Finally, the advent of the typewriter, an expanding economy, plus the shortage of men brought on by several wars, allowed women to take over the job of secretary. If any aspect of business has ever been entrenched in the mind of the public in a stereotyped fashion, it is the job of the secretary. She is either a man-eating pants chaser just waiting for the boss's wife to slip, or stays slim from being chased around her desk by every male from the boss to the mail boy, or is a dumb broad who holds her job through the grace of her magnanimous employer. These myths have been perpetuated by everyone concerned, from the man who talks of his office conquests, to the typewriter manufacturer who boasts of his new typewriter which will keep secretaries from making mistakes, to the woman who says, 'Oh, I'm only the secretary.'

"Most of the men in management positions today have grown up and received the majority of their business experience under the conditions just described. Is it any wonder, then, that they have trouble accepting the idea that there should also be a gold key to the women's restroom?

"It is not too difficult for man to accept the equal pay for equal work concept. It is the idea that woman can function in all types of positions, particularly management positions, that really causes him to wince and begin to talk of woman's emotionalism, her fluctuating appearance on the work scene, and her interest in things besides the good old Widget Manufacturing Company.

"The truth of the matter is that some of his fears are well founded. They happen to be equally well founded with respect to men, a point he carefully chooses to ignore, or, if the thought crosses his mind, he dismisses it at once. Men are certainly inclined to switch jobs and companies more frequently today, and at all ages we see a disinclination to put the company first and foremost on a list of personal priorities. These tendencies make him just as much an employment risk as his female counterpart.

"One of the real benefits, as a matter of fact perhaps the major benefit, of the Women's Lib movement is that it is making us look at women as individuals and not simply as a huge segment of the population, all of whom have the same characteristics, tendencies, and deficiencies.

"We are more aware of the tremendous waste of talent and ability which has been taking place in business as well as in the academic world, the government, and many other areas. In order to take advantage of this talent, we may have to cast aside many of the traditional approaches and to make it possible to employ more part-time women— not just in clerical or production work, but as managers, professionals, and technicians. We may have to develop leave of absence policies which actually encourage a prospective mother to come back to her job, and then develop ways to keep that job open for several months. Most of all, we must find ways to convince supervisors, managers, department heads, and senior management that women are capable of making bigger contributions and that the failure to both allow and stimulate these contributions is, in the long run, bad for society generally and for business in particular.

"In my opinion this is more likely to be done a step at a time, rather than through the controversial and illogical approach that the government has chosen through EEOC. The job of EEOC is really to keep us honest, to see that progress is being made and that we do continue to move forward. The individual who must be persuaded is, after all, male, and he is going to fight against what he considers to be an unrealistic and un-understandable approach.

"This brings us to the second word, *women*. If men and their beliefs are the most difficult things to change, women are their own worst enemies in the attempt.

"Anyone reading the paper or hearing the news would have to conclude that the great majority of women are downtrodden, tired of being at home, and just dying to be successful in a career. Not only is this a false picture, but it immediately puts the male on the defensive and makes him much more difficult to work with. Unfortunately the voices which create this impression are the most strident and drown out, with the help of the news media, the voices which present a more balanced picture.

"In spite of scientific advancements, it still takes approximately nine months to create a new human being and EEOC notwithstanding, it will still take time for women, no matter how competent, to acquire the skills necessary to be part of the management of a company. One woman manager, when asked what women coming into the business world should expect, replied, 'They should expect to work—it's the only way to make it.'

"I recently talked with a group of career women managers in our company and they were unanimous in their feeling that women should not be given preferential treatment, but rather should be given the same consideration and treatment as their male counterparts. They did acknowledge that women had some problems peculiar to women but felt that the responsibility of the company was to provide options and opportunities and that basically the individual woman had to come to grips with and provide the solution to the problems.

"In order for this equality of treatment to be possible, the individual woman has some decisions to make. She must decide if a career and career advancement are really important to her. Is she willing to put in extra time and effort to succeed? (Not because she is a woman, but because these are necessary ingredients in success.) Is she willing to put in extra time and effort because she is a woman and because, realistically, she is going to have to convince some male, somewhere, that she is capable of doing a particular job? Does she want responsibility and the problems that accompany it? Does she really feel that she is capable of reaching out and doing more? Does her self-image allow her to take on the tougher, more demanding types of work? It is important to bear in mind that self-renewal and development can be found in many ways— not just in one's job.

"Interestingly, many of the above questions must also be answered by the man who is evaluating his career progress and his future. This tends to lend credence to the theory that there is no difference in the process which a man or woman should and must follow in determining the course of his or her career. The woman's handicap is that she has few other women with whom she can share experiences and concerns, and from whom she can receive encouragement, and most men are not capable of this type of communication.

"How, then, do we help provide the opportunities that are desired? The traditional admonition when one wants to install a new program or concept in a company is that you must have backing from the top. This is true, but it is also an idea that is overrated. The number of programs backed by the president and thwarted by middle management is impressive indeed. To be truly successful, a program or concept has to be sold to all levels of management, and I don't mean just explained to them. Especially in this sensitive area, the department managers must be convinced that it will be to their advantage, to the department's advantage, and ultimately to the company's advantage for them to take a positive, active leadership role in helping qualified women to grow and succeed. This educational process is a time-consuming, frustrating experience in most instances, but it can be done and some companies are doing it.

"The life insurance industry has a workforce which is predominantly women and it has been one of the leaders in moving women into supervisory and then management positions. It has also been quick to recognize women's abilities in the technical and professional fields. Like every other industry, it is having difficulty, for reasons already discussed, in moving women into top-level positions. But the important thing is that such moves are being made, and in many companies where the actual move hasn't been made, the necessary preparation for such changes is under way.

"In my own company, while we do not as yet have women at all levels of management responsibility, there are very few types of work that women are not performing. The jobs filled range from supervisor to systems analyst, to investment analyst, to advertising manager, and so on and so on. Our company policy contains a statement: 'We will hire and promote based entirely on individual qualifications,' and we believe that we are doing exactly that.

"The women who want additional responsibility and growth are demonstrating that they can carry their end of the pole, and this is still the most convincing argument in favor of even more responsibility and growth for them. Incidentally, we also have many fine women and men who do not necessarily want additional responsibility and it is important to recognize that they also play a vital role in the operation of our company.

"And so the battle for equality will undoubtedly be fought vigorously. And it should be, for there are many things that are good and right about such equality. I just hope that victory is slow in coming to those who advocate total equality. I really do enjoy a nice pair of girl's legs in shorts or a skirt, . . . and I like to see a man seat a woman at the table, and nothing makes me more uncomfortable than the woman who flaunts her equality by using four-letter words and telling jokes that most of her male companions wouldn't.

"But then, I really believe that a woman's place is in the kitchen."

PepsiCo Executive

Many glowing words have been written about Joan Crawford's charm and acting talent, but this book is about working women and what makes them tick.

"What is she really like?" and "Does she really work?" were two questions asked by many people. I was impressed by the drive with which she does her job at PepsiCo. In 1972 she made more than a hundred appearances and spoke at fifty conferences. This means that she does not sit home and rest on her laurels but is out there working hard.

Miss Crawford brings a warmth to her job that few people have. She speaks of her experience in Birmingham, Alabama, where 80,000 people turned out in a driving rain to attend the opening of a new PepsiCo plant. She tells of spotting young children and babies caught up in the crowd. She asked that the youngsters be passed up to her and in between signing autographs and talking, she was able to maintain enough space behind her so that the youngsters wouldn't be crushed by the crowd.

This one episode emphasizes one of the important facets of her job. It helps erase the impersonal image, indicates that a company does care, and places the firm on a one-to-one basis with its customers.

When she talks of her work when she was on the board of directors of Pepsi-Cola, she again speaks of finding out what the job was all about and of working hard to succeed. After her husband's death, she came to the board knowing about Pepsi-Cola and its worldwide markets and says she was treated with respect and with a great deal of courtesy.

Miss Crawford's insistence on retaining her feminine charm while still doing a solid management job is worth emulating. She dresses beautifully, but more than that she has the other attributes of womanhood. She is a fine hostess and makes one feel at ease immediately. She has the tact and charm that many of the successful women in this book have developed. Men have these qualities too, but they often don't come across so clearly.

What does she think of more outspoken women's liberationists? She says they seem to be ashamed of being women and must be really unhappy people. She, like many of the women in the book, started with few advantages. Even with the breaks it was not easy to reach her current position. Her impatience with poor performance and her admiration for achievers underline her attitude toward women who talk a lot but don't really contribute anything.

She, too, worries about the "lost" young people and places much of the blame on the lack of parental guidance. She has plenty of admiration for the young people who have found their way and is all for the young women who are moving into management jobs with considerable ease.

Miss Crawford practices what she preaches. With her at the interview was young Mary-Jane Raphael, her manager of women's activities. The working relationship of these two women was most interesting to watch. Trust in a younger woman's judgment, appreciation of her talents, and quickness to sense her responses were only a few of the points observed. Important in a management job? Absolutely, say all the books and knowledgeable management people.

Miss Crawford has managed her home life well, too. The rigorous schedule of an actress did not cause her to neglect her children. Like many of the other women in the study she, too, juggled her schedule to allow for time with her children. Written into her contract at the studios was a 5:00 P.M. quitting time so she could have dinner with her children. It was important to her, and her children benefited, too.

Another characteristic Miss Crawford has is the discipline required by a management job. She lives with time schedules and with many demands, yet she made the time to schedule this interview. Her time is precious, and one feels that she uses it to the last second.

Another President's View

An interview with John Sheridan, president of Sheridan Associates, Chicago, reveals still more insight into how women are fitting into the work situation of today. As a consultant to management on labor relations, Mr. Sheridan travels a great deal and sees many situations. Here is how the picture looks to him.

"It seems to me that the women's liberation movement should be considered on two different levels—one on the outside and one in the work situation. The first seems to me a somewhat desperate movement dealing primarily with social issues. I am not so sure that the tactics being used are helping or harming the cause for women. The second movement toward a better work situation, toward equalization of salaries, and toward the utilization of talents is one that I am behind one hundred percent.

"There are many problems involved. I am aware of the prejudice that must be overcome. I am especially concerned with the idea of the 'token' woman executive. Her boss (usually a male) will usually do plenty of bragging that he is doing well by the women in his firm. He will say, 'Look at Ms. Green. She has been promoted from secretary to being public relations director.' On the other hand, Ms. Green is not happy with the situation either. She is asked to make speeches, to appear on panels, and to be the showcase woman on many occasions. She ends up resenting her promotion. If a promotion is made, it should be done honestly without all the extra fanfare that now often accompanies such an occasion."

Mr. Sheridan recently toured Russia, where he observed the work situation from many different angles. Contrary to the opinion held by many Americans about the large proportion of women doctors in Russia compared with the United States, Mr. Sheridan discovered:

"The majority of women doctors in the Soviet are really what we would consider head nurses or head technicians. The specialists and top doctors are still primarily men. In spite of all the publicity, women are still usually playing a supportive role.

"It is still surprising to see an all-woman crew in a steamroller gang on the streets. This means from the forewoman down to the women who are doing the hard physical labor.

"Another interesting sidelight—the second woman in our party was more than slightly pregnant. On the streets of Moscow she was treated very coolly. The women in the street gangs did their fair share of showing their disapproval.

"It seems that working women really are treated equally on the distribution of hard labor until they become pregnant. Then they become ladies of leisure and receive full pay while on maternity leave. In other words, the Russians have already granted this privilege, which the Equal Employment Opportunity [Commission] has included in its sex guidelines for American industry.

Mr. Sheridan had a few more comments to make about women in the labor movement here in the United States. He said that once a woman is sold on the issues, it is much harder to jar her loose from her position than it is a man.

The interview ended with this conclusion about women in management jobs: "We just can't afford to waste their talent, and it's high time that we begin to utilize it if we haven't already done so."

A Congresswoman's View

There are still comparatively few congresswomen in Washington. Those who are there do an outstanding job. Patsy T. Mink (D-Hawaii) is much concerned about the status of women. She concedes that progress has been made over the past ten years, but she says it has been very slow: "We must be constantly concerned with keeping the necessity of using women's talents before the policy-making level individuals whether they are in education, business, or government. Our future depends on doing this."

She is also very much concerned with the movement among educators and management executives. "It is easy to get any kind of job, but our concern is with upper-level jobs."

Congresswoman Mink says we can't divorce our social concern for women from the concern over management and educational opportunities. She states that in any movement there are bound to be wide differences of opinion on how to go about making progress. She feels that the social concerns and those for management progress complement each other.

Her concern for education goes back to the earliest school days, when children begin to learn their traditional roles. She wants even little boys and girls to get the idea that they are *people* and that their talents should be considered *equally*. For example, she is concerned with the depiction of physicians or other professional people as always being male. She was upset by a recent career film that showed women, ten times, behind a typewriter while males played the roles of doctors, lawyers, engineers, and so on. "It is time to stop this kind of propaganda. People shouldn't just be put into niches."

She predicts, too, that the constitutional amendment giving women equal rights will be ratified by enough states in 1973.

Congresswoman Mink does a lot of spadework in this area, and one wishes there were many more women in Congress. Perhaps the time will come soon.

A Former Senator's View

Here's what Margaret Chase Smith, formerly senior senator from Maine, says about women and their world.

"Just as the pioneering women made it much easier for women of our generation, the women in responsible positions of today will make life easier for the women who are coming behind us. Our thoughts and actions should be directed toward giving these women some sense of direction.

"As for the women's liberation movement, I believe everyone should have a right to her own opinions but do what she wants to do as long as it's kept clean. I again would like to emphasize the necessity for better direction for younger people.

"I have great faith in the younger generation and do not believe that there really needs to be a generation gap. I see many groups of young people both here in Washington and at home in Maine. I enjoy talking with them and they seem to enjoy visiting with me. We sometimes hit on subjects on which we may not agree, such as the seniority system here in Congress. I tell them that if they come up with a more workable way on this question and on others, tell me what it is and we'll try it out.

"I believe that there are fewer of the hardcore dissatisfied young people than there were even a few years ago.

When asked about the groups at the 1972 Republican convention, she said:

"In order to see the real American youths, you should have stood, as I did, for a half hour in the gallery autographing and observing. The young people were polite, bright, and exciting. There were some good ones outside the hall, too. I believe that the diminishing hardcore is beyond influencing or saving but they represent a minority of the young people of today's American youth.

"One of the honors I most cherish is the one making me an honorary member of the young people's group in the Republican party. Asked to be the keynote speaker at their convention, I was proud to be made one of them.

"I think the young people are talented and know much more than most of us did at a corresponding age. This, of course, includes bright young women as well as young men.

"I have great faith in the talents of people, and women, being people, should have opportunities on the basis of their qualifications and desires."

14

WHAT CAN WOMEN EXECUTIVES SAY TO THOSE ON THE WAY UP?

The majority of people, at least in the 1970s, have had to work until close to middle age before they attained success. Most older executives would honestly like to pass along their know-how to the younger people on the way up. There are many factors involved. Times and situations change and sometimes the old answers and the old ways are not enough to meet the complicated problems of today. The prospect of older women executives telling younger people how they did it when they were young or how they handled certain situations goes over like a lead balloon with the younger employee. Helping her with her problems tactfully is another matter. Most young people are eager to learn—the trick is to find the method of developing a two-way communication system that works.

Management Women and Their Children

Having children of your own may help, but even then bridging the generation gap is never easy. Many of the women included in the study have children of their own. Do they have the same problems other parents have with their young and teen-age children? Does this help them understand the problems of young executives better? Their comments should help us understand the women executives in the study. Here is what they say about their own children.

I think my children are proud of what I do and I hope that they make me more understanding of other young people.

My children often feel cheated. They would like to have had me home.

My daughter will be better educated—she goes to a better school than we otherwise could have afforded.

Some of the women feel that they have missed some of the real joys of motherhood by being away while their children were growing up. Others say they're really no good at keeping house, and staying home all the time would drive them up a tree.

Since this is not a psychological study in the interrelationships of mothers and children, we approached the subject another way and asked whether the respondent would want to have her daughter follow in her footsteps—go to the same college and do the same type of work.

Most, knowing the younger generation's drive for doing his or her own thing and because they probably have more broadminded views based on their experience in the working world, would leave the choice up to their daughters. One woman says, "I would send any child of mine to the school which provided the best courses that he or she wanted to choose."

Another states, "As a leader in extracurricular activities in a coed school, I made the transition to a male business environment easier than from a woman's college. I definitely want my daughter to attend a coed college and would encourage either a technical degree with an MBA or else a professional area."

As the youngest member in the survey said, "I would hope my daughter would want some professional training. If so, I would encourage her to attend a school away from her hometown, because I believe living away from home increases awareness and maturity."

Cutting the apron strings seems easier for the younger generation

—they are eager to get on their own. Their working mothers are probably somewhat more understanding than those who do not work, but to say they have really bridged the generation gap with their own daughters is problematical. They have high hopes for their children and understand their high ambitions. The mothers hope that they will work up to their capacities, but do not try to force them into the same colleges or to follow in their own footsteps.

Their plans for their daughters contrast somewhat with the almost happenstance planning of their own careers. When asked if she would plan her own career over again, one of them replied, "Plan it? Never! It is more fun *not planning*. Remember Burns—'The best-laid schemes o' mice and men [and women] gang aft a-gley.' And so it is when you try to plan someone else's life—you can dream all you want to about how great your children are, but they will make or break themselves." Trying to understand is about all adults—even management women—can do in trying to narrow the generation gap.

Advice to the Young

Here is good advice some of the management women offer to the younger generation.

(1) Get a degree in your field. (2) Become active in a few organizations. Preferably, devote your time achieving recognition in one organization in your field. Get an office. (3) Maintain your contacts and friendships even if it only means a card at Christmastime. (4) Never think (even if it may be true) that you are being held back because you're a woman. A lot of people use this as an excuse. (5) As my mother used to say, "Shoot for the moon and you'll hit a star."

Enjoy yourself. Don't compromise. Don't take yourself or "them" too seriously, but be serious about work and what it means.

Work like hell and don't give up. Don't settle for the nonexecutive (clerical) type of job. Don't learn to type. Learn as much as you can about everything and from everyone you work for and with.

Same advice I'd give to men—get trained. Don't expect to arrive too fast. Don't interpret everything on the basis of "How does it affect me?" Think big.

First, find out what you are fitted for by heredity and training. If there is a natural bent for science, mathematics, art, music, and so forth, it should be cultivated. Second, do what you like to do. Very important. Third, don't be afraid to really work.

Study, study, study—to be intelligent and to learn to think! Learn to communicate effectively both in speaking and in writing.

Keep fit physically, dress attractively, and groom immaculately. Enjoy life—be dynamic and enthusiastic.

Concentrate on good communications, learn to accept all people as people, not as men and women. Make friends with some of the men and establish a good rapport as colleagues so they can get to know you as a person.

Play hard and fair by the acknowledged rules of the business world.

Get the credentials for the job you want. Know what you want. Play it honest regardless of temptation—shortcuts do not pay in the long run. Do the job as an individual. Pay attention to your appearance. It helps anyone.

First you have to want to and want to very much. Set a goal. How much money you want to make is a good way of doing this. In x length of time I am going to be making x thousand a year.

Learn the job in depth and become totally competent in it. Work hard—never use sex, as such, but stay feminine and don't try to be one of "the boys." Be professional and dignified in the finest sense of the words.

These women do look for more specific help from the schools and hope that courses are more related to the future activities of their daughters. Many of the older respondents, even though praising their own colleges, found that they started toward the bottom of the management ladder because they had no special skills that might have been learned on the college campus.

They have had great pleasure from their children and have watched their education carefully. It is interesting that a recent survey showed that the working mothers in this study have some of the same characteristics as working mothers in the Soviet Union. "The more educated women were found to derive greater satisfaction and self-assurance from rearing their children and tried to make time for that purpose." [1]

Opinions About Younger Women Executives

What do successful women say about the younger crop of women executives?

I think it is fantastic that women are finally realizing that they have a right to be successful if they choose. However, the creation of successful women by guilty men or by those who wish to be "into" the women's liberation movement could definitely be detrimental.

They have greater expectations but this is partially due to women's lib. There have always been successful women but they had a low profile. For the foreseeable future, women will have more difficulty getting to the executive suite than an equally qualified man.

I think they are wonderful—and am thankful that they appear ready and willing to utilize the opportunities that have opened up for them over the past few years as a result of the various anti-sex-discrimination measures now on the statute books.

I think they are bright, aggressive, and have ability. Today's woman has her mind in business more than on homemaking, but not to the detriment of either.

The women who have had training and background make excellent executives; some who are being promoted to fill a void because they are women are not successful executives.

I am hopeful that more and more young women will enter the executive ranks of business. Youth is fearless.

I think that they are becoming more able to be feminine as well as productive and efficient.

Better than the previous crops. The drive for recognition of women has helped this.

Extremely enthusiastic and excited—the world is their oyster if they aspire and commit to top-level positions. They know themselves better—and are more accepted by their colleagues.

Their "consciousness" seems only half-raised. They often mistake aggressiveness, hardness, toughness, and promiscuity for liberation.

They may push too hard too fast. However, it's worth a try. Many are very bright.

By and large—great! More self-assured and eager to show what they can do.

I envy them—so bright, well-educated and with so much more opportunity for the more creative and challenging jobs.

Lacking in many qualities; inability to become company oriented. I feel loyalty is missing.

Great affirmative is that they are ready and eager to assume executive roles. Biggest danger is that they may be overeducated and underexperienced.

Good, but they aren't yet geared to thinking of themselves as "in for the long pull" or achieving the top.

Better equipped than I was to work toward executive row.

Will probably have a better chance of succeeding and have fewer hangups and inhibitions than their trailblazing predecessors.

For the most part enthusiastic and highly motivated.

In the legal profession I think they are good and getting better all the time, particularly since so many more are entering law school these days.

Afraid I've not met too many. I've met a few, though, who are quietly aware of their own worth—as individuals and as workers—and who do not consider it necessary to demand attention. They're mobile, too, and that helps. They don't consider it necessary to tie themselves too closely to a job, location, or particular male executive. They create a mood or attitude which I consider effective. On the negative side, I've found the lack of humor just awful.

Many women do not get serious about their jobs until they work long enough to want to continue to be in the work world, by choice.

I don't know enough of them, but I'm glad there are enough to be considered a crop.

I see real promise in many younger women. They are bright, well-trained and don't have a lot of the old stereotypes of "woman's role." Some are too prone to see sex discrimination where it really doesn't exist.

They have promising futures. If all prejudices and illegalities are wiped out, then job strengths and personal attitudes will be the only measures of success.

They seem more belligerent than my generation—ready to fight overtly.

If this relates to women in their mid-twenties I am singularly unimpressed with them. They are, I find, less compassionate, less risk-oriented, and overly preoccupied with themselves. It has been my experience that while they view themselves as executives or juniors, they behave like clock watchers and nit-pick, for example, about their benefits. A competent executive is free of this level of thinking and has moved to thinking beyond herself to others, and a contribution she can make.

I think if they stick to their guns and temper their militancy with some rationality, they should go places. More power to them. I also hope they can come up with an answer to dual responsibility.

Eileen Ahern pulls it all together with this statement, "I think they are well qualified and that they are going to have more opportunity to apply their ability and training than women in the past."

A review of the above statements reveals that most women executives are not catty or envious of their younger counterparts. As a rule they are impressed with the skills, talents, enthusiasm, and willingness to tackle anything. They are somewhat appalled by their lack of concern about the company, about their introspectiveness, and their lack of compassion. They admire the ability to move up and to move around—the flexibility that allows them to travel and to change jobs. On the whole, the younger woman ranks high in the opinion of the "trailblazing" women of the older generation.

In other words, most women now in management are making a real effort to understand, and young women shouldn't hesitate to work for them. They may understand the young woman better than a male could and will really try to help, especially if there is some talent and a willingness to use it. This is not saying that there aren't some bitches who are rough to work for, but if the young female executive is good in her field plus has a general compassion, she will have a much better chance than working for a male boss, especially if he is somewhat mediocre in his own talents.

The Pluses and the Minuses of the Young

From the woman executive's point of view, here are the pluses and minuses of the younger crop of junior women executives:

The pluses—

1. Smart.
2. Good-looking.
3. Well groomed.
4. Knows her talents.
5. Has been college-trained for specific management jobs.
6. Has read more broadly than the older executive had done when she first entered the workforce.
7. Knows what she wants in the management field—won't accept really mediocre jobs.
8. Is willing to learn and to accept constructive criticism.
9. Is able to move where the action is.
10. Is not tied to a specific job.
11. Tied to a skill, not a company.

12. Is used to freedom to express herself in a classroom. Does the same in the management meeting.
13. Is not a "yes" woman.

The minuses—

1. Too eager to get ahead. Minus the compassion of her older counterparts.
2. Can't make up her mind to be an executive—still clings to clock watching and useless chitchat.
3. Too mobile—will not get really interested in company per se.
4. Too conscious of her sex. Uses it more often than she should.
5. More interested in romance than the job at hand.
6. Demands rights to promotions without a track record to prove she can handle the situation.
7. Too sure her way is the only way to get a job done. Often more inflexible than older workers, who know that there may be many approaches to solving problems.
8. Unwilling to share detail work, especially if she thinks she is being assigned "women's" traditional work.
9. Likes to show off her brightness.

When the pluses are matched against the minuses the young female on the move has a lot going for her, say the older women.

Young Women Start Higher Today

Do young women have a chance to start higher up the management ladder? The answer is definitely yes. There are still a good number of male executives who are reluctant to hire smart young women in preference to less smart young men because these executives are sure the young women will get married and leave in a few years. The number of such diehards is getting smaller, as any recruiter on today's college campuses will agree. With the extra push on from legislators and from the women's liberation movement, companies are eager to get young capable women to fill executive trainee spots or to hire them according to their special skills. A top flight mathematical graduate, for example, skips the steps so many of her predecessors followed. The young chemist, the young psychologist, the young doctor, the young designer all have a chance to get to the top faster. Unfortunately, because some companies are attempting tokenism, just as happened in the hiring of some other minorities, there will be some women hired for jobs for which they are not really suited.

Studies Refute Common Beliefs

What about the manager's reluctance to hire the young, smart female college graduate? Is he more apt to lose the promising young female MBA before he loses the male from the same class?

Not so, says an article in *Harvard Business Review*.[2] The figures are based on 5,022 MBA graduates from 1965–1968. The overall rate of job changes, although the study shows it is not advancing, shows an appalling number of graduates lost from the first job at the end of the first year.

What about the women? More than 80 percent, a little higher than her male counterpart, entered business upon graduation. This indicates that in their first venture they were willing to enter corporate life. Nearly half of them, as compared with 20 percent among males, waited five years before marriage. This, as the study says, seems to dispose of the commonly held notion of women in business as husband hunters. The turnover rate was the same as for men, not higher as many management men would have believed. The survey goes on to point out that, coupled with recent census data predicting a shortage of top and middle managers by 1980, this finding reinforces the contention that women MBA's represent a largely untapped source of responsible, committed workers.

The article suggested that management use the same techniques for holding onto its young women executives as it uses to keep male managers. In other words, if you apply some of the "cures" you use to keep young male graduates—like offering better pay, listening to some of their ideas, giving them more responsibility, using realistic performance appraisals, and practicing two-way communication, you will be able to keep more of your much needed talent—both men and women. Incidentally, do you ask your men MBA candidates if they can cope with marriage and a career? It would be interesting to conduct a survey to see how many men's careers are fouled up by their wives. In evaluating the results of my survey, I found that the women whose husbands take their wives' careers in stride consider this one of the major factors in their successful climb to the top.

It is surprising, today, to see where you find surveys, studies, articles, diatribes, and most diabolic pieces about women. In *Scientific American*, which devotes much of its space to articles like "RNA-Directed DNA Synthesis" or "Geothermal Power" or the most esoteric scientific information, you'll find an article, "How Ideology Shapes Women's Lives." [3] The whole story is interesting, but a few excerpts are especially pertinent to this study. The report is based on a detailed questionnaire sent to the wives of graduate students. A sample of 1,012 wives who had attended college was selected for analysis.

The daughters of working mothers didn't seem to be marked by overeagerness to follow in their mothers' footsteps—many of them were happy to vicariously enjoy their husbands' achievements rather than make their own way in business.

The well-educated achievers, however, were eager to get their doctorates and to move up the ladder. Did it make any difference if they were first, third, or fifth children? Did they get all their encouragement only from their fathers? No, says the study. It does say that, despite some other studies to the contrary, the mother who achieves is as well admired as the father who achieves.

Mothers who were dissatisfied with the drudgery of housework were more apt to instill in their daughters a yen for a more fruitful life.

One distressing feature is the conclusion reached in this survey that the daughter of a mother who holds "contemporary" views is very lonely. Perhaps this is more than a hint to working mothers to pay as much attention as possible to the adolescent daughter, without trying to relive her own youth or trying to be forever young. Children really expect parents to behave like mature adults.

How much does this mean to young people? Should young women be upset because they are female instead of male? The successful women in this study contradict the studies that say that you can't be successful unless you are an only child or that your dominant father influenced you more than anyone else. Choose your statistics and you can probably prove anything.

Should you be upset about your rank in the family or where you were born? For example, if you are the second child of a family of eight, do you stand less of a chance than if you are an only child? If your parents were poor, are you doomed to failure? If you were brought up on the sidewalks of New York, do you have a better chance than if you went to a school in the Midwest? From this study it seems to make little difference.

Secretarial and Clerical Staff as an Executive Pool

Another management worry is the unrest among smart young secretaries and clerical workers. Almost all of them are women. Many have heard the pleas and promises of the women's liberation movement and are bugging their bosses for promotion. Men are conscious, too, that they should be doing something about promoting women and recognizing that they can do more than clerical and secretarial work. They are looking at this group as a potential source for executives.

Here is some fairly rough advice to the clericals, the secretaries, and the management men. Do you promote your young men from those ranks unless they have special skills, attributes, educational background, or know-how? Should you set up training courses to help some of these women up the ladder—especially in light of today's legislative pressure?

It may help to take an inventory to see what you have. If some of your women employees, particularly the young ones, are grossly underpaid and assigned work below their capabilities, then it is high time you did promote them. On the other side of the coin, a great deal of the effort to move up the ladder must depend on the individual's being willing to take the after-hour classes, the gruelling hours, and so on that it takes to become an executive. It is time that management gets this story across to young women who are loudly crying for advancement.

In a fast survey of graduate after-hour classes at New York universities, it was found that less than 5 percent of the students were women. Men are willing to spend this extra time to get what it takes to move ahead. Women, if they want these jobs, must be willing to sacrifice time and effort to obtain them.

It is hoped that if these women do make the extra effort they will find a more receptive management to give them a sincere crack at the next-level job.

Breaking out of the secretarial trap is rough, especially if you are a good secretary, but it can be done, as some of the women in this study have proved. If possible, a young woman is better off if she can get her training and education when young and find the job for which she is best trained. No longer is the usual road to management through secretary's row (if it ever was in the first place). Not that being *able* to be a secretary doesn't come in handy on many occasions, but it seems that the road to good jobs is more likely to come through solid college background, gradual advancement, and special skills.

Is a College Education Necessary?

Just how helpful is a college background? Are the young women in today's colleges aiming for a place in management? A few years ago the papers were full of the anti-establishment attitude of college students. There is no way of telling just how widespread this movement was, but it was well publicized. The mood seems to have changed and today's college students seem quieter and more concerned about their future. This does not mean that they have stopped questioning industry's practices. Far from it. But if the following views of two college students can be taken as typical, then management at least has a chance. It has much to do to communicate its story to the coeds, and perhaps management women should help in this cause.

To find out what the younger generation is really saying, two college students were asked to submit their views. The first was written by a sophomore at Princeton. It takes a bit of courage to publish it in its entirety, but here is the way it came when we "asked for it" from Carlyn Lynch. It is revealing as to what college is like today.

"The coed at a historically male university is yet in the process of finding an identity. Assuming she rejects the conventional stereotype of the typical coed she is pretty much on her own. Being one myself [one who has moved away from the stereotype], I have found that she is an entity displaying certain distinguishing characteristics.

"To examine the development of these characteristics through early experiences with the feminine mystique, present attitudes toward contemporaries and other women, and future ambitions will shed some light from the inside looking out.

"Until quite recently the Princeton student was wealthy and white (not to mention male). Now there is a large third-world program as well as a proposed goal of a 40 to 45 percent female student body. The class of 1975 ratio of men to women is 3 to 1. Nearly all women at Ivy League colleges are goal-oriented. To be here, they must be competitive, strong, bright, and directed. They are deeply intellectually committed to accomplishments. For most of them this means a professional career. A substantial number of the pre-medical and pre-law students are women. The Woodrow Wilson School encourages applications from those who are qualified, and the intensely academic life at Princeton points some women to a teaching career. In my first year at Princeton, I never heard a coed express a desire for a career in industry

"There are a lot of men who see themselves with MBA's from Harvard or Yale or Stanford, so it's not the university. Nor is it valid to explain this fact with a generally preconceived notion. Part of the explanation is obviously one's circle of friends. Being in architecture I encounter very few economics majors. However, one does run into them and they are all male. The solution then seems to be the attitude of women toward industry. Their notions are usually uninformed and uncomplimentary . . . they are vehement. They consider industry a catchall for those students who discover they have no particular talents or gifts, and have nothing in particular to do with the rest of their lives. Being strong-minded and opinionated—not to imply pigheaded—the Princeton coed is generally conscious of the natural abilities and strengths that have gotten her this far. She expresses violent ideas when discrimination is brought up. She feels she is gifted and is determined to make use of these gifts, shying away from the bloblike qualities of industry.

"In addition to the lack of personality of the industry image, there is also an excruciatingly awful stereotype of the woman in industry. The outstandingly successful ones are much admired either as successful types of the liberationist or as figures that are thoroughly identified with the coed's mind. These are the top echelons; the low echelons, armies of secretaries, are only a small cut below the gray pale of the ugly routine that seems to stretch almost to the top of industry. The coed has the idea of a Babbitt-like figure in a skirt who plods through her days—one exactly like the next—with marriage the ultimate goal in life. It is none too appealing.

"This is not to claim that this attitude is completely unchallenged on the college campus. Being the child of a woman who has chosen a career in industry, I consider myself more informed than most. Industry is not quite as amoebalike to me as to some of my friends. Regrettably, my views are not radically different, with the qualification that I consider most professions amoebalike. I fail to see any huge difference between routine office work in industry and researching dry law books day in and day out in preparation for someone else's brilliant briefs. Simplistic it may be, but it seems to me that the person makes or breaks any profession. The executive can shape the frame of a job rather than have it chained on her. It's almost an absolute to claim that an interesting life is made so by the virtue of the individual.

"The usual objection to industry is its lack of creativity. It is necessary, however, to realize that my idea of creativity is of something concrete, of a beautiful form that is arrived at through artistic training. None of the careful explanations I have heard concerning the unlimited creativity of the industrial scientist has convinced me at all. I realize that there are more drab careers in industry because that is where most of the jobs are, but I have found very few examples of creativity that did not appear to me to be manifestations of ambition or self-interest.

"Not only does industry stifle the mind of a woman, it is said, but it does affect her emotional life. Regrettably, women who work and leave the family must juggle priorities to an astonishing degree. "My family comes first" is the cant, but one discovers this is in the direst circumstances. The woman who will care for a very sick child often has not taken the time to stay with the child in his formative years. It is true that life is nicer if the mother has not dropped her career in midstream. The children wear nice clothes, do nice things, and go to nice colleges. I have no clear ideas that form themselves into definite opinions on this facet of a career. I do mention that every worker-woman should recognize it is a crucial question and think through it long and hard.

"Predictably, I have a lot more to say. However, life and the allotted space of the printed page run quickly by. I hate to write a definitive conclusion about the coed. Her strength is her individuality.

"Industry—we are a relatively calm group of people. We'll listen if you have anything to say."

Here is what a young woman freshman from the University of Michigan says. Ann Friend, like her counterpart at Princeton, looks for challenges. (Incidentally, both of the girls quoted are Merit Scholar Finalists. They are doing extremely well in college and surely exhibit great potential.)

"One of my basic assumptions is that I will be working for at least part of my life and, having worked in a low-skill commercial kitchen job, I know that I would be miserable in an unchallenging career. Therefore, if I want an interesting and stimulating job, I had best acquire the kind of education that will enable me to qualify for one. This is definitely not a joyless process—I thoroughly enjoy learning and [encountering] challenging situations.

"I think that the women's lib movement has made me more aware of alternatives to being a housewife, and I really feel that almost any career is open to me."

Can Young Women Develop the Qualities Necessary for Success?

The following discussion, based on the responses to this study, covers the qualities that seem necessary for a woman to be successful. Developing those qualities should help any woman who is eager to become a manager.

What are the main management characteristics that successful women seem to have? In general they probably are not much different from those of men. The most evident feature of the women included in the study is their perseverence in getting where they now are. Most of them had a long haul from their beginning jobs to the executive suite. Many of them started poor, but overcame all difficulties and are now successful.

There are surprisingly few gripes about the work involved in their current positons. The women are enthusiastic and full of action. As any other executive does, they work hard, put in long hours, and are conscientious about doing a good job.

They think their pay now is approximately the same as a man

earns for a comparable job, but almost all say that this is a fairly recent development. On the way up they have been paid far less than men for comparable spots and hold a certain amount of resentment either openly or in the back of their minds. Most admit, however, that unless they had taken jobs at a lower rate or a job "beneath" what a man would have started at, they would not now be on executive row.

Would they advise younger women to do the same? "If it means getting started in a place with a good management progression and if you can see the light at the end of the tunnel, go ahead. Don't let empty promises of fast promotions entice you if you have no concrete evidence that management means what it says."

Matching Talents to Jobs

The real difference today is that there is at least a start toward early matching of talents and jobs. Many of the women in the study depend on the good graces and consideration of a good male boss who recognized their talents. Will younger people have to do that? It is always important and helpful to have someone who is interested in your welfare and recognizes your talents, but younger women do not have to be quite so dependent on a sponsor in upper management. The extra help from farsighted individuals that older women executives often had to depend on is no longer crucial. Fitting talents to management jobs comes far faster to younger women than it did to their older colleagues.

The young women in the survey are also well aware that the management job is no sinecure. They, too, put in long hours, are enthusiastic about their jobs, and are less inclined to think they have ever been underpaid. (Except like everyone else, they, too, like a good solid salary check to match their talents.)

Have the women matched their talents to their jobs? Some of the older ones have, by a long, slow process.

"It took me 20 years before I finally found a job that takes almost all my capabilities."

"I really wanted to be a doctor but I ended up as an editor."

"The secretary's route made me spend too many years in detail. My real talents were not used for many years."

"I majored in math—I was a freak. Today I would have gone into the exciting world of programming and computers. Sure I'm a vice president of personnel and I'm satisfied with my job, but I still dream of what I might have been if I'd had a start in the mathematical field. Yes, it's too late to change now."

The professional women were rarities and had a hard time getting started, too. The list of law firms that wouldn't hire women was long and some women, even with outstanding grades, had a rough time getting started. Again, the perseverance paid off, but often over a rocky road of putting in longer time as clerks or even starting in another field.

The women admit that the road up hasn't been easy and the guard has had to be up. Even after being hired by an appreciative male who knew he could get more wits per dollar by hiring a woman, one woman was told, "The president doesn't really like women executives, so stay out of sight even if you have to jump into the closet when you know he might be coming." It's a far cry from then to the 1970s, when companies are really getting the word from the top down, "We might not get that government contract unless we have at least a few women on executive row."

The younger women in the survey have been luckier. Their talents are appreciated. They have been hired and continue to be trained for their special skills. Just a few examples are Jane Evans Sheer, president of I. Miller; Barbara Carstensen, inhalation specialist at Mercy Hospital in Toledo; and Sharyn Yanoshak, technical consultant, Cyphernetics Corporation. The girls in college know that they will be hired for their specialized talents and have their eyes set on careers that will match those talents.

The recruiters on college campuses interview both men and women for executive trainee positions and are well pleased when they snare bright, talented women for their companies.

The following quotes from younger women executives are indicative of their feelings about job-matching talents.

> My management has allowed me to shoulder as much responsibility as I can handle.
>
> My boss firmly believes in my intelligence and ability, and he has been responsible for promoting me.
>
> My company has long had a pervasive philosophy of promoting and accepting female executives.
>
> A woman must be talented—have brains and be able to produce. I've been accepted by my management on all three counts and I am pleased about it.

There are some who are aware that their problems are the same as those faced by women who have preceded them. They believe that some groups are just as chauvinistic even though they try to cover it—they have to be convinced that a woman can handle the job.

Today there may be a few "token" or "show" women on executive row, but few companies can afford to keep executives on the payroll who do not carry their own weight. The women in the study are not the "token" women who may begin to show up in very top jobs because of outside pressures to make the firm look as though it's in compliance with government regulations and doing its best for the women's liberation movement.

The women in the study are doing a good solid job of attending to their work and even though there are some dreams of what-might-have-been if they had started where the younger women are starting now, there is no excuse given for not doing a conscientious job.

Performance Factors for Success

To catch the flavor of what the women are saying, here are their opinions about the qualities and performance factors that have made them successful.

> *The same qualities that make a good male executive. Knowledge of the job, willingness to make decisions, willingness to admit being wrong (occasionally), and ability to delegate.*
>
> *Willingness to accept responsibility, leadership, dedication, and administrative skills. Relatively few women will accept the consequences of their decision making. I suppose this could be said of any executive—generally a woman has more staying power and resilience than a man.*
>
> *The qualities that make anyone a good executive—perhaps an added bit of persuasiveness, tenacity, and objectivity.*
>
> *Hard work, knowledge of the business, and ability to communicate with people.*
>
> *I think that a woman must have the same qualities and performance record as a man (that is, aggressive, tactful, hard working, ambitious, desirous of excellence, and so forth).*
>
> *Hard work, constant learning, and luck. Technical competence, and ability to open my mouth when necessary—and more important, to be silent when necessary.*
>
> *Basic honesty—keeps her mind on the job—treats everyone with directness and respect.*
>
> *You must understand the man you work with—don't bruise his ego.*
>
> *(1) If we have become an exec, we have usually had to analyze situations and people. This helps us in making decisions. (2) In interviewing, either through sympathy or a sharing of thoughts, ideas,*

and so on, she can usually learn more about either the prospective employee or a current one.

A willingness to have stretch and ability to be creative, a respect for human beings, an awareness of the needs and dignity of people, an open-mindedness to new ideas, integrity, and willingness to take risks, a confidence and willingness to provide full support to subordinates, objectivity, a tough skin, the ability to admit a mistake, the acceptance of democratic participation to a point, but the ability to take a firm position where indicated, the ability to understand the true meaning of accountability and live it. If you think yourself a mature, competent executive, then act it.

Self-assurance, a sense of humor, willingness to give and take criticism, honesty in dealing with people, tough-mindedness, not looking for magnifying slights or prejudices.

Most of these women have the same skills in organizing, delegating, performing, inspecting, and regrouping as men do. The recognized management skills are not the sole province of male managers.

Factors That Cause Trouble for Women

Which skill do women have the most trouble developing? Delegation seems to be the most difficult. Most of them claim to be perfectionists. They just can't stand to see the job not done as well as they can do it. Too often they are accustomed to detail and hate to let go. They recognize, however, that unless they learn to delegate they will not be the best of managers. It is something they tell younger women to watch, to learn early in the game.

Women, too, find it hard to let go of pet projects or something they really think needs doing in a certain way. Perseverance or stubbornness? It really is tough to let go of something you believe in. Evidently the women in the study were right most of the time in holding on—their bosses still keep them around. It would be interesting to see how many projects have been saved by this *perseverance* of talented women. They sometimes drive male executives crazy by this bull-dog "stubbornness." Often it is said that males are apt to abandon ship too early—the women have rescued projects that shouldn't be scuttled.

Are younger women any different? They probably will be able to delegate better, but it's questionable whether they will lose the perseverance that characterizes the older women.

The women executives in this study are not a bunch of babies. They have talent and are using it. They are aware that they have this

talent. Do they flaunt it? No more than men. But by necessity women
have had to prove their worth even more than men. Are they hard-
boiled? Not if the quotes in this book have any validity. They are concerned with making the best of their own talents. But are also concerned, as any other true executive is, with developing and utilizing
other people's talents.

Because they are still in the minority on executive row and the
spotlight exaggerates any failures, they are apt to work even harder and
to be even more conscientious than their male counterparts.

They are loyal to their companies, their peers, and their subordinates. However, because they have had to fight their way up they know
when they have hit the wall of intolerance in one company and will
move elsewhere if their talents are not recognized. To some of the
women in the study, moving up meant moving out.

The younger executives in the study have the same gutsy enthusiasm as the older women. They may be more restless—ready to move out
faster when opportunity knocks, more confident of their talents but outstanding in these talents, which wise managements have recognized
early and rewarded well.

It is a rather sad fact of life that it took some of the women so
long to be given the responsibilities and pay they deserved. It was a
waste of talent, but most of them are happy that they are finally in jobs
they feel they deserve and can handle. They know, too, that this is not a
problem peculiar to women, but they feel that it has been more acute
for them.

There is a warmth and enthusiasm in their willingness to share
their experiences (as their participation in this study shows) minus any
blistering attacks on males, and in their eagerness to help other women.
It is true there are a few unkind words about the younger generation
and probably a few from the younger about the older, but on the whole
there is a shared understanding that you don't step on another's toes to
get ahead, either male or female.

It may be that the women in this study constitute a select group
and that most women executives aren't this warm and generous.

The study has been made, however, to show that there are topflight women executives and professionals with all the concomitant attributes. They want to bridge the generation gap and are asking the cooperation of the younger women coming into the field to help them
communicate. It's a two-way street between the young and the old, and
neither should neglect to understand what the other is thinking or
doing. It's a sad fact of life that there is misunderstanding between the
older worker and the younger, but the older women in the study are saying, "We hope we have something to give. Try us and we'll share. We

can help you over the hurdles with no strings tied to the offer if you will let us."

And a final plea to men or women who are responsible for helping women use their talents. Take a chance on them. They really can do the job—those firmly held by men as well as those always held by women. Take a chance on this exciting new crop of young women. They are a talented group. Your patience will be rewarded.

This book leaves many challenging questions unanswered. Where we go from here remains to be seen, but women themselves, through their own efforts and with the help of legislation and enlightened managements, must and will continue their fight for first-class citizenship and first-class jobs in management.

APPENDIX A
Quizzes for
Women and Men

For Women

1. What do I really think of my own talents?
2. Am I willing to make the most of my talents?
3. Do I resent the fact that men seem to have the best jobs, the best chances of promotion, and the most exciting challenges?
4. How am I trying to improve my own position—more education, more research, better attitude?
5. Do I look at everything emotionally instead of making some well-thought-out plans?
6. When did I last read a book pertaining to the jobs I'd like to hold?
7. Do I continually think of myself as a secretary, as a helper, as a crutch instead of being the actual person doing the higher-level job?
8. Do I pass the blame for not having a good job off on someone else—my parents, the boss, the school I attended, and so on?
9. Am I willing to do the hard work necessary to hold a responsible job?

10.   Am I willing to work as a member of a team to accomplish a worthwhile project?

11.   Am I willing to help others on the way up, particularly other women?

12.   Am I willing to fight for my rights on equal ground and on the basis of what I have done and can do in the future?

For Men

1.   Do I consider hiring competent women for top-level jobs?

2.   Am I willing to pay a woman the same salary as I would a man doing the same job?

3.   Do I consider women for promotion to top-level jobs?

4.   How much talent have I wasted over the years by not hiring and promoting competent women?

5.   Have I underpaid competent women doing good jobs?

6.   On major projects do I automatically assign the routine work to women?

7.   Do I give women credit where credit is due?

8.   Am I willing to concede that a woman can equal or even beat me at my own job?

9.   Am I through giving lip service to the idea that women can work as well as men, and really mean it when I say: "I'd like the best person available for this task"?

10.   Am I informed about the curricula in the colleges graduating women? Can I do something to see that the curricula are geared to today's management needs?

11.   Am I bringing up my daughters to fit into this modern world rather than trying to turn back the clock to have them try to live in the past?

12.   Am I willing to be more sympathetic to the effort women are making to improve their lot?

APPENDIX B
Questionnaire Used
for This Study

Dear———:

We live and work in what is essentially a male-dominated world; yet many women have succeeded in management. I am writing a book on women executives because despite all the books on women, I don't believe any of them gives true insight into the management job as seen by a woman on the inside.

I'd like to cover such aspects of the woman executive's job as her relationships with male colleagues, her playing of many "roles," her feelings about her career, plus other broad-gauged perceptions of women in business.

Because you are a successful management woman, I'd like you to fill out the enclosed questionnaire. I'd like to sit and talk with you, but hope the information from the questionnaire will get me started. Your help will be very much appreciated.

Sincerely,
Edith M. Lynch

223

On-the-Job Factors

1. Present position; description of responsibilities.
2. Jobs held previously (stepping-stone jobs).
3. Who helped you attain your present position? What was his (or her) job? Did you work directly for him or her? How did he or she help you?
4. What do you think are women's chief hangups on the job?
5. What are or were the chief hangups about women executives of the men who are or were your colleagues or bosses?
6. What qualities, performance factors, and so on make a woman executive successful?
7. Are the qualities necessary to a woman executive's success different from those required of a man? If so, please comment in detail.
8. What do you think of the new crop of women who seem headed for executive positions?
9. Do you feel that women are too emotional to hold executive jobs? If so, please comment in detail.
10. Comment on the fact and fiction of women's weeping.
11. Do men hate to work for women? If so, why?
12. Are men reluctant to hire or promote women? If so, why?
13. "What can you expect—she's a woman!" What are your reactions to this comment?
14. What does it mean to you when a male executive says that you think like a man?
15. How do you react when a male executive suggests that you take the notes or serve coffee at a meeting? Please give your reasons.
16. Do you let your male colleagues or business contacts take the dinner check, pay for the taxi, carry your luggage? Please comment on this problem.
17. How do executive travel requirements affect the woman executive?
18. How do you feel about the belief that women by nature are incapable of making logical decisions?
19. How do you feel about men referring to women as "broads," "dolls," "chicks," and other similar expressions? How do you react when your male colleagues use these terms?
20. On the job, you probably have encountered embarrassing, humorous, or irritating situations with respect to being a woman executive in the male-dominated world. Please describe them.
21. (a) Why do you think you've made it?
    (b) List your primary executive assets.
    (c) What if anything holds you back from future achievements?
22. What advice would you give a young woman with brains, drive, ambition, and personality as to how best to succeed in the male-dominated executive world?
23. On the basis of what you now know of the executive world, if you had it to do over again, would you handle your career differently? If so, how?

Job-Related Personal Factors

1. Home and children
    (a) As a working woman, have you successfully resolved any problems in handling these responsibilities?
    (b) Is your husband cooperative?
    (c) What do your children think about your working?
    (d) Is travel a problem in relation to family responsibilities?
    (e) When a job relocation is required, how do you and your husband decide whose job takes precedence?
    (f) Describe any other problems involved in holding an executive position.
2. Education
    (a) Which college or university did you attend; why?
    (b) Did choice of school make a difference in your career?
    (c) Would you want your daughter to have the same education you had? Why, or why not?
    (d) To which college or university would you send her?
3. Who, excluding your business contacts, influenced your career the most?
4. Describe your off-the-job interests (clubs, philanthropies, and so on).
5. What are the biggest personal problems you, as a woman executive, have encountered on the job? For example, has someone else usually taken credit for your work because you are a woman?
6. What observations do you have about the role of sex? For example, what would you do if a man, thinking you needed his influence to get ahead, asked you to sleep with him? Do male executives feel that you are a challenge sexually because you are a woman executive? What are your views about becoming romantically involved with a male colleague? Please comment freely on this whole issue.
7. If you think it worthwhile, get your boss's opinions about women executives.
8. If possible, get opinions about women executives from your subordinates.

APPENDIX C
What Has NOW Accomplished?

What has the National Organization for Women (NOW) specifically and the new feminist movement in general accomplished on behalf of women since 1966 when they came into existence?

The celebration on August 26, 1972, of the 52nd anniversary of the passage of the 19th amendment, which gave women the right to vote in 1920 after nearly a century of struggle by the first wave of feminists, is an appropriate time for the new movement to inventory its progress.

NOW's comprehensive, *but by no means exhaustive*, inventory of the new feminist movement's accomplishments includes:

In General—

1. We have raised the consciousness of the country to sexism as a public problem.

Dated August 1972.

2. We have changed women: whether they are for or against us as an organization or a movement, they have a new self-confidence and they are doing more! And a 1972 opinion survey shows that now 48% of all women favor our goals and only 36% oppose them. Only a year ago 42% were in opposition to our efforts.

3. We are changing men, too! The same survey showed that 49% favor our efforts and they have begun to think and act differently.

4. We have begun to create new definitions, styles, and patterns of leadership, unique to the feminist movement, that may in the future provide models for other movements as well as for organizations and institutions in society at large—though this development is the least perceived by the media and general public.

In Employment—

1. We compelled the Equal Employment Opportunity Commission (EEOC) to act on sex discrimination cases; before NOW came into existence, they were ignoring complaints of sex discrimination.

2. We pressured President Lyndon Johnson to extend to women the Executive Order banning discrimination in government and in employment by federal contractors.

3. We persuaded the EEOC to revise their guidelines on sex discrimination to prohibit advertising in sex-segregated classified ads and we have influenced many newspapers (sometimes by court action) to de-sexregate their Help Wanted advertising columns.

4. By legal support of courageous women, we have substantially expanded employment opportunities and rights for both women and men by helping to destroy antidiluvian definitions of "women's work" and "men's work."

5. We are helping to remove the restrictive application of so-called protective labor legislation to women, which kept them out of many jobs and restricted their opportunities for promotion, and are helping to extend genuinely protective laws to all workers—men and women.

6. We are destroying sexist employment "standards" arbitrarily imposed only on women that have been used to bar them from employment—such as having pre-school age children—unless the standards are applied to men as well.

7. We have opened up employment opportunities for women in fields from which they were barred only by sexist practices, such as broadcasting, where women must now be included in the affirmative hiring and promotion programs for radio and television that are required by the Federal Communications Commission.

8. We compelled the Secretary of Labor to issue Revised Order 4 in 1971, which requires federal contractors to devise and implement affirmative hiring and promotion programs for women.

9. We are compelling educational institutions which receive federal funds to devise and implement affirmative hiring and promotion programs for women.

10. We have established caucuses in virtually every professional field to press

for the hiring and promotion of women and virtually every profession has been compelled to respond by including women in and promoting them on the basis of their (long-ignored) qualifications.

11. We have inspired the formation of other organizations which are now pressing the special interests of women in specific areas of employment, such as stewardesses and media women, and we have stimulated the formation of women's caucuses within individual companies to press for the end of discriminatory company policies and practices.

12. We provided the critical lobbying support for the successful passage of the EEOC Enforcement Act of 1972, which gave the Commission significant new means for fighting discrimination in employment on behalf of women and minority groups.

13. We succeeded in 1972 in accomplishing a long-time goal of extending the Equal Pay Act of 1963 to executive, administrative, and professional personnel as part of the Higher Education Act of 1972.

14. We have drawn attention to the denial of equal opportunity in employment for women teachers by filing charges (May 1971) under Executive Orders 11246 & 11375 against the public school system (elementary and secondary).

15. We have succeeded in persuading the EEOC to issue guidelines that require companies to pay women while on maternity leave, as they would for any other temporary disability and companies must offer women their jobs back after maternity leave.

16. We are succeeding in getting Affirmative Action Programs to eliminate sex discrimination in employment in individual companies and in institutions of local government.

17. We have filed charges of sex discrimination in employment against the *Fortune* 500 largest companies and aided and abetted the EEOC in moving against AT&T—"the largest single oppressor of women in the country."

18. We pressured the Office of Federal Contract Compliance into ruling that companies must make public their affirmative action programs for women and minorities so that we can monitor each company's progress in terms of their own stated goals.

19. We are working to include household workers under the federal minimum wage law and raise the minimum wage.

20. In coalition with welfare rights groups, we are succeeding in getting a new focus on women in poverty and creating an awareness that "the poor" in our society are mainly women—80% of the people on welfare—and we are challenging the practices of government agencies in "manpower" training programs that give preferential treatment to men.

21. We are succeeding in opening up new opportunities for women in employment in such fields as law enforcement where studies already show society as a whole may benefit also by a reduction in violence—evidence suggests that women tend to defuse volatile situations and provoke less hostility than men.

22. We are succeeding in getting women appointed to the boards of directors of corporations where their presence may have a humanizing effect on business practices and encourage greater ecological responsibility.

23. We lobbied successfully in behalf of the Health Manpower and Nurse Training bill of 1972, which forbids sex discrimination in health occupations.

24. We lobbied and testified in behalf of the Emergency Public Service Employment Act of 1971 and have since had to challenge the excessive preference to veterans encouraged by the Department of Labor's guidelines which have subverted the goals of the bill to help *all* the unemployed.

In Education—

1. We have raised the professional aspirations of women throughout the country and encouraged the entry of women into previously exclusionary or "quota'd" fields such as medicine, law, dentistry. In 1971 more women entered law school than the total that registered in the past ten years. And we are compelling their acceptance by pressuring the Department of Health, Education & Welfare (HEW) to enforce compliance with nondiscriminatory standards required of institutions that wish to continue receiving federal funds.

2. We have stimulated the addition of Women's Studies Programs in high schools, colleges, and universities around the country and are succeeding in having women rewritten into courses in such fields as history, sociology, literature, etc. We are also succeeding in having the image of women in textbooks reflect her participation and accomplishments in a variety of roles in our society.

3. We are succeeding in destroying sex segregation in courses such as shop and home economics at the high school level.

4. We are succeeding in eliminating nepotism rules in academic hiring that have traditionally discriminated only against academic women married to academic men.

5. We are influencing school counselors to guide their students into fields based on their abilities regardless of their sex and to counsel their women students to prepare for the reality that they will be working for extended periods whether or not they marry and should be prepared to support themselves and their dependents.

6. We have filed sex-discrimination complaints against nearly 300 colleges and universities and are succeeding slowly but surely in compelling them to comply not only with the law of the land but with their own humanitarian rhetoric.

7. We substantially aided the passage of amendments to the Higher Education Act of 1972 which include in their provisions prohibitions against sex discrimination in any educational program or activity receiving federal funding, from pre-school and elementary school through graduate and professional institutions, though we opposed the anti-busing provisions of the Act.

In Religion—

1. More women are assuming positions of leadership in religious life, becoming ministers and rabbis, and heading national religious organizations.
2. Religious misogyny has begun to collapse from the weight of its own contradictions and pressure from religious feminists.

In Politics—

1. NOW members have been instrumental in the organization and development of the National Women's Political Caucus (NWPC) and state and local caucuses.
2. A member of NOW and former member of its national board of directors, Congresswoman Shirley Chisholm was a candidate for the Presidency of the United States.
3. The growing power of the new feminist movement can be measured by women's impact on the 1972 conventions of the major political parties. At the Democratic Convention, 40% of the convention delegates were women, triple the 13% at the '68 Convention; the Democratic Platform includes the most comprehensive plank on women's rights ever included in the platform of a major party; women chaired important committees as well as sessions of the convention itself; a woman—Sissy Farenthold of Texas—came in a respectable second in the voting for a vice presidential candidate; and for the first time in history, a woman—Jean Westwood of Utah—is a chair*person* (note that title!) of the Democratic National Committee. At the Republican Convention, 30% of the convention delegates are women, a significant increase from their 17% representation in '68; and a woman—Anne Armstrong of Texas—who has served as cochairman of the Republican National Committee, was the first woman to keynote a major national political convention.
4. More women are running for office in the 1972 campaigns: 40 women are in contention for seats in the House of Representatives; four are running for the U.S. Senate; two are still candidates for gubernatorial offices; and there is a substantial increase in the number of women running for office at state, county, and city levels.
5. Pressure from NOW and other feminist organizations has compelled the appointment of women to government agencies at every level.
6. NOW and other women's organizations are compelling the recognition of women as a notable force in American history in the planning of the 1976 Bi-Centennial Celebration.

In Family Life—

1. A new involvement of men in family life is becoming evident as the new feminist movement breaks down the sex-role stereotypes that have inhibited their participation in the past.
2. New qualities to the relationships between women and men are becoming apparent, based on egalitarianism and mutual respect rather than dominance and submission.
3. NOW specifically and the feminist movement generally have created a new climate of opinion on women's right to have or not have children; motherhood is rapidly disappearing as the barometer of "fulfillment as a woman," and marriage without children is becoming socially acceptable.
4. We have succeeded in making the issue of developmental child care centers a matter of national debate and we succeeded in getting legislation that would have initiated the establishment of such centers through both houses of Congress, only to have it vetoed by President Richard Nixon.
5. We have begun to have an impact on sexist child-rearing practices that inhibit the natural development of both boys and girls by artificial definitions of masculine and feminine behavior.
6. We have so far successfully opposed H.R. 1, the administration's so-called Family Assistance Plan, because of its provisions for forced labor of mothers with dependent children at 75% of the minimum wage which perpetuates the existing exploitation of women by employers; for denial of aid to mothers trying to enhance their earning ability by full-time study; and for its emphasis on reducing the cost of welfare without reducing the poverty problems of welfare recipients, as well as for its failure to recognize that the poverty of welfare families is the result of the transference of women's financial dependency from husbands/fathers to the state.

In the Law—

1. We are close to succeeding in achieving legal equality for women under the Constitution with the passage—after 49 years of consideration—of the Equal Rights Amendment by Congress and with ratification to date by 20 states; 18 more are needed.
2. In the context of the new feminist movement, precedent-setting court cases —some brought by NOW and other feminist organizations and others by individual plaintiffs—are succeeding in establishing women as full persons under the law—not as inherently subordinate, second-class citizens. Among such court decisions are: the ruling by the Rhode Island Supreme Court in 1972 that the State Constitution does not, as was argued, give a man the right to beat his wife "in accord with his fundamental right to punish her;" and the case of *Reed* v. *Reed*, in which the U.S. Supreme Court ruled unanimously that an Idaho law giving automatic preference to males over females, when

both are equally qualified to serve as estate administrators, violated the 14th Amendment, which guarantees equal protection under the law.

3. We have half-succeeded in getting jurisdiction over sex discrimination for the U.S. Civil Rights Commission in a bill that passed the Senate on August 4, 1972, but must still pass the House of Representatives.

4. Stimulated by the new feminist movement in general and NOW specifically, concepts of marriage, divorce, and family law are now in the process of being redefined for the benefit of both men and women.

5. Since 1966, 16 states and the District of Columbia have liberalized abortion laws to give women greater control of their own bodies.

6. In cases designed to set legal precedents, NOW has moved against sex discrimination in public accommodations and won—from McSorley's to the "tables down at Morey's."

7. NOW lawyers have been successful in winning cases—that had previously been lost at the trial level—on appeal for working women under Title VII: *Weeks* v. *Southern Bell* set the precedent, affecting thousands of women, that an employer must open all jobs to women applicants unless he can prove that all or substantially all women are not able to do the job and a NOW member, Lorena Weeks, was the first woman to obtain complete monetary relief (over $30,000) plus placement in the job of switchman at an increase in pay of approximately $60 per week; *Bowe* v. *Colgate-Palmolive Company* was a class action suit which attacked arbitrary job assignments in plant as well as lines of seniority.

8. NOW also filed amicus briefs in *Thorn* v. *Richardson* in which priority for male, as opposed to female, welfare recipients for training under the federal government's WIN program was held invalid; *Daniel* v. *Commonwealth of Pennsylvania*, which struck down a state statute imposing heavier criminal penalties on women than on men for the same crime, and *Dr. Ina Braden* v. *the University of Pennsylvania*, the first class action suit ever filed against a university for women faculty members because of sex discrimination.

In Images and Attitudes—

1. We have raised the consciousness of the country to the stereotyped images of women that are pervasive in the media and in advertising and in 1972 began to see the first signs of change—and variety—in image.

2. We have freed large numbers of women from the constraints of "fashion"— more and more women are making a free choice of what to wear and how to look on the basis of what is uniquely suited to their personal style and individual lives.

3. Responding to the stimulus of the new feminism, secure men have begun to redefine "masculinity" to include and even emphasize the so-called feminine characteristics of nurturance, compassion, gentleness. What is emerging for both women and men is a creative new synthesis of so-called feminine and masculine characteristics into characteristics desirable for all human beings regardless of sex.

4. Under the impact of the new feminism, the theory and practice of psychology that have traditionally made maleness the norm and femaleness a deficiency, an incompleteness, even an abnormality, have begun to crumble and a new psychology is being constructed that does not "adjust" women—or men—to stereotyped roles and that recognizes that women are human beings with an inherent right to develop to the maximum of their potential and that both men and women have a right to define and express their own sexuality.

5. In the first attempt to force the Federal Communications Commission (FCC) and the general public to recognize the role television plays in creating and reinforcing sex role stereotypes, NOW filed a petition to deny the license renewal of WABC-TV in New York on the grounds of consistent failure to cover serious women's issues and a disparaging portrayal of women's role in society as reflected in overall programming and commercials as well as for failure to provide equal opportunity for women in employment.

6. We are effectively changing sexist customs and language by successfully promoting the use of such terms as "Ms." and "chairperson" (as opposed to "chair*man*"), and "humankind" (as opposed to "*man*kind").

APPENDIX D
Women Who Participated in This Survey

Eileen Ahern

Coordinator, Industrial Relations Research, Continental Can Company, New York

Formerly: research associate and consultant, American Management Association; regional personnel officer, War Labor Board; training specialist and employment interviewer, Bureau of Employment Security; contributing editor, *Personnel Journal*; author of *Collective Bargaining in the Office, Handbook of Personnel Forms and Records*, and numerous articles on personnel and labor relations.

NOTE: Not all the participants are listed; some wished to remain anonymous.

Jane M. Alexander, Esquire

Attorney at Law, Alexander and Alexander, Dillsburg, Pa.; Director of Bureau of Foods and Chemistry, Pennsylvania Department of Agriculture, Harrisburg, Pa.
  Formerly: general law practice.

Carol D. Ayres

Planning Technician II, City of Atlanta, Model Cities Program
  Formerly: personnel assistant, Atlanta City Personnel Department; medical assistant; special claims approver, John Hancock (Medicare Contract); quality analyst, Retail Credit Corporation.

Grace Bechtold

Executive Editor, Bantam Books, Inc., New York
  Formerly: reader-editor, Doubleday Book Clubs; editorial secretary.

Helen Delich Bentley

Chairman, Federal Maritime Commission
  Formerly: maritime editor, *Baltimore Sun;* reporter, *Ely Record.*

Joan B. Berkowitz

Project Director, A. D. Little, Inc., Cambridge, Mass. (engineering research and management consultants)
  1955–1957 Postdoctoral fellow, Yale University.

Margaret Bowes

Vice President (Personnel), Kings Lafayette Bank, Brooklyn, N.Y.
  Entire career at Kings Lafayette Bank: assistant vice president, manager (junior officer), personal loan department; auditor; executive secretary; commerical loan clerk; head bookkeeper; bookkeeper.

Barbara M. Boyle

President, Boyle, Kirkman Associates Inc., New York
    Formerly: at IBM, manager, special programs; systems engineering manager (Eastern and Central Europe); marketing manager and assistant branch manager; systems analyst.

Claire Carlson

Professional Engineer and Attorney in her own professional practice
    Formerly: at Westvaco corporate headquarters, project engineer, project manager, and real estate manager.

Barbara Carstensen

Chief Inhalation Therapist and Cardio-Pulmonary Technologist, Mercy Hospital, Toledo, Ohio

Betsy Carstensen

Co-manager, 500-acre farm
    Formerly: chemist, University of Oregon Laboratories.

Catherine Cavalli

Controller, National Retail Merchants Association; Treasurer, NRMA Enterprises
    Formerly: assistant controller, NRMA

Margaret Carter

Training Director, Gimbel Bros., New York
    Formerly: personnel coordinator, National Alliance of Businessmen, Washington, D.C.

Catherine Case

President, Gidding Jenny Department Store, Cincinnati
Formerly: vice president in charge of merchandising; buyer, every type of ready-to-wear clothing.

Eileen Casey

Personnel Director, Group Health Insurance, Stamford, Conn.
Formerly: at Teleregister Corp., director of industrial relations; assistant to the director of industrial relations; secretary to the director of industrial relations.

Dorothy D. Chappel

Director, Personnel Plans and Programs, IBM World Trade Corporation, New York
Formerly: at IBM, manager, personnel plans and programs; personnel programs manager; headquarters personnel manager; administrative manager, Office Products Division, Headquarters; personnel assistant; services supervisor, Office Products Division, Headquarters.

Leila L. Colmen

Personnel Director, Institute of International Education, New York
Formerly: benefits manager, worldwide youth-serving organization; personnel manager, health research agency; recruitment specialist, scientific agency.

Coline Covington

Editorial Coordinator, *Glamour Magazine*, The Conde Nast Company, New York
Interrupted career for 14 years to raise family. Served six years as newspaper reporter, two years as woman's page editor, and held part-time publicity jobs.

Carolyne K. Davis (R.N., Ph.D.)

Chairman, Baccalaureate Nursing Program, Syracuse University
    Formerly: assistant chairman, baccalaureate nursing program, Syracuse University; teacher of nursing; pediatric and surgical nurse.

Jacqueline Delafuente

Urban Affairs Counsel, F. W. Woolworth Co., New York
    Formerly: attorney, F. W. Woolworth Co.; general law practice.

Arneta K. Dow

President, Dow Sales, Inc., Branford, Conn. (arts and crafts)
    Formerly: supervisor of arts and crafts products; business administration teacher.

Pamela Duncan

Systems Engineer, IBM
    Formerly: associate systems engineer, IBM.

Betty Ann Duval

Manager, Personnel Development, General Foods Corporation, Morristown, N.J.
    Formerly: related jobs at General Foods; at RCA, corporate training and development; training administrator, division level; training supervisor, plant level; training, hourly workers, plant level.

Wendy Duval

Sales Estimator and Forecaster, Avon Products, Inc., New York
    Formerly: personnel administrator/project coordinator, Avon; personnel administrator, Avon; Personnel Assistant, O and M Ad Agency.

Evelyn G. Enteman

Trust Officer, American National Bank and Trust of New Jersey (Financial Planning Department), Morristown, N.J.
Formerly: trust administrator, American National Bank and Trust; at Irving Trust Company, trust administrator; investment analyst; executive secretary to head of Wall Street office; administrative assistant to trust administrator.

Dorothy Flynn

Personnel/Office Manager, Chemicals and Plastics Group, Borg-Warner Corporation, Chicago
Formerly: at Borg-Warner, secretary to vice president of administration; administrative assistant to the vice president; executive secretary, Norge Division.

Linda R. Franklin

Director, Personnel, Education and Volunteers, Community Service Society, New York
Formerly: director of personnel, Jewish Theological Seminary of America— negotiated contracts, prepared and presented arbitration cases; responsible for recruitment, training, wage and salary administration; graduate student adviser and curriculum planning; co-director, Seven Sisters Colleges vocational workshops, Barnard College (Carnegie Fund grant to conduct workshops for helping women graduates reenter labor market).

Ann Friend

Freshman, University of Michigan

Jean Friend

Homemaker and Community Leader; active in Four-H Club work; officer in Parent–Teacher Association, home economist
Formerly: home service adviser, utility company, Saginaw, Mich.; full-time researcher, food and nutrition staff, Michigan State University; at Michigan State University, teaching assistant, staff; graduate assistant, food and nutrition department; high school teacher, home economics and science.

Helen Galland

Vice President and General Merchandise Manager, Bonwit Teller (department store), New York
> Formerly: at Bonwit's, associate general merchandise manager; divisional merchandise manager (two divisions); divisional merchandise manager (one division); buyer.

Mary Garzoni

Corporate Vice President, Chas. A. Stevens & Co. (department store), Chicago
> Formerly: senior vice president, Chas. A. Stevens; pension and profit-sharing specialist, Herman Zischke Organization; secretary, store planning and display, Sears, Roebuck and Co.

Mary S. Girard

Vice President, Corporate Personnel, Ohrbach's, New York (retired, 1972)
> Formerly: At Ohrbach's, corporate personnel director; personnel director, New York and Newark stores; personnel manager, Newark Store.

Anita D. Goldberg

Rehabilitation Counselor and Administrative Assistant to Rehabilitation Center Director, Kings Park State Hospital, New York
> Formerly: rehabilitation counselor, Northeast Rehabilitation Hospital; research assistant, United Cerebral Palsy, Queens; staff specialist—Personnel, Autometric Corp. of America (New York and Alexandria, Va.); personnel clerk, Bulova Watch Co.

Margaret A. Green

Dean of Students, Borough of Manhattan Community College of the City University of New York
> Formerly: dean of students, Butler Community College; counselor and associate professor, Staten Island Community College; coordinator of women's

residence hall, Louisiana State University; activities counselor, City College of City University of New York; head counselor, Morrison Hall, Indiana University; teacher and high school counselor, Portland, Oreg.

Lorle Guntsch

Service Adviser, Ohio Bell Telephone Company, Toledo
Formerly: at Ohio Bell, instructor; service assistant; long-distance operator.

Guin Hall

Urban Affairs Supervisor, New York Telephone Company, New York
Formerly: deputy commissioner, New York State Department of Commerce, in charge of Women's Program Division; reporter, feature writer, *New York Herald Tribune;* U.S. Coast Guard SPARS; assistant buyer, Portland, Oreg., department store.

Aileen Hernandez

Self-employed as consultant/lecturer on urban affairs and public relations; Western representative/consultant to the National Committee Against Discrimination in Housing; chairone, National Advisory Committee, National Organization for Women (NOW)
Formerly: President NOW; commissioner, Equal Employment Opportunity Commission; assistant chief, California Division of Fair Employment Practices; education and public relations director, Pacific Coast Region, International Ladies' Garment Workers Union; assistant education director and organizer, Pacific Coast Region, International Ladies' Garment Workers Union; teacher, adult education, University of California at Los Angeles; research assistant, Department of Government, Howard University; newspaper columnist.

Bette Heydrick

Office Manager, Al Heydrick Associates, Lighthouse Point, Fla.
Formerly: secretary to agency vice president, Pan American Life Insurance Co., New Orleans, La.

Carol Ivansheck

Personnel Director, Frederick Atkins, Inc. (buying office), New York
  Formerly: employment manager, Frederick Atkins; assistant to manpower
  manager, Genesco; assistant personnel interviewer, Franklin Simon (department store); records clerk, Interstate Department Store.

Alice Ready Kehoe

Director of Nursing, Clinton Nursing Home, Bay Shore, Long Island,
N.Y.
  Formerly: charge nurse, 40-bed floor, 25-bed private pavilion, St. Joseph's
  Hospital, Yonkers, N.Y.; supervisor of night nurses, 220-bed general volun-
  tary hospital.

Marion S. Kellogg

Consultant, Marketing Management Development, General Electric
Company, General Electric Service; also consultant to outside com-
panies, lecturer, seminar leader—Europe, Africa, and South America.
Member, corporate staff
  Formerly: manager, employee relations, Flight Propulsion Laboratory, Cin-
  cinnati; physics instructor, Brown University. Author of four books.

Alice Gore King

Executive Director, Alumnae Advisory Center, Inc. (founded to help
graduates of Seven Sisters Colleges and Universities)
  Formerly: assistant head, the Brearley School (New York City private school
  for girls); personnel supervisor, Pratt and Whitney Aircraft; vocational adviser, Bryn Mawr College.

Constance W. Klages

Vice President, Battalia, Lotz & Associates, Inc. (executive search firm)
  Formerly: senior consultant and head of research, Battalia, Lotz & Associates; consultant and research manager, Battalia, Lotz & Associates; manager, Research and Survey Division, Commerce and Industry Association

of New York; wage and salary analyst and supervisor, employment, Univac Division of Remington Rand Division of Sperry Rand Corporation; personnel assistant, Institute of State Education.

Nancy Knox

President, The Renegade Corporation (men's shoes importers) Division of Genesco, New York
Formerly: Co-founder, Jags, Unlimited (men's shoes); partner, Clark-Knox (overseas consulting company); assistant fashion director, I. Miller.

Jean Lang

Chairman, Department of Retailing, Webber College, Babson Park, Fla.
Formerly: twelve years' experience in merchandising (seven years with a large department store and five years with a specialty ready-to-wear clothing and accessories store); high school teacher.

Elizabeth Coryllos Lardi, M.D.

Pediatric Surgeon, Long Island, New York; in charge of pediatric surgery at Nassau County Medical Center
Formerly: Private practice as third "man" in pediatric surgery group. After her second child, went into private practice. Assistant professor of surgery in charge of pediatric surgery, Flower and Metropolitan Hospital (New York Medical College).

Ann Laskey

Homemaker and High School Teacher
Formerly: Elementary school teacher; secretary, Champion Spark Plug, Toledo, Ohio.

Catherine Laskey

Freshman, University of Michigan

Patricia Leonard

Placement Manager, Hal-Ba Personnel Associates (employment agency), New York
Formerly: Held jobs as sales representative or in personnel areas.

Hermine Levine

Editor, Prentice-Hall, Inc., Englewood Cliffs, N.J.
Formerly: writer on labor relations, The Conference Board; freelance writer specializing in personnel; secretary, American Arbitration Association.

Carlyn E. Lynch

Sophomore, Princeton University

Mildred McLean

Production Manager–Advertising, General Learning Corporation, New York
Formerly: production manager–advertising, Silver Burdett Company (textbook publishers), a division of General Learning Corporation, Morristown, N.J.; administrative assistant to the director of advertising, Silver Burdett Company; personnel director, Martindale-Hubbell, Inc.; controller, Overlook Hospital, Summit, N.J.

Mary S. McMahon

Director, Management Development and Communication, The Equitable Life Assurance Society of the United States, New York
Formerly: director, Communications Consulting Service, Equitable; professional consulting staff, Rogers Slade and Hill (management consultants), New York; editor and community relations assistant, Hyatt Bearings Division, General Motors.

G. G. Michelson

Senior Vice President for Employee and Consumer Relations, R. H. Macy & Co., Inc., New York
Formerly: at Macy's, vice president for consumer relations and labor relations; vice president for employee personnel; administrator, employee relations department; councillor, employee relations department; manager, employee relations department; assistant to the labor relations manager; member of the executive training squad.

Jean M. Moore

Manager, Equal Opportunity Affairs, Atlantic Richfield Company, Los Angeles
Formerly: equal opportunity coordinator, New York; secretary to financial vice president.

Betty Southard Murphy, Esquire

Partner, Wilson, Woods and Villalon (law firm), Washington, D.C. Active in all D.C. courts. Has argued in nine of the eleven U.S. Courts of Appeals and the U.S. District Courts of Maryland, Massachusetts, Maine, Georgia, Louisiana, Florida, and Washington, D.C.
Formerly: attorney, National Labor Relations Board, enforcement branch; freelance reporter in Europe and Asia.

Peggy A. Ogden

Store Manager, Ohrbach's, Westbury, Long Island
Formerly: personnel manager, Ohrbach's; personnel adviser, Ohrbach's; assistant to personnel manager, Ohrbach's; personnel adviser to Girl Scouts of America; assistant to the personnel director of Institute of International Education; assistant director of YMCA Counseling Service, Hartford, Conn.

Shirley O'Neill

Attorney, Sullivan and Cromwell (law firm), New York
Formerly: at Sullivan and Cromwell, senior associate in Trusts and Estates

Department—drafted, planned, and administered decedents' estates. Joined Sullivan and Cromwell right after law school.

Hilda Pedersen, M.D., M.B., Ch.B., F.F.A.R.C.S.

Assistant Professor of Anesthesiology, Columbia University (clinical medicine, administration, instruction of resident doctors and medical students)
> Entire career in medical field: Mount Sinai Hospital, New York; Edinburgh University School, Scotland; McGill University, Montreal; Stanford University, California.

Rita A. Perna

Assistant Vice President, National Fashion Coordinator, Montgomery Ward, New York
> Formerly: stylist, Alden's (retail mail order); stylist and assistant fashion coordinator, Spiegel's (retail mail order); fashion coordinator, Abraham and Straus (department store).

Esther A. Peterson

Consumer Adviser to the President, Giant Food Inc. (Washington, D.C.-based supermarket chain)
> Formerly: special assistant for consumer affairs to President Johnson; also chairman of the President's Committee on Consumer Interests; assistant secretary of labor; executive vice chairman of the President's Commission on the Status of Women; director of the Women's Bureau, U.S. Department of Labor; legislative representative of the Industrial Union Department, AFL-CIO; assistant director of education of the Amalgamated Clothing Workers of America; taught women workers in industry, Bryn Mawr summer school; teacher, Winsor School, Boston (private girls' school); teacher, Branch Agricultural College, Cedar City, Utah.

Mary-Jane Raphael

Director of Consumer Affairs, PepsiCo, Purchase, N.Y.; Manager of Women's Activities; Coordinator of Joan Crawford's Business and Publicity Schedule
> Formerly: conference officer at UN during 1969 General Assembly; women's travel director, Shell Canada Ltd.

Eva Robins

Labor and Industrial Relations Arbitrator, New York
Formerly: deputy chairman, Office of Collective Bargaining of New York City; staff member and arbitrator, New York State Mediation Service; assistant vice president and assistant director of industrial relations, Pioneer Ice Cream Division, The Borden Company.

Michaelyn Robison

Assistant to the President, The Cyphernetics Corporation, (computer time-sharing company), Ann Arbor, Mich.
Formerly: secretary to the president of Cyphernetics; high school teacher.

Alice Rohloff

Treasurer, Rohloff Bros., Inc. (alfalfa mill and distributor), Trowbridge, Ohio
Formerly: elementary school teacher.

Maryellen Schwarz

Homemaker and Tax Accountant
Formerly: tax accountant and estate administrator, Kelley, Drye, Warren, Clark, Carr & Ellis (law firm), New York; tax accountant and estate administrator, Sullivan and Cromwell, New York (law firm), personal shopper for Best and Co. (department store).

Jane Evans Sheer

President, I. Miller (retail store), New York
Formerly: fashion coordinator, I. Miller Design Studio; handbag and hosiery buyer, I. Miller; assistant shoe buyer, I. Miller; assistant to the director of the Transnational Division, I. Miller; Genesco management trainee.

Jean Head Sisco

Vice President of Personnel, Woodward & Lothrop (department store), Washington, D.C.
> Formerly: personnel director, suburban and corporate personnel departments, Woodward & Lothrop; assignment supervisor for part-time workers (sales supporting staff), Marshall Field, Chicago; personnel trainee, Time, Inc.

Donna Smith

Director of Counseling, The Fashion Institute of Design and Merchandising, Los Angeles
> Formerly: director of fashion merchandising institute and placement director of fashion institute; stylist, Peter Pan Swimwear; fashion coordinator for film and TV; freelance for Filmfair Studios.

Rhoda M. Stewart

Vice President, Administration, Chemicals and Plastics Group, Borg-Warner Corporation, Chicago (retired, 1972)
> Formerly: at Borg-Warner, director of materials distribution, Marbon Chemical Division; purchasing agent; priorities manager.

Janet J. Thomas

Homemaker and freelance editor
> Formerly: elementary school teacher; secretary and bookkeeper.

Virginia S. Varnum

Management Librarian, American Management Association
> Formerly: personnel and information specialist, industrial and labor relations, National Association of Manufacturers; editor, management information, National Firemen's Institute; specialist, labor relations research, Western Electric Company; high school teacher.

Maria Vescia

Vice President, International Division, Airwick Industries, Inc., Carlstadt, N.J.
Formerly: manager, Export Department, Airwick Industries; assistant to the export manager, Airwick Industries; vice president, Foregger International, Inc. (worldwide sales and marketing of anesthesia apparatus and accessories); manager, export department, Foregger International; secretary to the president, Foregger International.

Judith P. Vladeck

Partner, Vladeck, Elias, Vladeck, and Lewis, (labor law firm), New York
Formerly: Associate, at present firm; associate, Conrad and Smith (law firm).

Cynthia C. Wedel

Associate Director, Center for a Voluntary Society, Washington, D.C.; also president, National Council of Churches
Formerly: associate general secretary, National Council of Churches.

Judith Weinberg

Personnel Officer, New York City Community College, Brooklyn, New York
Formerly: personnel director, Glemby Corporation (leased beauty shops, 6,800 employees, international corporation); personnel director, Astron Corporation (electronics).

Harriet Wilinsky

Retail Consultant, Filene's (department store), Boston
Formerly: sales promotion manager, vice president, Filene's; ad manager, fashion director, Filene's; ad manager, copywriter, E. T. Slattery Company.

Beatrice F. M. Wilson

Manager, Employment Services, Allied Chemical Corporation, Morristown, N.J.
> Formerly: secretary of volunteers, New York Hospital, Cornell Medical Center; personnel trainee, R. H. Macy & Co.; personnel director, Davison (Macy affiliate); consultant in personnel and employee relations, The Bowery Savings Bank; member of board of education, Madison, N.J.; chairman of personnel, finance and negotiating committees, vice president and president of the board of education.

Judy Wilson

Manager, Programmed Instruction; Editor, Self-teaching Guides, John Wiley & Sons, Inc., New York
> Formerly: started career as secretary.

Margaret Scarbrough Wilson

Chairman, President, Chief Executive Officer, Scarbrough's Department Store, Austin, Tex.
> Formerly: at Scarbroughs, assistant to the president; department manager; part-time employee in the store while attending high school.

Sharyn Yanoshak

Working toward MBA at University of Pittsburgh, on leave from her position of technical consultant, Cyphernetics Corporation (computer time-sharing company), headquartered at Ann Arbor, Mich.
> Formerly: systems programmer, IBM; data processing trainee, Franklin Computer Associates; manager, customer services, Virtual Computer Services; girl Friday and salesgirl while attending high school.

NOTES

Chapter 1

1. *The New York Times,* August 26, 1972.
2. Press release, ECOSOC 3274, United Nations, May 25, 1972.
3. *Congressional Record,* March 22, 1972.
4. Ibid.
5. *Congressional Record,* March 21, 1972.
6. March 20, 1972.
7. March 17, 1972.
8. September 14, 1971.
9. February 13, 1972.
10. February 27, 1972.
11. Prepared twice a year by the Section on the Status of Women, the United Nations Secretariat, May 1972, p. 58.
12. *The New York Times,* July 31, 1972.
13. Random House, New York, 1970, p. 396.
14. Ibid., pp. 397, 417.

15. Ibid., p. 417.
16. United Nations *Development Programme Service Bulletin*, Vol. 2, No. 2, 1972.
17. *Monthly Labor Review*, Table 2, "Employment Status by Color, Sex, and Age," June 1972, p. 80.
18. *Fact Sheet*, Women's Bureau, U.S. Department of Labor, Washington, D.C., 1970.
19. U.S. Department of Commerce, Bureau of the Census, *Current Population Report*, No. 80, p. 60.
20. From a private conversation.
21. Elizabeth Waldman and Kathryn R. Gover, "Children of Women in the Labor Force," *Monthly Labor Review*, July 1971, p. 19.
22. AMA, 1971, p. 175.

Chapter 2

1. April 28, 1972.
2. AMA, 1971, p. 45.

Chapter 4

1. July 27, 1968.

Chapter 5

1. The first three books cited were published by AMA (1965, 1967, and 1972); the last two, by Gulf Publishing Company, Houston, Texas (1968 and 1969).

Chapter 8

1. Elizabeth Waldman and Kathryn R. Gover, "Marital and Family Characteristics of the Labor Force," April 1972, pp. 4–8.
2. Janice Neipert Hedges and Jeanne K. Barnett, "Working Women and the Division of Household Tasks," April 1972, p. 13.

Chapter 10

1. McGraw-Hill, New York, 1971; British publisher, MacGibbon and Kee Limited, 1970.
2. Ibid., p. 102.
3. Ibid.
4. Ibid., p. 108.

5. Ibid., p. 109.
6. Ibid., p. 131.
7. Random House, New York, 1970.
8. Ibid., p. 34.
9. Ibid., p. 307.
10. Ibid., p. 346.
11. Ibid., p. 448.
12. Ibid., p. 482.
13. Ibid., p. 560.
14. Ibid.
15. Ibid., p. 562.
16. Pegasus of Bobbs-Merrill Co., Inc., New York, 1971, p. 11.
17. Ibid., p. xii.
18. Ibid.
19. Ibid., pp. x–iv.
20. Ibid., p. 35.
21. Ibid.
22. Ibid., p. 152.
23. Ibid., p. 154.
24. Ibid., p. 159.
25. Ibid., p. 183.
26. Ibid., p. 195.
27. The Macmillan Company, New York, 1968.
28. Ibid., p. 9.
29. Ibid.
30. Ibid., p. 201.
31. W. W. Norton & Co., New York, 1963, p. 335.
32. Ibid., p. 364.
33. August 27, 1972.
34. Ibid.
35. Term paper, "The Women's Liberation Movement," May 1972.
36. *The New York Times,* March 5, 1972.
37. Op. cit.
38. David McKay Co., Inc., New York, 1968.
39. Lyle Stuart Inc., Secaucus, N.J., 1970.
40. "Secretary Image: A Tempest in a Typewriter," March 7, 1972.

Chapter 11

1. *Federal Register* No. 111, June 9, 1970.
2. *Federal Register* No. 234, December 4, 1971.
3. *Diaz* v. *Pan American World Airways, Inc.,* 3 EPD para. 8166 (5th Cir. 1971); *Rosenfeld* v. *Southern Pacific Co.,* 3 FEP cases 604, 607, 608 (9th Cir. 1971). For other court cases on bfoq see *Weeks* v. *Southern Bell Telephone Co.,* 408 F. 2d 228 (C.A. 5, 1969); *rev'g in part* 277 F. Supp. 117 (S.D. Ga., 1967); *Bowe* v. *Colgate-Palmolive Co.,* 416 F. 2d 711

(C.A. 7, 1969) *rev'g in part* 272 F. Supp. 332 (S.D. Ind., 1967); *Cheat-wood* v. *South Central Bell Telephone and Telegraph Co.*, 303 F. Supp. 754 (M.D. Ala., 1969).

4. Sec. 1604.2, EEOC Rules and Regulations, 37 *Federal Register* No. 6835 (April 5, 1972); *Rosenfeld* v. *Southern Pacific Co.*, 3 EPD para. 8247 (C.A. 9, 1971); *Richards* v. *Griffith Rubber Mills*, 300 F. Supp. 338 (D.C. Ore., 1969); *Local 246, Utility Workers Union of America* v. *Southern California Edison Co.*, 3 EPD para. 8100 (C.D. Calif., 1970); *Caterpillar Tractor Co.* v. *Grabiec*, 63 LC para. 9522 (D.D. Ill., 1970); *Ridinger* v. *General Motors Corporation*, 3 EPD para. 8175 (S.D. Ohio, 1971); *Garneau* v. *Raytheon* Co., 3 EPD para. 8153 (D.C. Mass., 1971).

5. *Phillips* v. *Martin Marietta Corporation*, 3 EPD para. 8088 (U.S.S. Ct., 1971).

6. 37 *Federal Register* 6835, April 5, 1972.

7. See *Bartmess* v. *Drewrys U.S.A., Inc.*, 442 F. 2d 1186 (C.A. 7, 1971), *cert. denied*, 92 S.Ct. 2746 (U.S.S.Ct. 1971); *Rosen* v. *Public Service Electric and Gas Co.*, 409 F. 2d 775 (C.A. 3, 1969), 3 EPD para. 8242 (D.C. N.J., 1971), 3 EPD para. 8073 (D.C. N.J., 1970). These decisions conform to the principles expressed in Sec. 1604.9 of the Commission's guidelines on sex discrimination.

8. See *Doe* v. *Osteopathic Hospital of Wichita, Inc.*, 334 F. Supp. 1357 (D.D. Kansas, 1971).

9. See *Schattman* v. *Texas Employment Commission.* [Recently the Supreme Court decided not to hear this case. This means that the Texas Employment Commission was not guilty of discrimination in its maternity policies. However, the case was decided before EEOC included state and local governments. This is the main reason the Supreme Court would not hear the case, letting stand the Appellate Court decision sustaining the Texas Employment Commission].

10. EEOC press release No. 7–8, June 30, 1971.

11. Equal Opportunity Report No. 1, "Study of Employment of Women in the Federal Government," 1967, 1968, 1969, 1970; Report No. 2, "Job Patterns for Minorities and Women in Private Industry, 1966," 1967.

12. EEOC press release No. 71–21, December 3, 1971.

Chapter 12

1. Robert Levy, "The Woman Who Wasn't There," June 1972, pp. 63–64.

2. Ibid.

3. "A Good Woman Is Hard to Find," August 6, 1972.

4. Ibid.

5. Ibid.

6. Ibid.

7. AMA, 1972, p. 21.

8. Ibid., pp. 22–23.

9. Ibid., p. 31.

10. Alfred A. Knopf, Inc., New York, 1970.
11. Laurence J. Peter and Raymond Hull, William Morrow and Company, Inc., New York, 1969.
12. James Menzies Black, AMA, 1964.
13. James Menzies Black and Edith M. Lynch, McGraw-Hill, New York, 1967.
14. World Trade Academy Press, Inc., New York, 1965.
15. Felix M. Lopez, Jr., AMA, 1970; McGraw-Hill, New York, 1965.
16. AMA, 1971.
17. Felice N. Schwartz, Margaret H. Schifter, Susan S. Gilloti, "How to Go to Work When Your Husband Is Against It, Your Children Aren't Old Enough, and There's Nothing You Can Do Anyhow," *McCall's*, March 1972.

Chapter 14

1. *The New York Times*, May 6, 1972.
2. John A. De Pasquale and Richard A. Lange, "Job-hopping and the MBA," November–December 1971, pp. 4–13.
3. Joan Lipman Blumer, January 1972, p. 28.

SELECTED READING

General

de Beauvoir, Simone, *The Second Sex*. New York: Bantam Books, 1968 (paperback); first published in Paris, 1949.

Chafe, William Henry, *The American Woman: Her Changing Social Economic, and Political Roles, 1920–1970*. New York: Oxford University Press, 1972.

Flexner, Eleanor, *Century of Struggle: The Woman's Rights Movement in the United States*. New York: Atheneum, 1970 (paperback); first published in 1959.

Hole, Judith, and Ellen Levine, *Rebirth of Feminism*. New York: Quadrangle Books, 1971.

Janeway, Elizabeth, *Man's World, Woman's Place: A Study in Social Mythology*. New York: William Morrow, 1971 (also in paperback).

Kanowitz, Leo, *Women and the Law*. Albuquerque: University of New Mexico, 1968 (paperback).

Loring, Rosalind, and Theodora Wells, *Breakthrough: Women into Management.* New York: Van Nostrand Reinhold, 1972.

Sullerot, Evelyne, *Woman, Society, and Change.* New York: McGraw-Hill, 1971 (paperback).

Anthologies

Gornick, Vivian, and Barbara K. Moran, eds., *Woman in Sexist Society: Studies in Power and Powerlessness.* New York: Signet Books, 1971 (paperback).

Theodore, Athena, ed., *The Professional Woman.* Cambridge, Mass.: Schenkman Publishing Company, 1971 (also in paperback).

Bibliographies

Astin, Helen S., Nancy Suniewick, Susan Dweck, *Women: A Bibliography on Their Education and Careers.* Washington, D.C.: Human Service Press, 1971 (paperback).

Drake, Kirsten, Dorothy Marks, Mary Wexford, *Women's Work and Women's Studies, 1971: An Interdisciplinary Bibliography.* New York: Barnard College Women's Center, 1972. Available from KNOW, Inc., P.O. Box 86031, Pittsburgh, Pa. 15221.

Westervelt, Esther Manning, Deborah A. Fixter, Margaret Comstock, *Women's Higher and Continuing Education: An Annotated Bibliography with Selected References on Related Aspects of Women's Lives.* New York: College Entrance Examination Board, 1971.